Children Reading Print and Television

This book is dedicated to my parents, Albert and Anita Robinson, who gave me my delight in narrative.

Children Reading Print and Television

Muriel Robinson

The Falmer Press

(A member of the Taylor & Francis Group)
London • Washington, D.C.

UK   Falmer Press, 1 Gunpowder Square, London, EC4A 3DE
USA   Falmer Press, Taylor & Francis Inc., 1900 Frost Road, Suite 101,
        Bristol, PA 19007

First published in 1997

**A catalogue record for this book is available from the British
Library**

ISBN 0–7507–0682 1 cased
ISBN 0–7507–0636 8 paper

**Library of Congress Cataloging-in-Publication Data are available
on request**

Jacket design by Caroline Archer

Typeset in 10/12 pt Times by
Graphicraft Typesetters Ltd., Hong Kong.

Printed in Great Britain by Biddles Ltd., Guildford and King's Lynn on
paper which has a specified pH value on final paper manufacture of not
less than 7.5 and is therefore 'acid free'.

Contents

List of Transcription Symbols

} }	Two or more people speaking simultaneously
[]	Comment added by me in the middle of a speech
()	Comment added by me elsewhere, usually to do with mood/action
. . .	(at end of speech) Speaker interrupted
. . .	(at beginning of subsequent speech) Interrupted comment continued
. . .	(elsewhere) Pause
[. . .]	Omission
[class teacher]	Name removed for anonymity
(unclear)	Clarity lost because of tape quality/overlapping voices/other noise
italics	Action/dialogue from screen or section read aloud from text (also used for book and programme titles within text)
MR	The researcher

Preface

This book is based on my doctoral thesis, but, in order to render it more readable, the thesis has been extensively rewritten and certain sections have had to be omitted or summarized. Those readers who find the theoretical frame a little light as a result are referred to the original thesis for a much fuller discussion, including a consideration of existing research on children, television and reading. Similarly, the original thesis contains a full methodological justification and complete transcripts. I would be very happy to enter into debate about these aspects of my work (or indeed any other aspects).

I am indebted to the Centre for Mass Communication Research at the University of Leicester for giving me permission to reproduce here in chapters 4 and 5 some sections of my unit for their distance learning MA in Mass Communications (unit 45: Children and Issues of 'Media Effects').

The transcripts in the text of the book are numbered using the numbering system for the thesis and a full list of transcripts is included as an appendix, together with a brief summary of transcription conventions. I have included the line references from the thesis, in part for the benefit of any readers wishing to read the full transcripts but also to give a sense to readers of this book of the location within each transcript of each extract.

The fieldwork leading to the data used in the book was carried out in a British state primary school situated on a large council estate with 8- and 9-year-old children. There are some incidental details about the school and the children in the text, but a detailed description has been omitted to preserve confidentiality. For that reason, too, I will only thank the class teacher and headteacher for their invaluable help without naming them. Thanks are also due to my supervisor, Dr David Buckingham, and to all the friends and colleagues who supported me through the process, in particular to my husband Richard Mosiewicz for endless patience and support (and many cups of coffee), and to Iain Rushton for technical advice on word-processing. But especially I need to thank Alexis, Ashley, David, Kelly, Natalie, Neil, Rikky and Sarah, whose contribution is central to my work and without whom there would be no book.

Muriel Robinson
January 1997

Chapter 1

Everyday Discourses about Children, Television and Reading

I have been an avid reader of stories in books and comics for almost as long as I can remember. Although I derive great pleasure from finding new authors and encountering their stories for the first time, I also have a core of well-loved books to which I return on a regular basis. Here the pleasure comes not so much from predicting the outcome but from seeing a familiar pattern unfold or from having time to enjoy the way the book is written. In the past, apart from occasional repeat showings, the only way to re-experience stories which I encountered first on television was through book versions of the story. When the television version had been taken from the book, this was usually a satisfying experience; when the book came from the television script, it was usually a disappointment. I think I assumed that this was inevitable; how could a television script have sufficient depth to generate a complex polysemic written text? Had we not acquired a video recorder, I might well have carried on believing this to be the case.

With the arrival of our video, however, came the possibility of re-viewing certain programmes. When John Byrne's drama series *Tutti Frutti* was shown for a second time, we decided to record it, and found ourselves watching it almost compulsively. In the first few weeks during and immediately after transmission we watched it repeatedly, almost to the exclusion of any other television. This experience led me to reconsider my earlier views about narrative and to speculate about the different possibilities available to televisual and printed stories. I could see that in my re-watchings of *Tutti Frutti* I was deriving the same satisfactions as in my re-readings of favourite novels; I could watch the interweavings of the various storylines, appreciate the way in which characters were presented, and savour the distinctive language patterns. Moreover, whereas in printed fiction the author/narrator might reveal the thought processes of all or some of the characters, here I had to work much harder to decide for myself the stances of the characters towards each other, towards the specific events of the series and towards life in general. There was an added dimension of visual and aural information alongside the words, giving extra possibilities for the creation of a secondary world. In other words, although the discourse might be televisual rather than written, there was still a complex story to be told and the story was told in such a way as to create what was for me a very satisfying, complex narrative.

Talking about this with colleagues, I began to speculate about the ways in which children might learn to make sense of narrative in the different discourses they encounter. Might there be ways in which their understandings of narrative in general were enhanced by all their encounters with narrative in whatever form? For many of my generation, television arrived in our homes when we were already at school and either reading or learning to read, but for almost all children today television is among their earliest experiences and provides some of their first encounters with narrative, long before formal schooling: one survey for the *Radio Times* found that almost a third of children begin to watch regularly before their first birthday (*Daily Telegraph*, 28 August 1991). Might early experiences of television actually support later encounters with stories in books?

This book is an attempt to answer some of the questions that I found myself asking as a result of my encounter with *Tutti Frutti*. The ideas explored here come from the research I undertook for my PhD, and so at times I shall be considering the theoretical frames available to us from the wider research tradition. Before looking at these, though, it is important to explore more fully the everyday, 'common sense' attitudes to television and to reading which are prevalent in Western society, and so the next section of this chapter does just that.

(As I wrote this book, I considered updating the examples drawn from the media which illustrate my arguments. However, since any set of examples would be history by the time of publication, let alone by the time of reading, this seemed to be of little value. What I would recommend is that readers of this book look for themselves at what the papers are currently saying about reading and television, not so much to see how far attitudes have changed but to see whether what I say here about the logic underlying attitudes is still dependent on 'common sense' beliefs about the world.)

Everyday Opinions: Common Sense or Cultural Construct?

Even for those of us engaged in research, everyday opinions as expressed in the media play a key role in influencing our view of the world. We may reject the opinions or attitudes we find expressed or we may agree with them, but we are unlikely to ignore them, especially if they are to do with anything which is a part of our daily experience. Many of these views that we encounter in the national newspapers and in books written for the lay person take certain key cultural concepts as 'given' common sense, beyond question. But what do we mean by 'common sense'? Where does it come from? Is it the same in all cultures?

These questions have been explored by Barthes (1973a) in his examination of myth as a depoliticizer and naturalizer of our view of the world. For Barthes, everyday attitudes are part of our semiological system; he suggests that they are really myths created by each society. Through his investigation of the ways in which aspects of everyday life such as wrestling, children or new cars are given symbolic meaning by their representations in our lives, he suggests that what these myths do is to naturalize history. By naturalizing the history or intentions behind the sign, its constructed nature becomes hidden and its power is increased:

> What the world supplies to myth is an historical reality, defined, even if this goes back quite a while, by the way in which men have produced or used it; and what myth gives in return is a natural image of this reality. (Barthes, 1973a, p. 142)

Thus myth has a depoliticizing action, which acts to suggest that concepts such as family values or the work ethic are universally held and natural, rather than created by a particular culture at a particular time and consequently capable of challenge and change.

Barthes shows how, as a result of this depoliticization, the concept of the bourgeoisie, for example, has become so unproblematic as to be 'exnominated'. It is no longer named but is taken as a natural state so that bourgeois values are seen as normal values:

> The whole of France is steeped in this anonymous ideology ... everything, in everyday life, is dependent on the representation which the bourgeoisie has and makes us have of the relations between man and the world. These 'normalized' forms attract little attention, by the very fact of their extension, in which their origin is easily lost. (Barthes, 1973a, p. 140)

In the same way, many of the often very problematic concepts to do with popular culture could be seen as exnominated by the way in which they are taken as natural. As a result, these concepts are kept outside the debate, which then operates as though there were universal agreement about such matters as the role of the family, the value of tradition, of the responsibility of parents to be involved in their children's education, and of the cultural importance of reading. This changes the nature of the argument or opinion built on the exnominated concept, giving it a false authority. When we engage in the debate, unless we consider the basis of the exnominated concepts, we are still arguing from false premises, even if we are contradicting the original opinion which began the debate.

Barthes' recasting of common sense as myth does much to emphasize the ways in which our common-sense views are part of our semiological system, reconstructed as fact rather than values. It is not that the exnomination resulting from myth prevents our discussing these matters. Rather, it changes the nature of the discussion:

> Myth does not deny things, on the contrary, its function is to talk about them; simply, it purifies them, it makes them innocent, it gives them a clarity which is not that of an explanation but that of a statement of fact. (Barthes, 1973a, p. 143)

Thus the ways in which people writing about television and reading bring common-sense views into the debate gives these views power as fact rather than as opinion for their audience.

Of course I too start from a position in which my everyday beliefs are to a large extent bound up in a culturally constructed common-sense system, and to ignore this would be to fail to look sufficiently at the context of my own work; moreover, the possibility exists that these beliefs, even though based not on universal truths (assuming such things exist) but on less scientific grounds, may still have something of value to offer. The anthropologist Clifford Geertz, who has shown how what we take as common sense in our culture may be very different from common-sense views in a different culture, emphasizes this possibility when he discusses the beliefs of Australian aboriginals about the ways in which their land took on its physical characteristics. He shows how the aboriginal belief that a particular creek was formed, for example, by a primordial kangaroo's tail or snake's belly, does not stop the creek from possessing certain natural characteristics. Whether we believe this or have a different view, in both cases the creek will still operate according to some of the forces of nature: 'water runs downhill in both of them' (Geertz, 1983, p. 86). In other words, I may feel that some views about television and reading are based on theories at least as hard for me to believe in as those about Australia in the dreamtime, but that is not to say that there is no truth in their utterances. When we work out a calculation, there may be times when we use the wrong formula but still end up by chance with the right answer. My aim in this research is not to refute the claims of those whose views are presented below but to go beyond the 'thinness' of everyday life in which 'the world is what the wide-awake, uncomplicated person takes it to be' (Geertz, 1983, p. 89) to explore in more depth what actually happens when children are watching television or reading and to examine the relationship between these two activities.

What I wish to do here is to explore everyday attitudes to children, television and books, both to record the key attitudes expressed in the national and local press and in books which have been written for parents or for a general audience, and to begin to uncover those concepts that are taken as beyond question by the key protagonists in the debate. At the same time, I shall be looking at the ways in which opinions are presented to see what counts as evidence and who claims the right to speak authoritatively. By doing this, I hope to establish which ideas are central to my own investigations and which need exploring in a more academic and systematic way.

Television and Reading

Arguments seeking to draw comparisons between television and reading draw on many exnominated ideas about family, about culture and about learning. The arguments themselves tend to revolve around starkly expressed oppositions to do with high and popular culture, active and passive learning and verbal and visual experiences, with television on the less favoured side of the equation.

One opinion to the forefront in popular debate about the interrelationship of television and books is that books are intrinsically better than television because reading is a more worthwhile activity. Books are seen as part of a cultural heritage, which it is automatically important to pass on to the next generation, whilst television viewing is seen as trivial: the foundations for such views are not explored but remain part of the exnominated ideology of those commenting.

For former Education Minister, Michael Fallon, this means an assumption that it is better for his young son to experience books than television:

> I discourage Peter who is $2\frac{1}{2}$ from watching any TV. When I am home, I read to him. (*The Sun*, 14 May 1991)

For some, the emphasis is on television as a barrier to reading, taking up time that could be more profitably spent, with parents at least partly to blame for allowing children to spend too much time watching television and for setting a bad example by watching television themselves instead of reading. Typical of many comments in this vein is A.N. Wilson's claim that:

> There are now far too many lazy parents who do not read themselves and who find it easier to plonk their children in front of a television set as a way of shutting them up, than to read to them before bedtime. (*Daily Mail*, 8 January 1991)

This not only again relies on a shared, unquestioned understanding of the superiority of reading as a cultural experience but also makes many assumptions about parenting and childcare, which again are part of Wilson's ideological stance rather than naturalized 'truths'.

One of television's sternest critics, Marie Winn, extends this view beyond the cultural debate to argue that television is not only culturally less significant, but that it can take us away from our daily responsibilities (though there is no mention of the rights that might normally accompany such responsibilities, nor any acknowledgment that there may be different interpretations of such a concept as responsibility):

> In this comparison of reading and television viewing a picture begins to emerge that quite confirms the commonly held notion that reading is somehow 'better' than television viewing. Reading involves a complex form of mental activity, trains the mind in concentration skills, develops the powers of imagination and inner visualization; the flexibility of its pace lends itself to a better and deeper comprehension of the material communicated. Reading engrosses, but does not hypnotize or seduce the reader from his human responsibilities. Reading is a two-way process: the reader can also write; television viewing is a one-way street: the viewer cannot create television images. And books are ever available, ever controllable. Television controls. (Winn, 1985, p. 66)

This image of television as dominating lives at the expense of other activities is also a key part of Jim Trelease's case for banning or severely limiting children's viewing. Although Trelease's main concern is with the effects on reading, he also picks up the notion of responsibilities: thus we learn that one of the benefits of his own family ban on television was that household chores were now done 'without World War III breaking out' (Trelease, 1984, p. 106).

Winn's view of reading, as expressed above, draws on a metaphoric view of the mental activity required for reading which has its origins in the gymnasium. This view of reading as a fundamentally active process, putting the brain through a regular workout, is one that recurs frequently in the arguments about television and reading, with television yet again seen as less worthwhile. Michael Fallon's anxieties about *Neighbours* (see below) seem to stem from a view of children as 'passive, unimaginative voyeurs' (*The Sun*, 14 May 1991).

Winn has no doubt that television watching requires only 'passive intake' (Winn, 1985, p. 7):

> Television images do not go through a complex symbolic transformation. The mind does not have to decode and manipulate during the television experience. (Winn, 1985, p. 59)

This is contrasted with her view of reading as

> ... learning to transform abstract figures into sounds, and groups of symbols into the combined sounds that make up the words of our language (Winn, 1985, p. 57)

Trelease makes a similar case, emphasizing the differences he perceives:

> Compared to reading, television is still the more passive of the two activities. In reading, educators point out, a child must actively use a variety of skills ... Television requires no such mental activity. (Trelease, 1984, p. 102)

Such views recur frequently in press reports, and just as here take for granted the value judgments about the relative worth of activity and passivity for children's development. For Winn, the dangers of passivity are accompanied by the risk of addiction in the viewer: television is seen as a 'plug-in drug'. She suggests that the cumulative effect of too much television could be neurological impairment caused by 'excessive stimulation for the right-hemisphere forms of mental functioning' (Winn, 1985, p. 49) and that television watching is a compulsion as real as drug addiction, with physical withdrawal symptoms as well as psychological effects.

Whereas Winn and Trelease see television as beyond redemption, others, whilst embracing the notion that television is potentially harmful, suggest ways of promoting reading through television, such as checking the daily programme schedules in the newspaper, thus using the less desirable habit to increase the potential for the desired mental activity of reading. This is one of the key strategies of an organization called Reading Is Fundamental, Inc. (RIF), who in their leaflet *TV and Reading* also suggest looking out for magazine articles about favourite television shows and for books which have been on television. That they do still see viewing as less desirable is clear from the inclusion of such strategies as making a game of 'reducing the amount of time your family spends watching television' (RIF, 1985).

A subtle variation on this argument is to suggest that one of the reasons why television viewing is so much less valuable than reading is that whereas reading requires verbal skills, viewing is a visual activity. Trelease, for whom 'television is the major stumbling block to literacy' (1984, p. 97), believes that one of the reasons for this is the way in which television is a visual rather than a verbal experience:

Television presents material in a manner that is the direct opposite of the classroom's. Television's messages are based almost entirely on pictures and our emotions in response to those pictures. Conversely, the classroom relies heavily on reading, the spoken word, and a critical response to those words, not just raw emotion. (Trelease, 1982, pp. 100–1)

Here again there are huge assumptions of shared, unquestionable views about the importance of schooling and the appropriateness of current classroom practice.

The visual nature of the viewing experience is explored at some length by Winn, who suggests that children's cognitive development may be affected by television watching, since it deprives them of the opportunity to use language by being so essentially nonverbal. She argues that the passivity of the viewing experience is proof that it is a nonverbal activity:

If during those formative years . . . children engage in a repeated and time-consuming nonverbal, primarily visual activity . . . might this not have a discernible effect on their neurological development?

This question requires consideration because there are reasons to believe that television viewing is essentially such a nonverbal, visual experience in the lives of young children. (Winn, 1985, p. 49)

Here again there are assumptions about the nature of child development and about parental responsibility which are never explicitly examined but which are used to give weight to the view of television as inducing an unhealthy lack of activity and reading as mental aerobics.

Television, then, is represented in everyday terms as a passive, visual activity which is inherently less worthwhile than the active verbal work which is reading. But how far do these assumptions hold when we examine the ways in which reading and television are discussed separately?

Reading

In the debate about television and reading, reading itself is seen as unproblematic. The idea that the nature of reading itself might be subject to a similar debate is not voiced. In fact, the reading debate, which goes back many years, has been re-energized and brought into the public arena over the past few years by a series of claims and counter-claims about standards and methodologies. As represented by the press, this debate is also set out as a series of oppositions. In some cases, these are used to promote one side of the debate at the expense of the other; whilst in others, the two apparent extremes are there so that a middle position can be justified at the expense of one or sometimes both extremes. The debate is of particular interest here because of the new dimension it gives to the arguments about television and reading. If there is not the assumed underlying agreement about reading (and in particular learning to read) which has been one of the exnominated features of the television–reading issue, then many of the arguments about television need to be seen in a new light.

The different stances on reading have been characterized by the press as 'Phonics' versus 'Real Books', 'Traditional' versus 'New' and in some cases 'Phonics' versus 'Look and Say'. Coverage ranges from apparently objective descriptions of contrasting-pairs of classes to opinion columns and reports of ministerial comments. Further developments of this suggest the idea of reading as work, as opposed to reading as play, and of teachers and schools versus parents and real life. Press accounts typically lack a detailed examination of the various methodologies they report, and it would be inappropriate here to spend too much time preempting the consideration of the reading process to be found later in this book by a detailed analysis of the inaccuracies of these accounts. However, this lack of careful presentation of the different approaches is worth noting, since it is through the resulting polarization that people outside the teaching profession encounter this debate.

One typical example begins a description of two local schools' practices, written to the headline 'Two sides of the story in big reading debate', thus:

> Jolene, four, started school last week. Already she has read her first book. She can't recognize a word of the print before her, but that is not important.
>
> For Jolene is a student of the new 'real books' approach to reading. (*Evening Argus*, 15 September 1990)

The second school's approach is introduced via the photo caption: 'Tina Davidson takes a reading class at St Luke's school, which uses traditional teaching methods' before its appearance in the second half of the article:

> Roger Red-Hat, Billy Blue-Hat and their friends in the Village of Three Corners are almost part of the family for seven-year-olds at Brighton's St Luke's School.
>
> The pupils have followed the villagers through a series of exploits since they met through the most basic of introductions three years ago.

Although the body of the article sets out fairly dispassionately the approaches of each school, and stresses the good test results of the 'real books' school, the two descriptions quoted above highlight the idea of 'real books' as something exotic and strange as opposed to the familiar security of Roger Red-Hat. This image of exoticism was reinforced in an attack on teaching methods reported in the *Daily Mail:*

> The scandal of poor reading standards in Britain's schools was officially revealed last night by Education Secretary Kenneth Clarke.
>
> He said badly organised staff using trendy methods were at the heart of the 'deplorable' problem . . .
>
> He particularly criticised the controversial 'real book' teaching method — in which children are surrounded with literature so that they learn to read by soaking it up — as 'curious and odd'.

> He stressed that in future all teachers must use a mix of methods, including the more traditional 'phonics' in which children sound out letters, parts of words and whole words, for example cuh-ah-tuh — cat. (*Daily Mail*, 10 January 1991)

Running as a sub-theme to the opposition between supposedly traditional and newer methods of teaching reading is the notion of the need for discipline and hard work:

> Never mind trendy big words like 'creative expression' and 'natural development'. Let us get back to basics and put it so that every well-taught seven-year-old in the country should be able to understand:
> > *All girls and boys must learn to read and write.*
> Alas, that is just what all too many of them fail to do . . .
> There is only one sensible conclusion: Teachers can and must do better. Ken Clarke, the Education Secretary, is determined to see that they do . . .
> Schools will be told to organise classwork in a more orderly way. Reading ability will be taught, not left to grow like Topsy. (*Daily Mail* editorial, 10 January 1991)

This links the reading debate to the wider education context, tying changes in reading methodologies to a deeper concern about teaching and learning; to reinforce this, the *Daily Mail* story about Kenneth Clarke quoted earlier features an insert of three previous headlines about education, captioned 'The *Mail*'s campaign for better teaching' (10 January 1991).

The opposition between the approaches used in some schools by supposedly misguided teachers and the more common-sense attitude of people outside schools also grows from the methodological debate. Thus Clarke is quoted as saying, 'As a *layman* [my italics] I do express some of Mr Turner's scepticism about modern methods' and is said to have 'placed the blame squarely on schools' (*Daily Mail*, 10 January 1991). A.N. Wilson, in another article for the *Daily Mail*, talks of 'the crazy American system known as Real Books' being on the increase, suggesting 'The rot starts in the training colleges where these batty theories are propounded' and contrasting this with a description of those who agree with him as 'sensible people' (*Daily Mail*, 8 January 1991).

So, for the public at large, reading is presented as something which requires work, where apparently basic skills of matching sounds to letters are being neglected, and where teachers and their advisers are endangering literacy standards by introducing new, 'batty' theories. Parents themselves come in for some criticism here for not taking sufficient interest in schools' approaches, and thus allowing this situation to arise, and for not providing a good enough example:

> Yet how many parents of primary school-aged children could begin to identify whether the method by which their offspring are taught to read is based on identifying individual letters and their sounds or acquiring a repertoire of whole words? Moreover, it is not only schools which educate. Parents also teach children — for example the habit of not reading and of lounging in front of screens. (*Independent* editorial, 2 July 1990)

Again, throughout these views runs a theme of an accepted, universal norm of family life and of societal values. The value of tradition is among these exnominated concepts, together with the notion of school as work and of parents as guardians of the next generation. Although a more complex view of reading emerges here that to some extent exposes the view generally held in the television–reading debate as over-simplified, there are still many ways in which these exnominated concepts build up certain 'given' truths which then act to substantiate opinions based on them.

Television

Just as there are more views about reading than are represented in the television–reading debate, so television provokes a wider range of everyday opinions than might be supposed from the views reported above. Soap opera as a genre provokes some of the most diverse responses and it is useful to consider these for the light they shed on the more unified view of television found in the television–reading debate.

Soap operas regularly occupy the top of the viewing statistics and they equally regularly attract criticism. Some of the fiercest complaints have been about the moral outlook and image of family life presented by British soaps such as *Brookside* and *EastEnders*. Here the underlying concepts of what counts as acceptable family behaviour and how far any real families conform to the stereotype assumed by the critics are rarely explored and are almost completely exnominated. Mary Whitehouse has made frequent, widely reported complaints about *EastEnders*, which she sees as 'a violation of "family viewing time"' (Buckingham, 1987, p. 146) and as providing 'dangerous models of behaviour, which young people might be led to imitate' (p. 148). Peter Dawson, then general secretary of the Professional Association of Teachers, continued this attack, describing *EastEnders* as an 'evil influence' which 'projects as normal highly deviant forms of behaviour' (*The Guardian*, 2 August 1989). Neither of these critics suggests that their own views of normal behaviour may be open to debate.

The objections above are to do with notions of morality and behaviour norms which Whitehouse and Dawson take as universal, but the attacks on soap operas from the right also raise the issue of quality, which again is seen as generally agreed and beyond question. Fallon's attack centred on the Australian series *Neighbours*:

BAN TRASHY NEIGHBOURS
It makes our kids dunces, says Minister
    Top TV soap Neighbours should be BANNED because it is 'junk', a Government Minister said last night.
    Michael Fallon, 39, who is Minister for Schools, claimed the hit Aussie series is turning millions of children into dunces.
    He said: 'I would like to see Neighbours banned. Children learn nothing from these junk programmes which dull their senses, making teachers' jobs even harder.'
(*The Sun*, 14 May 1991)

Later in the article we learn that Fallon himself prefers to watch 'the news, the occasional good play and Inspector Morse', which presumably count as quality, though this is left implicit.

This leads to a qualification of the main view of television as less desirable than reading; just as reading is not seen in the same way by all, so within television output there are some programmes which are seen as better than others. However, even soaps are not universally condemned. In the context of a double-page spread exploring the ways in which soap operas reflect the real world with particular reference to religion, *The Universe* reported the view of the Roman Catholic Bishop of Motherwell that parents should use soaps as a positive vehicle for family discussion of moral issues:

> The bishop praised programmes such as *Neighbours, Home and Away* and the BBC's *Grange Hill*, set in a fictional London secondary school.
>
> He says parents should discuss the characters and issues with their own children as a means of discussing Catholic morals and opinions . . . 'If parents simply dismiss the programmes as rubbish and turn off the TV, their children can easily turn it on another day. What is needed is for parents to continue the debate by introducing the Catholic view and compare that to what the programme shows.' (*The Universe*, 5 May 1992)

Not only do we now have a view that suggests that not all television is of low cultural worth, but also one which suggests that even those programmes generally seen as being 'popular' rather than 'highbrow' can be worthwhile, though again here the debate is not so much about the nature of social behaviour as a construct but makes assumptions about the universality of certain views.

The positive benefits of soaps are also stressed by Maire Messenger Davies, for whose daughter the fictional death of a favourite character in *Brookside* appeared to be a positive emotional experience:

> Elinor . . . is an experienced soap opera viewer and these experiences seem to have taught her how to recognise and cope with the emotions aroused by fictional drama in a way that would not have been possible if she had had less experience with the genre. (Davies, 1989, p. 94)

Davies's more positive attitudes have beneath them an image of television watching as a more active process than that which we have so far encountered, and as something which is both visual and verbal:

> Apart from visual skills, the other major skill required to make sense of television is verbal ability. Television is so often described as a visual medium that there can be a danger of forgetting that it is a verbal medium too — often delivering material in highly complex sentences, with unfamiliar vocabulary and references, even in children's programmes. (ibid., p. 15)

> . . . children are neither meek, nor passive, nor uncritical. (ibid., p. 55)

Again, however, embedded here are exnominated attitudes to adolescence and emotional development as well as to the nature of learning which are not presented for critical reflection but are taken as read.

These different attitudes to television, children and the television watching experience show that the neat consensus about television taken for granted by so many is a chimera. It also reveals the extent to which these attitudes are based on what is presented as common sense but which is better described as a series of cultural assumptions.

The Focus for this Study

This exploration of 'common sense' views on television, reading and the relationship between the two has revealed many inconsistencies and contradictions between the various debates. There is one consistent feature, though, which deserves attention, and that is the lack of any acknowledgment of the role of narrative. The personal experience that has brought me to this study was essentially to do with narrative; as I shall argue, narrative can be seen as particularly significant in the development of literacy and in all our meaning-making endeavours as human beings. In these everyday debates, its role has all but disappeared; in my own study, narrative will play a central and very visible role.

I began this chapter by describing my own discovery that the implicit distinction I had accepted between narratives in books and on television had been brought into question by my own experience. From this experience, I raised the possibility that learning to read narratives might be in some ways a process that transcended media boundaries. In the middle part of this chapter, I have attempted to show how my original position has echoes in the cultural attitudes to reading print and television encountered in everyday discourse, and to suggest that these everyday common-sense views are cultural constructs which gloss over many apparent contradictions and which need more careful exploration if we are to arrive at a better understanding of how we become readers.

In this book, through my review of the existing body of knowledge, and through a detailed study of the ways in which one group of children go about the business of making meaning from printed and televisual narratives, I attempt to provide what Geertz (1983) has called a 'thicker description' of the ways in which children read these two media on which more effective pedagogical principles can be built. I begin this in Chapter 2 by reviewing the different traditions that have informed our understanding of the reading process, and by summarizing existing work that has sought to explore the relationship between reading books and watching television. This review of the literature is extended in Chapter 3 as I consider the relationship between culture and language, and more particularly the role of narrative in this relationship and in the reading process. These two chapters lead to a more precise formulation of my research questions as I move from the very broad base set out above through a more systematic consideration of this base to a focus on the nature and function of narrative in the reading process.

Subsequent chapters set out and analyse the data from the fieldwork. The gradual focusing in on narrative of the first three chapters is deliberately echoed by a move from a consideration of the broad social and cultural context within which the children in the study are becoming readers of television and print through a consideration of the expectations the children bring from these contexts to the reading or viewing situation to a study of the strategies used by the children when reading specific narratives.

It is important to explain the meanings I am giving to certain terms. The words 'reading' and 'literacy' have been the subject of much debate over the years. Both carry a complex series of connotations, particularly in terms of their associations with media education. The debate about the extension of the term 'literacy' to a wider meaning of competence in one of a whole range of areas (as in such expressions as television literacy, computer literacy, and even emotional literacy) is not helpful to this study; for the sake of clarity, I shall use the term 'literacy' to refer to print literacy only. 'Reading', however, I shall use to include the interpretation of televisual and print messages, not to deny the undoubted differences between the two media, but to emphasize that both are for me active processes. Where I wish to distinguish between the interpretation of television and of print, the context will make this clear.

The everyday assumptions explored above suggest three areas in which exnomination has played a significant role in shaping the debate. Throughout, the precise role of the reader is left unconsidered, as are the exact significance and function of the text and the role of the family and wider community. These roles of reader, text and community in the reading process will act as the frames of reference as I turn to a review of the theoretical background to this topic.

Chapter 2

How Do We Read?

If everyday notions about reading and television are, as I have suggested, drawn not from some innate and obviously valid common sense but from a series of myths and cultural constructs, it becomes important to ask what we know about the reading process from the vast body of existing educational research. This chapter can in no way offer a comprehensive exploration of the existing research, but it does set out to offer a way of considering the issues by bringing together ideas from a range of traditions that address the respective roles of reader, text and community in the reading process.

The Pedagogic Tradition

The Role of the Reader

Although there have been literate English-speaking societies for hundreds of years, formal reading instruction of the majority of the population is comparatively recent; in England, for example, dating back only to the nineteenth century. As formal instruction became more widespread, however, so did the fierce methodological debates about reading that continue today.

The earliest debates took a view of learning to read as a question of memorizing certain physical features of language and using these features to decode text. Where the different protagonists disagreed was over the relative importance of recognizing words on sight ('look and say') and of using the sounds of language ('phonics'), particularly in terms of the role of the very young or beginning reader. The first major attempt to conduct an objective assessment of this debate (Chall, 1967) concluded that children who began with a systematic phonic programme had an advantage, but since this could only be shown to be the case up to third grade, and since Chall herself showed the research data available to be of variable quality, the strength of this conclusion has been called into doubt (Adams, 1990, pp. 31–41). I would argue that no attempt to provide a conclusive answer that only considered these two facets of reading could hope to succeed; more recent developments have shown how simplistic a view of the reader's role was taken by these early studies.

Chall's study, though inconclusive, extended the parameters of the debate by talking about 'code-emphasis' and 'meaning-emphasis' (Chall, 1967, p. 307). More recently cognitive psychology has challenged the views of learning inherent in Chall's position. Drawing instead on Kelly's construct theory (Bussis Chittenden, Amard and Klausner, 1985, pp. 12–20), researchers who had closely observed readers in action suggested that meaning is paramount from the beginning; their view was (and is) that the task of the reader is to extend their existing understanding of the text through constant testing of what they are reading against prior knowledge. The feedback thus provided helps to refine the mental view of the text and of reading in general. Thus children might start by making an approximate interpretation of a text and will then move gradually to a more exact identification as they draw on prior experience to make more accurate predictions.

Particularly significant here is the work of Kenneth Goodman (1969) who analysed thousands of examples of adults and children reading to draw conclusions about the crucial role of errors or miscues in helping to refine reading ability. Goodman concluded that the space to make mistakes was a key factor in the learning process, since only by making errors did learners gain the necessary feedback to refine their mental model of what reading entailed. For Goodman, the emphasis shifts from rote learning to a more creative process in which readers draw on a range of cue systems; syntactic cues (knowledge about their own language system) and semantic cues (existing knowledge of the way the world works) taking precedence in the early stages over word recognition. Goodman's undeniably significant intervention in this field has focused attention on the apparent opposition between a 'top–down' and 'bottom–up' approach. Many writers have (not entirely justifiably) criticized the apparent lack of attention given to what Goodman calls the grapho-phonic cue system (1969, p. 65). However, this is yet another area in which more recent work has suggested that this oppositional approach may be unhelpful.

Firstly, a major longitudinal study of young readers' approaches to reading (Bussis et al., 1985) challenged the existing rather over-generalized views of learning. Whilst providing a detailed description of the categories of knowledge they believed support proficient reading, the study challenged the idea that any of these categories needed to be developed before the others could be learned. Rather, they saw the task of the reader as:

> . . . the act of orchestrating diverse knowledge in order to construct meaning from text while maintaining reasonable fluency and reasonable accountability to the information contained in writing. (Bussis et al., p. 67)

The reader engaged in such an orchestration must be drawing simultaneously on visual and verbal information, and on information from the code, from the semantic understanding and from the context.

Such a view is expressed again in the most recent and most comprehensive study to date. Taking as a framework Rumelhart and McClelland's (1986) model of reading as parallel processing, Adams suggests that what the reader has to do is to draw on the mental ability to process context, meaning and orthographic and phonological information in a way that allows each 'processor' to interact freely with the others to interpret text. This moves us on considerably from the crude arguments of the earlier debate; however, neither Adams' view of the role of the reader nor those of earlier theorists can work when held in isolation from their various stances on the role of text and of environment and community.

The Role of the Text

Just as there have been different interpretations of the role of the reader, so the text is seen differently by different theorists; but here the range of perspectives is if anything slightly more complex. For many, the main emphasis is on the linguistic structure of the text and its role in inhibiting or assisting the developing reader (Schonell, 1951, p. 56; Morris, 1981, p. 23). Such experiments as Pitman's Initial Teaching Alphabet have focused on the role of the text in providing orthographic and phonological knowledge and have tried a variety of methods of altering or marking traditional orthography to make the English spelling system more accessible.

Alongside such concern about word count and repetition of common sounds there has been some slight attention to content and the need for children to enjoy the stories. A typical approach would be the view expressed by the author of *Janet and John*, where we are told that 'Neither of these factors [content quality and vocabulary control] can be sacrificed to the other' (Munro, 1954, p. 12) in a manual that devotes one page to content and fourteen pages to vocabulary control and repetition. Interestingly, many of those who have contributed most significantly to the debate on the role of the reader have also paid scant attention to the question of the role of the text, beyond criticisms of the artificial language and limited stylistic range of some reading schemes (see, for example, Goodman, 1987, p. 246) and rather generalized exhortations to use a broader range of texts including children's literature (pp. 264–5). However, others have seen other implications for the role of content of texts, and here there are some surprising bedfellows.

For the Victorians, the role of the text was to inculcate sound moral beliefs, and early primers were crammed with moral tales and improving messages. The text was seen as having great power to influence young readers. Although more recent scheme books for young readers do not on the whole emphasize their moral content, the issue of books as sources of influence is by no means forgotten. In place of the Establishment efforts to use content to control societal attitudes, there has been a steady growth of left-wing criticism of the ways in which children's books, and particularly schemes, have reinforced attitudes seen by the left as politically and ideologically untenable. Whilst this is a genuine cause for concern, and whilst the more subtle arguments expressed by some writers in this area undoubtedly extend the debate beyond the rather simplistic approach of the politically correct checklist, a view of readers as simply soaking up messages from text seems problematic whether one is deliberately putting in right- or left-wing perspectives, and is not much more helpful as a way of understanding the role of text in its interaction with the beginning reader than the earlier stress on vocabulary and syntactic control.

More significant here is the view of Paulo Freire (see, for example, Freire and Macedo, 1987). Whilst his work has been largely with adults rather than with children, his stance on content for beginning readers makes an important point about the interaction between text and reader and the necessary conditions for success. Briefly, he emphasizes the need for the text to be saying something of real value to the person trying to read it so that the beginning reader may take ownership of literacy and make it their own. Thus for the adults with whom he works in South America, whose daily lives contain much injustice and hardship, there is a need for the earliest texts encountered to offer a way of representing reality that can be recognized by the learners and which suggest that literacy might be an agent of change. This moves us from a view of text as dictating to the reader to one in which the role of the text is to interact with readers in something akin to an equal partnership.

There have been other substantial advances in this area that have considered the role of the text in a way which allows a role for the reader. Foremost among these must be Carol Fox's research into young children's oral narratives (Fox, 1993), in which she shows the ways in which stories read to young children had a direct influence on their own storytelling. Here the text takes on a new role in which it is interacting with the reader to teach lessons about the way that all texts work, about the nature of written language, and about the ways in which stories are an integral part of our lives.

Meek has built on the research of Fox and others to suggest that the text, specifically the picture book, is an important reading partner in the learning process and that the kinds of texts we give young children will influence much more than the vocabulary they learn or even their attitudes towards gender roles and the like. Meek shows how in modern children's books the illustrations teach children complex messages about the multilayered possibilities of narrative long before they could cope with these messages in written form. The use of such polysemic texts as *Rosie's Walk* (Hutchins, 1969) help children to learn just what a complex business reading can be:

> Gradually the reader learns that the narration is made up of words and pictures, together. The essential lesson of *Rosie's Walk* depends on there being no mention of the fox, but the reader knows there would be no story without him. Nowhere but in a reader's interaction with a text can this lesson be learned. It is a lesson we take with us from wherever we first learned it to our understanding of Jane Austen. (Meek, 1988, pp. 12–13)

Thus the role of the text takes on a new significance in which the crucial factor is the interaction of the reader with the text; each story encountered alters the information already in our heads, and since we as readers bring as much to the text as it brings to us, the nature of our response will reflect our individual learning styles. But there is an extra dimension to be considered in addition to this complex interaction of text and reader: the role of the community.

The Role of the Community

For those for whom learning to read is seen as involving a large degree of skill development, the crucial question to do with community is the way in which the teacher teaches. If one's view of reading suggests that a high degree of technical understanding is necessary, then trained personnel are likely to be seen as the only significant others in the beginning reader's attempts. For many years, teachers were seen as the only adults who could make a useful contribution to a child's development:

> So often faith for the future has been placed in new materials for the children. Now more than ever before we realize that the understanding and expertise of the teacher is the more important factor in gaining real success for the children. (Moyle, 1972, p. 6)

Whilst not denying the importance of the teacher, recent writers have shifted the emphasis so that the teacher's energies are channelled into different directions. Even Adams, who perhaps takes the most interventionist stance, suggests a more collaborative approach:

> Overall, the best instructional strategy for orthographic development is to induce children to focus on the likely sequences that comprise syllables, words, and frequent blends and digraphs. As the children become familiar with these spelling patterns, their ability to syllabify will naturally emerge along with the automaticity with which they will recognize the ordered spellings of single syllables. (Adams, 1990, pp. 134–5)

The role of the teacher here is to help the child to learn by guiding, rather than by teaching directly through drills and rules.

Those who, like Freire, see reading the text as inextricably tied to context, have a different outlook: for them, reading is much more a social act, both influencing and being influenced by the reading context. Freire presents two models of education; banking and *conciêntização* or conscientization (Freire, 1972). The banking model of education comes from a view of the teacher as the one with knowledge which has to be deposited in the child; this gives a passive role to the learner and also suggests that knowledge exists independently to be deposited and withdrawn. Freire argues that such a model preserves the inequalities of the status quo and demonstrates a misunderstanding of knowledge itself, which is dynamic rather than static. He argues for a process instead of conscientization in which the learner takes an active part in knowing rather than accepting transferred knowledge. This implies a shared experience between teacher and taught in which both become learners working together to explore knowledge through their experience of one another and the sharing of prior experience. A parallel can be drawn with the work of Vygotsky, who argued that we learn best when working in a collaborative situation being led by a more able co-learner (Vygotsky, 1962).

If we accept a view of learning based on Vygotskian or Freirean principles, then the role of the adult changes significantly. Rather than the only adult who can help being the highly trained specialist, anyone with even slightly more ability in reading can play a part in helping a child to learn to read. This has particular significance for the role of parents and family in reading, but it also changes the nature of classroom interaction, with more stress placed on ways of supporting the child as an active participant and of modelling the reading process, as exemplified by Liz Waterland (1988).

Parental involvement in reading has grown considerably over the last two decades. It has been shown that systematic attempts to involve parents in the reading partnership have consistently resulted in improved reading levels of the children concerned (Topping and Wolfendale, 1985, p. 5), regardless of the method of instruction involved. If home–school collaboration is so effective, it seems clear that there is a role for others in the learning situation; child and book together will be less effective than child, adult and book.

Reader, Text and Community

Although our understanding of the ways in which young children learn to read has increased considerably over the last fifty years, we still do not have sufficient information to be sure that the reading debate has an end in sight even among researchers, let alone in everyday opinion. What still remains to be seen is how far parallel processing is an adequate formulation of the relationship between information taken from the page and prior knowledge brought to bear on the print. There are also many more questions about the precise role of the text in this process — that Meek's work has raised but which remain unresolved — and others about mediating influences such as parents and in particular peers and siblings which need urgent attention. Alongside all this, Adams' conclusions that past methods of teaching sound–symbol relationships are probably not adequate raises the question of which methods will most effectively enable children to make active use of such relationships. As I turn to a consideration of literary theory, these unresolved issues act as a backdrop to the research in this area.

Perspectives from Literary Theory

In order to understand the ways in which children make sense of narratives, it is not sufficient merely to consider what we know about the pedagogical tradition. Alongside this there is a need to explore the field of literary theory to show how it can provide some answers to the question, 'How do we read?'

The Role of the Text

When considering pedagogy, the role of the reader was the first issue to be considered by researchers; in literary theory, the text has been seen as most important.

For the early literary theorists the ordinary reader was given a relatively powerless role, with the main emphasis on the correct interpretation of the author's message as explained by experts or on learning the correct cultural values. For Leavis and his followers, the text held a message that correct reading would reveal, and this message was not so directly to do with any superficial notion of plot as with the transmission through a canon of great literature (defined by Leavis) of certain (largely undefined) values and beliefs. These were not so much specific views as a general moral awareness.

For a writer to be a part of the canon, this awareness had also to be a part of their own value system. Thus Leavis justifies Austen's place in the canon by explaining that:

> She is intelligent and serious enough to be able to impersonate her moral tensions as she strives, in her art, to become more fully conscious of them and to learn what, in the interests of life, she ought to do with them. Without her intense moral preoccupation she wouldn't have been a great novelist. (Leavis, 1962, p. 7)

The purpose of reading literature was that it was perceived to have a beneficial effect on the reader's character; as Eagleton has remarked, 'it made you a better person' (Eagleton, 1983, p. 35). Nor did the growing influence of those who believed in 'close reading' or 'practical criticism' return any power to the reader. All that mattered was the text itself; no contextual or historical knowledge, no hint of the author's intentions gleaned from other sources was allowed to interfere with the search in the text for the meaning. Any associations brought to a piece of literature from prior knowledge were seen as dangerous, offering the reader the possibility of an easy way out of the interpretative struggle:

> Far more than we like to admit, we take a hint for our response from the poet's reputation. Whether we assent or dissent, the traditional view runs through our response like the wire upon which a climbing plant is trained. And without it there is no knowing at what conclusion we might not have arrived. (Richards, 1973, p. 315)

Although the reader has to take an active role here, it is very constrained; the view comes through that reading is a search for truth that needs to be hard work if it is to be successful.

This somewhat constrained position for the reader has much in common with the similarly tight approach to beginning readers held by many of those considering schooled literacy. There are clear parallels, too, in that the text was in both cases seen as relatively unproblematic. The task of the reading primer was to transmit information about the act of reading; the task of literature was seen variously as the transmission either of the cultural heritage or of the author's intentions. Although literary texts were undoubtedly held in higher regard than the primers in terms of their cultural value, both were seen as relatively transparent and straightforward, and as relatively powerful in the reader–text relationship.

While British and American critics argued about the respective importance of the work and the author, a very different approach to the role of the text was developing in Europe. The work of the Russian Formalist school and of the structuralists led to approaches in which the text and its form were central, to the exclusion of author and reader and with an emphasis away from the intentions and moral values of the work and towards an approach in which all texts were equally worthy of structural analysis.

Growing out of structuralist and formalist textual analysis are other developments in the field of literary theory which have significantly changed our understanding of the text–reader relationship. Firstly, new views of the power of the text have developed out of the fields of reception theory and semiotics:

> The implication that the ideal reader is a *tabula rasa* on which the text inscribes itself . . . makes nonsense of the whole process of literary education and conceals the conventions and norms which make possible the production of meaning. (Culler, 1981, p. 121)

As Culler stresses, we need a much more sophisticated view of the interaction between reader and text if we are to understand how we learn to read literature. At the same time, the idea that studying the form of the text alone would lead to an increased understanding of the reading process was re-examined. Those developments in literary theory which have moved us away from an overly simplistic understanding of text–reader relationships have particular relevance as we strive to understand the ways in which children learn to make sense of narrative.

Structuralist and semiotic theory led to the idea that authors of texts have to convey their desired meanings by using a set of codes that will enable a text to speak to a reader sharing these codes (see, for example, Barthes, 1990). Eco (1981, p. 7) suggests that authors do this by assuming what he calls a 'model reader'. This might sound very close to the view above of the reader passively absorbing this message, but in fact Eco argues that the text helps to create its reader, by presupposing certain competencies in the reader. These are made sufficiently explicit by the text for a reader without these competencies to be able to unconsciously infer their necessity and assume them:

> Thus it seems that a well-organized text on the one hand presupposes a model of competence coming, so to speak, from outside the text, but on the other hand works to build up, by merely textual means, such a competence. (Eco, 1981, p. 8)

This correlates closely with Meek's view that the books given to beginning readers play a crucial part in teaching them to read. Eco argues for two categories of texts which he calls open and closed. Closed texts are produced by authors who do not take account of the fact that the reader may be interpreting a text from a different background of codes than that intended. Open texts, on the other hand, are paradoxically more closed, since they assume an ideal reader rather than an average one:

> They [closed texts] can be read in various ways, each way being independent from the others . . . This cannot happen with those I call 'open' texts: they work at their peak revolutions per minute only when each interpretation is reechoed by the others, and vice versa . . . An open text, however 'open' it be, cannot afford whatever interpretation . . . It is possible to be stupid enough to read Kafka's *Trial* as a trivial criminal novel, but at this point the text collapses — it has been burned out. (Eco, 1981, pp. 9–10)

This moves us forward in terms of an understanding of the text and its role in helping the reader to read it, but it does little to redress the power balance; the text is still more powerful than the reader.

However, the text cannot act in isolation. Barthes' cultural code in particular relies on a range of knowledge gained from beyond the text. Each new text builds on all our previous experience of texts — both the texts of our lives and the previous narratives we have encountered — so that our understanding of each text is mediated and enhanced by the other stories it evokes. Intertextual messages work to alter our readings:

> 'Intertextuality' thus has a double focus. On the one hand, it calls our attention to the importance of prior texts, insisting that the autonomy of texts is a misleading notion and that a work has the meaning it does only because certain things have previously been written. Yet in so far as it focuses on intelligibility, on meaning, 'intertextuality' leads us to consider prior texts as contributions to a code which makes possible the various effects of signification. (Culler, 1981, p. 103)

So each text we read is read in the light of all our prior reading, and all our prior reading is in some way read anew in the light of the new text.

Here, the question of each text as a part of some literary canon becomes relevant. If texts presume prior knowledge of other texts in their reader, they can set up a prescriptive approach to reading, just as the need to learn certain words in order meant that beginning readers who had not read the earlier books in a reading scheme could be disenfranchised; without the correct sight vocabulary, the next book would be unreadable. Here, intertextuality could be seen as setting out a canon of accepted works which need to be read if later references are to be understood. In the case of children's literature, a clear example of this would be *Each Peach Pear Plum* (Ahlberg and Ahlberg, 1980), which assumes prior knowledge of a canon of folk and fairytales drawn from a European tradition. Unless children are familiar with these characters, the story loses much of its resonance. What needs to be considered is the extent to which intertextuality constrains readers who do not share the textual and life knowledge of the writer, and the ways in which an understood, unarticulated canon acts in comparison to more clearly articulated attitudes to required reading held in the past.

Although there remain many questions here about the precise ways in which the text acts on the reader, it seems clear that the text is not the transparent, straightforward transmission of information from the author to the reader, but that text itself is complex and polysemic, relying on interaction with the reader for the shared creation of meaning.

The Role of the Reader

As the text takes on this polysemic, intertextual appearance, so the role of the reader changes from that of someone who is relatively constrained to a more active interpretive position. Once we admit that any narrative carries a range of potential meanings, then the reader is no longer the passive decoder of the true meaning behind the words but the active selector of meaning. The problem here is to decide how the reader can balance the prior knowledge and experience they bring to bear on the text with the boundaries of the text itself so that their reading can be seen as acceptable.

Reception theorists have a view of the text as something that is only complete when read. For Iser (1974), the text had an indeterminacy which left the reader to complete the blanks to create a meaning. At a basic level, the connections to be made would be those that filled in the gaps in the plot created between chapters, or as the narrative is disrupted by a change of storyline or narrator, but this also works at a deeper level. Iser's stress on the joint roles of anticipation and retrospection has much in common with the psycholinguistic emphasis on prediction and retelling. However, whereas Goodman et al. (1987) focus almost exclusively on the task of the reader, Iser also stresses the role of the text. This text acts as a limit to the power of the reader for the reception theorists. Iser talks of an ideal reader, but this ideal can be seen as very much a product of Western European education for whom there will be little clash of codes between reader and author. This leaves the power fairly securely with the text; the reader's role is actively to construct the text, but to arrive by doing so at a correct reading.

For Fish, on the other hand, the text is much less in control; it is the reader who creates the text by reading it, and the reader will determine the meaning by this reading. The text can hardly be said to have meaning without the reader:

> A sentence is never not in a context. We are never not in a situation. A statute is never not read in the light of some purpose. A set of interpretive assumptions is always in force. A sentence that seems to need no interpretation is already the product of one. (Fish, 1980, p. 284)

Lest we should see this as a totally anarchic position, Fish claims that readers are not at liberty to interpret text in any way they choose, but that they are controlled by an interpretive community (1980, pp. 14–15), a concept to which I return below. However, the reader here is certainly more powerful than the text, which only exists once read. The question that remains is how far, if at all, readers are constrained by the text.

Scholes (1989), though unhappy with the notion that there are no textual limits to the range of possible meanings, has challenged the idea that there is ever one meaning unaffected by time or social constraints:

> In every act of reading the irreducible otherness of writer and reader is balanced and opposed by this need for recognition and understanding between the two parties. As readers we cannot ignore the intentions of writers without an act of textual violence that threatens our own existence as textual beings. But neither can we ever close the communicative gap completely — and in many cases we must acknowledge that the gap is very wide indeed. (Scholes, 1989, p. 51)

Ultimately, for Scholes, the crucial factor is that there should be a reconciliation of theory and practice so that we can continue to strive for a better understanding of the relationship between text and reader:

> If we have no Truth with a capital *T*, we must stop using the notion of such Truth — in whatever guise — to measure what we then take to be our failure to attain it. But we must not give up distinguishing between truth and lies within whatever frameworks we can construct to make such determinations. Within such frameworks, some readings are better than others and some texts are better than others, for reasons that we must keep trying to articulate. Finally, of course, we must keep on reading, keep on rewriting the texts that we read in the texts of our lives, and keep on rewriting our lives in the light of those texts. (1989, pp. 154–5)

Here there are clear echoes of the call by pedagogical theorists to allow texts to teach children about reading and to allow children to make sense of texts by drawing on their prior knowledge of life and of other reading experiences.

The Role of the Community

The role of the community has received comparatively little attention within literary theory, although the presence of a community of readers is often not far from the surface:

> . . . learning to read is an interpersonal activity: one sees how others respond, grasps intuitively or through explicit demonstration what kinds of questions and operations they deploy. (Culler, 1981, p. 124)

The main contribution here which sheds light in particular on the ways in which children might be influenced by the community as they become readers is the work by Fish mentioned above on interpretive communities, together with the various responses to this work.

It has to be said that Fish's use of this concept is problematic, largely because his own definitions are slippery. He suggests that:

> Interpretive communities are made up of those who share interpretive strategies not for reading (in the conventional sense) but for writing texts, for constituting their properties and assigning their intentions. (Fish, 1980, p. 171)

This leaves a great deal to the imagination. There is nothing here to explain whether people may belong to more than one community at once or how they come to be in a community to begin with. Nor is there any sense of how wide or narrow the community might be or of its physical limits. Later amplifications do not help very much. Fish tells us that membership is flexible and unstable:

> ... interpretive communities are no more stable than texts because interpretive strategies are not natural but learned. (1990, p. 172)

This seems to imply that it is possible to change communities, to learn new ways of interpreting; yet at other times the community is seen as deterministic, so much so that individual readers are effectively 'community property', the community having the power to 'enable and limit the operations of his [the reader's] consciousness' (Fish, 1990, p. 14). If the community exercises such thought control, how do individuals manage to break away and move beyond these limits? Nor is it clear how one may identify particular communities, other than by the evidence of shared interpretations. In other words, because we are in the same community we share an interpretation and because we share an interpretation we are in the same community. Fish himself admits that we cannot identify membership clearly:

> ... how can any one of us know whether or not he is a member of the same interpretive community as any other of us? The answer is that he can't, since any evidence brought forward to support the claim would itself be an interpretation ... The only 'proof' of membership is fellowship, the nod of recognition from someone in the same community, someone who says to you what neither of us could ever prove to a third party: 'we know'. (1990, p. 173)

Scholes sees the interpretive community as too deterministic a model and so rejects it in favour of a more individual approach:

> Where Fish sees interpretive communities remotely controlling acts of interpretation by individuals suffering from the illusion of freedom, I see individuals with many codes, some more and some less relevant, trying to see which ones will serve best in dealing with structures that have their own necessities. (Scholes, 1985, p. 162)

Whilst I would agree that, as defined so far, Fish's theory of interpretive communities is largely unworkable and in the end unhelpful, I would not reject it but would argue instead for a redefinition of community which allows for a dialectic relationship between individual members and the community as a whole. This would also allow examination of the ways in which the 'many codes' Scholes believes we are able to draw on are made available to us and the respective roles of individual and society in this process.

Active Readers in Partnership

Although here we have seen a much higher degree of attention to the reader–text relationship than was evident in most of the pedagogical debate, there are still many

questions to be answered, particularly from a perspective which seeks to understand how we *become* readers. We do not learn from this tradition how we learn to
be active readers who can use a codified and intertextual printed message to derive
a polysemic text, nor how the somewhat ill-defined notion of an interpretive community might be relevant within a classroom. Although such researchers as Fry
(1985) have stressed the crucial need for children to feel 'themselves to be part of a
community that reads' (p. 94), we still know little about the ways in which children
take on membership of what Smith (1988) has dubbed 'the literacy club'. With these
unanswered questions in mind, I turn to the third theoretical tradition which attempts
to show how we read.

Reading Media Texts

If I am to be able to compare the ways in which children make sense of narratives
from the different media of print and television, then my exploration of the question,
'How do we read?' cannot be limited to what we know about printed texts. It must
also raise the question of reading other media, in particular television, to consider
what light media research can provide.

Although this section is organized around the divisions I have used above to
consider text, reader and community, the overlaps and inconsistencies apparent in
these divisions in the earlier parts of this chapter are again evident here. This may
seem paradoxical, given that much media research has tended to concentrate on
either the reader or the text, with little consideration of any interaction:

> One tradition of work (in film cultural studies) has concentrated on the semiology
> of the text/image and the problem of textual meaning, only latterly registering the
> problematic status of the 'reader' to whom the text is addressed, and that largely
> in isolation from the social context of viewing. On the other side, the sociological/
> leisure studies perspective has concentrated (as has much of the broadcasting
> organisations' own research) on counting patterns of viewing behaviour with scant
> regard for how meanings (and thus choices) get made in this process. (Morley,
> 1986, p. 13)

However, the explorations in film cultural studies referred to here by Morley draw
heavily on traditions of literary theory and thus enter again into the overlapping
concerns of text and reader.

Just as the division of earlier research between text analysis and audience
behaviour is problematic here, so is my earlier distinction between individual
viewers and their community. The nature of the process of viewing television is
more obviously social than that of reading a printed text. It is as likely that we will
watch a television narrative with other people simultaneously as it is that we will
watch it alone. Television has a physical presence which can be seen as more
dominant and demanding than a book. If I wish to watch television, any other
person who wishes to be in the same room will be in some way influenced by my

decision; a decision to read a book would not be likely to impose the same constraints. The separation between reader and community cannot be as sharply defined here, then, as it was in my earlier considerations of the reading process, although, as will be seen in this section, little media research has addressed this adequately so far.

The Role of the Reader

Above, as I considered the ways in which children become readers and the ways in which we as adults make sense of printed texts, the notion of code was significant. The early debates in reading focused on ways of helping children to crack the physical code of written language; later arguments show how other codes of meaning also need to be a part of the process. Goodman's work showed how mistakes in decoding provide important information for the learner. Barthes' codification of narrative shows how written texts systematically help the reader to create a meaning by drawing on our understandings of semiotic and cultural systems — the codes beyond the marks on the page, the connotations created by the denoted symbols. Similarly with televisual texts there are those who argue that what the text does is to use a system of codes to provide the reader with the necessary structure to create a meaning.

There has been much research into the physical characteristics of television which can be seen as having some parallels with research into children's understanding of the sound–symbol relationships of written English discussed above. Anderson and Lorch (1983) found that certain features of television (such as women's and children's voices and laughter) would attract children back to the screen, whereas others (for instance, men's voices and solo singing) reduced attention to television output. Similarly, certain visual attributes maintained children's attention to the screen whilst others were likely to lead to a loss of attention. Their findings lead them to suggest that television texts could exploit such features if children are to read them more attentively. Although the extrapolation of generalized views about television viewing in real life from laboratory-based work must be treated with caution, there are potentially significant ideas here.

Huston and Wright (1983) focused on the formal features of television, such as auditory and visual techniques, which they analysed to assess the information provided and the ways in which children learned to use such information. Their conclusion has marked similarity with the views of those researching the acquisition of print literacy:

> Television literacy develops not only as a consequence of growing cognitive skills, linguistic competence and world knowledge, but also a consequence of learning the forms and formats that constitute the medium's critical features. (p. 65)

In other words, for Huston and Wright, reading television entails using information gleaned from the screen as well as non-visual information brought to the text. What is rendered unproblematic by this account and that of other research into form and content reported by Bryant and Anderson (1983) is the meaning itself, which is seen largely as a straightforward message to be interpreted, rather than something to be made in collaboration between text and viewer.

One important attempt to analyse televisual form and its relevance for comprehension is that of Salomon, who suggests that in order to make sense of television (and of life) we draw on a set of pre-established mental schemata which then act to help us interpret any situation by highlighting its salient features (Salomon, 1981, pp. 55–74). He argues that children bring to the televiewing experience a knowledge of the language of television and knowledge of the world (Salomon, 1983). Their stage of cognitive development will also ensure that they identify certain parts of the message as more significant than others and that they have particular ways of giving meaning to messages. However, schemata are also subject to change and can thus be altered by television itself; the structure of what is being watched also plays a part in helping children to make sense of what they see. This does not happen in a straightforward way, but rather the less well structured a text, the greater the amount of invested mental effort and the greater the comprehension. This is very similar to the psycholinguistic view of reading print argued for by Goodman.

In her argument for improved television literacy training, Dorr (1983) stresses the constructed nature of meaning, drawing heavily on Salomon's schema theory. Children's readings are seen as potentially different from those of adults, with a clear emphasis on a developmental process. Clearly this work, together with other current research on form and content, has at its centre a child who is given an active role in constructing meaning; the degree to which the child can control the text is, however, as much in debate as the relationship between adult reader and printed text discussed above.

Bryant and Anderson's summary of the research underway shows not only the wide range of work being undertaken to investigate attention and perception but by what it does not mention reveals an important absence, within this body of research, of perspectives drawn from the work being done in other areas of media theory which draws on literary theory. This in turn echoes the limitations noted above in the work of Adams and other researchers which fails sufficiently to take on the roles of text and community.

The most recent research into children and television has begun to open out the view we have of the role of the reader. Hodge and Tripp's (1986) study explores the real responses of the children they researched and attempts to describe the active nature of these children's role in making meaning from television. Although there is a strong reliance on semiotic theory and the idea of the viewer needing to decode messages to take meaning, this is set in a frame which also acknowledges the importance of the social context and the implications of this for the research context itself.

Buckingham has also shown the role of the reader as more complex and interwoven with the role of text and community. Working with a group of media teachers, he orchestrated a series of research projects which began to offer a 'thick description' (Geertz, 1983 and elsewhere) of school children and students making meaning of a range of media texts (Buckingham, 1990). He has also provided a more detailed examination of the ways in which individual children operating in complex social contexts interact with texts (Buckingham, 1993a).

These attempts to broaden out the research base to provide a more adequate understanding of the role of the reader emphasize the limitations of attempting to discuss this in isolation from the role of text and community. As I consider the various stances on the role of the text, we will see how far these too attempt to move beyond these boundaries.

The Role of the Text

Work on the role of the text in media falls into two broad areas which have had little to do with each other. On the one hand, there has been a great deal of content analysis and effects research into such questions as ideological and moral influences exerted by television. There are echoes here of the debates in Victorian times and among radicals today about the inherent dangers of certain children's books, and again these come from a variety of sources, all of which tend to see the viewer as relatively powerless and passive and which concentrate on content analysis. Early content analysis attempted to provide objective evidence about the actual incidence of certain types of content in various media; Berelson's work, for example, attempted to show the amount of time spent by Americans 'in the presence of culture' (Berelson, cited by Tunstall 1970, p. 19). More recent content analysis, however, has been more overtly political in design; for example, the work of the Glasgow University Media Group (see, for example, Glasgow University Media Group, 1976).

Developing out of content analysis came a tradition of examining the impact of exposure to media on the audience. Early work in this area tended to suggest a simplistic cause and effect mechanism, with television as a 'magic bullet'; however, work by Lazarsfeld in the 1940s (Lowery and De Fleur, 1988) in particular showed the relationship to be less straightforward than was previously imagined, stressing instead the ways in which personal contacts were more influential than media images.

The other strand of work considering the role of the text is potentially more helpful in terms of my own question. This is the work undertaken by media theorists into the role of the text which echoes the efforts of literary scholars over the past century. Direct parallels can be drawn here in the gradual development of a range of positions on the respective roles of reader and text. The limitations of the earliest work have been shown by David Bordwell, who criticizes its lack of attention to the spectator of a film as an active participant:

> The theories of filmic narration discussed in the last two chapters have little to say about the spectator, except that he or she is relatively passive . . . The passivity of the spectator in diegetic theories generally is suggested not only by the extensive

borrowing of mimetic concepts of narration but by the use of terms like the 'position' or 'place' of the subject. A film, I shall suggest, does not 'position' anybody. A film cues the spectator to execute a definable variety of operations. (Bordwell, 1988, p. 29)

Bordwell goes on to set out a view of the spectator's role which has close parallels with Goodman's view of the reading process described above. He suggests (1988, pp. 32–3) that the viewer has to use a range of cues which he divides into 'perceptual capacities', 'prior knowledge and experience' and 'the material and structure of the film itself' which he sees as actively developing the viewer's ability to read this and other films, just as Meek (1988) suggests that young children learn important lessons about reading from the texts themselves.

Allen's work on soap opera draws out an important dimension in the relationship of reader to television text (Allen, 1985, p. 73), particularly to such extended texts as soap operas, by stressing the changing nature of the prior knowledge and experience brought to bear on the text if that text itself is read over a period of time (possibly over years). Just as the viewer of a soap opera is encouraged to believe in the continuing existence of the fictional community between episodes and to fill the gaps — in Iser's term, to complete the narrative — so the temporal gaps between episodes change the viewer's stock of life knowledge as he or she grows older alongside the serial. This may be a particularly significant factor for younger viewers as they learn to read television, since their knowledge of the world is likely to be changing and growing more rapidly than that of older viewers.

Moving the debate to a discussion of the part such signifiers as camera shots and close-ups play in our overall understanding of televisual images, Fiske (1987) develops his understanding of the interacting roles of text and reader. He stresses the codes of television and the ways in which we need to be aware of the collaboration such codes facilitate:

Codes are links between producers, texts and audiences, and are the agents of intertextuality through which texts interrelate in a network of meanings that constitutes our cultural world. (1987, p. 4)

He suggests that such a complex system of codification works at three levels at least (but is ultimately too interwoven for any attempt to separate out the different strands to be successful), and that television is just one site for such a process of encoding:

The point is that 'reality' is already encoded, or rather the only way we can perceive and make sense of reality is by the codes of our culture. (Fiske, 1987, p. 4)

However, Fiske sets out certain codes that are particularly applicable to television within his framework. Taking as a starting point what he calls social codes, which would be part of our general encoding of life, he shows how these then have to be encoded at a second representational level through technical codes which transmit 'conventional representational codes' of narrative, character, setting and so on, which are then given some kind of coherence at a third level through ideological codification.

Fiske does not suggest that there is a right way of decoding the text; that, if only we apply the right formula to each code, we will arrive at the correct meaning as set out by the producer. Rather, he stresses the ways in which the encoding of television provides us with a potential to make our own meanings, which may be those anticipated by the producer or may be quite different (1987, p. 84). He sees television as essentially polysemic and ultimately unstable:

> The television text is, like all texts, the site of a struggle for meaning. The structure of the text typically tries to limit its meanings to ones that promote the dominant ideology, but the polysemy sets up forces that oppose this control. (Fiske, 1987, p. 93)

The reader draws on the various codes to arrive at a meaning. Here there are clear parallels with Barthes' analysis of the codes in written text.

There are other links with Barthes in Fiske's use of the concept of intertextuality as central for both reader and producer, providing as it does a shared potential for making sense of the new text. He defines this by drawing on Barthes' description of culture as 'a web of intertextuality' (Fiske, 1989, p. 64), seeing:

> . . . a meaning potential that exists in the spaces between texts, a cultural resource bank that texts and readers can draw from and contribute to equally but differently. (p. 65)

Despite this stress on 'equal but different', there do seem to be implications here that certain viewers may be at a distinct advantage, just as with intertextuality in print; the sum of what has been already read, or in this case seen/read, will be different for each one of us. This difference may be particularly significant for those learning to read; the unanswered (because unasked) question concerns the ways in which less experienced viewers learn to use this resource bank and how far it is possible to make sense of programmes without sufficient funds in the bank to make sense of intertextuality in texts.

Although these accounts do take on the idea of the viewer as an active participant in meaning making, most of those described so far share with much literary theory a theoretical perspective unsubstantiated through research with real readers. Some more recent investigations into reader response have attempted to set these theoretical considerations into real contexts by investigating the views and responses of viewers to particular texts.

This work also moves away from a view of the individual response to consider the role of groups and to examine the kinds of interactions that take place in group discussions of particular texts. Radway's (1987) work on women as readers of romance starts by drawing on Fish's notion of the interpretive community but the study itself focuses on the ways in which romance novels are produced, distributed and read by groups of women rather than on the ways in which meanings for the novels are negotiated within the groups. Hobson's work on *Crossroads* (1982) and Ang's investigation of the reasons why people watched *Dallas* (1985) tend to focus less on the nature of the meanings made by individuals and more on the enjoyment and involvement with the characters and narrative. Buckingham's work on *EastEnders* (1987), however, moves beyond this, combining a close textual analysis of the series with an examination of the ways in which it is mediated to viewers (see below) and with an analysis of transcripts of discussions with groups of regular viewers which reveal the different meanings given to the series by different viewers. This approach is also evident in his later work (see, for example, Buckingham, 1990; 1993a).

As indicated above, Hodge and Tripp also extend the debate in their consideration of the ways in which children make sense of television, moving us away both from theoretical debate about potential meanings to a research project investigating these and from a reliance on laboratory experiments to a closer consideration of viewing in a less artificial environment. They offer not only a detailed examination of the ways in which children deal with visual and verbal elements of television but set this in a broader context by drawing on semiotic theory and by considering the impact of the school as interpretive community. They articulate the need for a more thoughtful analysis of materials used in television research, and begin to attempt to provide this by a semiotic analysis of the cartoon film *Fangface* which they used in their experiment. This has the advantage of allowing attention both to potential meanings and to the technical production of such meanings. Their work incorporated not just an investigation into the role of the text as provider of potential meanings and the ways in which the children selected from these, but also a consideration of the other factor which has been a preoccupation within this chapter, namely, the social dimension.

In their conclusions, they acknowledge that their work was of the kind that opens up a debate rather than providing definite answers, but they do suggest that children are actively constructing their understanding in a way very reminiscent of the ways in which they learn to decode print, namely by learning through what might be called modality miscues. Alongside this notion of the reader's role as one in which meanings are created we again find a view of the text as polysemic and potentially contradictory:

> Children's television typically carries dominant ideological forms, but also a range
> of oppositional meanings. (Hodge and Tripp, 1986, p. 215)

They stress the inevitability of mediation, showing how meanings are reconstructed through social interaction, but emphasize the need for more direct involvement in this process by parents and teachers, seeing schools in particular as sites where children's opportunities for increasing their understanding of televisual texts are extremely limited, with damaging consequences. Overall, this work by Hodge and Tripp seems to move forward research into television and children in a way that draws on many of the concerns raised not just by different workers in media studies but by those engaged in the pedagogical and literary theory debates described above.

The Role of the Community

These last examples of research into the actual meanings created by readers as they strive to make sense of texts all raise the question of the viewing community, whether this is the immediate family or those present at the moment of viewing, or the interpretive community of work or school in which the viewing experiences of past and future are contextualized. I move now, then, to a consideration of audience research and what it has to tell us about the various ways in which television texts are mediated to us through the community.

The earliest work on audiences has been referred to briefly above in terms of content analysis and effects research allied to this. Although largely accepted as methodologically flawed, particularly in its failure to explore sufficiently the link between the media and the opinion leaders who were felt to influence friends and colleagues, Lazarsfeld's Decatur Study (Lowery and De Fleur, 1988) is significant in its emphasis on the role of social interaction as a key factor in people's use of the media. Radway's (1987) study, which shows how influential the woman book-seller is in the ways in which the book purchasers relate to the novels, supports Lazarsfeld's principle that there are key personalities who act as mediators of media texts. This idea has important implications for those involved in helping children to become readers, though Radway's study provides an insufficient account of the ways in which these people themselves take up this power position or how they themselves relate to texts before mediating them. More recent work has attempted to take a more explicitly social view of audiences, as Moores' (1993) study has shown.

Particularly significant in the development of a view of the role of the community in the television viewing process has been the work of David Morley, beginning with his study of audiences for the evening news programme *Nationwide* (Brunsdon and Morley, 1978) which attempted to move beyond broad cultural groupings and to take on the interpretive community of the viewer by defining different audiences' responses in terms of certain characteristics of each group. Although this and the *Family Television* project (Morley, 1986) are limited by over-simplistic divisions of audiences into homogeneous groups, they have acted as catalysts for more sophisticated attempts to explore the ways in which the viewing community acts as interpretive community. Later work (Morley, 1992) attempts a more subtle analysis of audience which starts from the home viewing situation, exploring uses of a range of information and communication technologies within the home, to show how each household went about creating and sustaining its autonomy and identity, though again the material so far published tends to set the role of the family against the role of the culture in which the family is situated, rather than taking a view in which the tension between these two is seen as a dialectic (see, for example, Morley, 1992).

This, then, is the problem for all ethnographically influenced studies of social groups; how to define the group in such a way as to maintain the identity of both group and individual and to explore the relationship between the two in a way which sees this relationship as dynamic and mutually constructed. Buckingham, suggesting that the limits of work coming from the Cultural Studies tradition are to do with the scant empirical data on audiences on which such work draws, has begun to rectify this by bringing together work (Buckingham, 1993) which attempts to show how a variety of families situate themselves and are situated as they use a range of media products. Richards considers the ways in which young girls 'use television and other media in their enactment and exploration of possible identities' (Richards, 1993, p. 25); Gillespie (1993) shows how cultural and in particular religious beliefs act both to constrain and enable one Asian family's readings of two versions of *The Mahabharata*. When such studies are set alongside work on media education which also seeks to consider the ways in which students negotiate shared meanings and learn about the reciprocity of production and consumption (Buckingham, 1990), we can begin to see a social theory of television emerging that may help us towards a deeper understanding of the need for studies of television viewing to take into account the role of the community.

The role of the community can be partly understood as one of mediation. Buckingham has suggested that mediation is a crucial part of the relationship between text and audience:

> The relationship between a text and its audience is never direct. On the contrary, it is always mediated in various ways. (1987, p. 116)

Family units are just some of the potential mediating forces; Buckingham (1987) shows clearly how other media such as the daily press and women's magazines act as mediators between the text of the soap opera *EastEnders* and those trying to read the programme (pp. 116–53). Sometimes this mediation will act to support the reader by providing extra information which can be added to Fiske's cultural resource bank. At other times, as in the case of inaccurate speculation about plot developments, the mediation acts to interfere with the smooth production of meanings by the individual reader, and even when press predictions are more accurate, they may make it harder for young readers to develop their own predicting abilities; why try to work out what might happen when one can read it in *The Sun*?

Beyond speculation about characters and actors, the media also provide mediation through secondary texts. Children's programmes in particular often have innumerable secondary texts ranging from books and comics that retell the story or tell new stories about familiar characters to products such as mugs and teeshirts which reinforce key characters or concepts by isolating and repeating them. Occasionally this does happen for a printed text, but usually only when the first secondary text has been a televised version (as in the case of *Thomas the Tank Engine*, for example, where the books had been available for many years but which, once televised, spawned a whole series of further secondary texts). These secondary texts may have a particular mediating role in terms of heightening awareness of intertextuality and thus need to be seen as a part of the community within which children learn to read television.

Bringing It All Together

In each section above considering media research, the most fruitful work has been shown to be that which looks beyond the immediate focus — whether this be on reader, text or community — to see how this is just a part of the overall viewing experience. Just as the questions that seem to need most urgent attention in the pedagogical and literary theory debates focus around this interaction, so here both the most pressing concerns and the most promising research have the same central concern.

How We Read — More Questions than Answers

Although we do have access to a vast body of research into the reading process, the questions asked so far do not necessarily address the significant issues. As a result, even those questions that are being asked are not being answered satisfactorily in terms of a wider view of the reading process. There are connections that have not been made and questions that remain unanswered. As I review the three fields I have brought together here, I can discern large areas of overlap in terms of implicit attitudes and explicit borrowing and development of theory. However, I can also see emerging certain key questions that remain unresolved and which I believe my own data, explored in the following chapters, may illuminate.

The first of these concerns the question of the interpretive community. How people become part of such communities, how adults and the contexts in which children encounter literacy and television influence children's initiation as readers, and the precise roles of those most significant members of the community seem to be key themes running through my investigations here, from Leavis's notion of the intellectual elite controlling the canon to Radway's bookseller facilitating women romance readers. We need more information about the ways in which children take on understandings of reading a whole range of media and the extent to which their social experiences shape these understandings.

Beyond this broad question about the nature and role of interpretive communities comes the question of the canon. If, as has been suggested here, the text is an active participant in the reading process, and if part of this participation comes through intertextual resonances, then the role of the canon becomes problematic. It has been argued (see, for example, Eagleton, 1983) that a canon of the kind suggested by Leavis and Eliot, in which a small academic elite determine which books are worthy of inclusion and study, is less than ideal, and I would certainly want to support such an argument. However, if we are to some extent turned into readers by the books we read, then it may be that there will inevitably be a group of books that it will be necessary to read to understand other books, or at least in order to have access to the widest range of possible meanings in other books. This could be seen as an implicit canon, which might even be more elitist than one which is clearly named and therefore challengeable. For the children in my study, who are still becoming readers of both televisual and printed texts, there perhaps needs to be some guidance and support from the interpretive community as to which texts might be enjoyable, if not as to which might be most worthwhile. It does not seem to be sufficient to challenge the values and assumptions of the traditional canon of English literature without in some way suggesting alternative and less elitist ways of introducing novice members of the literacy club to the range of texts available.

The idea of a canon, be it prescribed or spontaneously arising, points up the need to consider the respective role of text and reader in making meaning. How children learn to make meanings from a range of texts, both in terms of their ability to categorize different texts and to draw on prior experience to understand the genre and the specific text, has yet to be established in a way that will uncover the links and discontinuities between media. The specific forms of mediation that will most successfully build on children's existing competencies remain unclear. The evidence we do have (see, for example, Bussis et al., 1985) suggests, though, that there is no one answer to this; rather, individuals have different preferred ways of learning and different prior experiences to bring to bear on the text.

The three main areas highlighted above (community, text and reader) will form key elements in my own study; however, to take them in isolation and without further discussion would be unsatisfactory. It is the interaction between individual and community and between people and texts, in all its complexity, that needs to be considered, but to do this from the base so far established would omit some important dimensions. The role of the community and the ways in which children become active members of a whole range of social groups needs to be set in a broader context. In addition, the particular role of narrative as a prime mover in all this has yet to be established, and this will involve a consideration of language, thought and culture.

Chapter 3

Language, Thought, Culture and Narrative

In the last chapter, I suggested that in order to construct meaning when we read printed or televisual texts, we draw on three sources of information: the text presented to us, the prior life and literacy experiences we have brought to the text and the social context in which both text and reader are positioned. The meaning we create comes then out of the interaction between text, reader and community; but behind these lie language, thought and culture and the interactions between them, and in this chapter I want to move to explore these concepts. This chapter also provides a more precise focus on narrative, a crucial site of interaction for these concepts, and asks what we have to do to read narrative. Without language, though, there would be no narratives, printed or televisual, and so I begin by attempting to show what language is and how it influences and is influenced by thought and culture.

Language, Culture and Thought

What Is Language?

A common definition of language used by my undergraduate students is that it is a system of communication. At one level this is undoubtedly true, but it is also fundamentally unsatisfying. We do use language to communicate, but we also use it to block people out, to prevent communication. We use it to communicate not just in the sense of transmitting information within the words we use, but to share social expectations, to convey social attitudes, to build community, to maintain cultural norms or to challenge them. We use language to discover who we are and what we believe, to make connections with others who have a similar world view and to persuade others that our world view is more real than theirs. 'Communication' seems inadequate to account for all this, but what other ways of describing language might be more fruitful?

For early linguists such as Saussure, language was first and foremost a symbol system. That language is a symbol system is as obvious a truism as that it is concerned with communication, but what does that mean, and what are the specific implications of that for my study here? Saussure (1974) argued that the symbols or signifiers of language are arbitrary, with no inherent connection to the signifieds that with the signifiers go to make up each sign, but this arbitrariness can be misleading. For Saussure's attempts to examine language as a system outside of this messiness, synchrony was a useful concept; for those of us attempting to consider language as a part of our reality, it can be problematic. Although in synchronic terms the link between signifier and signified may indeed be arbitrary in almost all cases, our experience of language is not synchronic but diachronic; we encounter the concreteness of Saussure's *parole*, rather than the possibilities of *langue*, and we are a part of the complex and even messy way in which language is constantly changing and growing. In our experience of language, then, it is hardly possible to capture language outside its diachronic existence.

Volosinov (1973) has questioned Saussure's division of language into diachronic and synchronic, since the synchronic form has no real meaningful existence, being outside time. He argues that language can only be studied in a way that takes into account the 'social psychology' of the culture in which it is used. Hodge and Kress (1988) build on this critique of Saussure's work to emphasize that we use language in situations that are embedded in time and space. They suggest that there are many ways in which our choice of signifier is heavily motivated (Hodge and Kress, 1993). As we learn language as children, for example, or when we choose to use one from a range of possibilities, our choices are clearly affected by such factors as the limits of our existing vocabulary or by social convention. As diachrony has hidden the origins of particular words, our motivation in choosing words may be obscured. Where we have a choice of particular signifiers to describe signifieds, then, it may demonstrate too limited an understanding to regard choices as arbitrary simply because we are no longer aware of the word's etymology. If we consider the example of our use of words of French origin to describe animals as we eat them (pork, beef, mutton) as opposed to the use of Saxon terms for the same animals running around in fields (pig, cow, sheep) — which originated in the relationship with the signified (that is, the Normans ate them while the Saxons tended them) — we can see that this usage cannot be seen as entirely arbitrary. What may seem to be a neutral and arbitrary system when studied as *langue* becomes highly motivated and culturally specific as *parole*. If, then, we wish to understand the relationship between language and culture, the study of language as a formal symbol system will not be sufficient.

This symbol system which we call language, then, is not separate from our culture but is a part of it. Neither can it be seen as entirely separate from thought, since running through all our encounters with language is a search for meaning. No sooner does a linguist come up with an example of a syntactically correct but meaningless sentence (such as Chomsky's 'colourless green ideas sleep furiously') than someone comes along behind to attempt to produce some possible if obscure interpretation. Those expressions deemed phatic by linguists not only carry a social meaning (so that we can interpret the hesitations of everyday speech as meaning 'I wish to keep speaking although I am still trying to think what to say next') but also are often credited with a more precise meaning, so that social greetings such as 'How are you?' are interpreted more frequently than most questioners desire as a genuine request for a detailed account of the responder's physical, mental and emotional health. But language cannot be seen as a mere psychological tool. As we strive to create meaning out of the utterances which we hear, or as we attempt to use language to share a desired meaning with others, we are operating in a real context that will also act on the interpretative act. We tend to read into any situation the meaning we are expecting to find there, and these expectations come from our social understanding of the world. Nor are we simply interpreting in a fixed context; the context itself is at the same time being created and defined by our intervention.

Culture and Reality

This brings into question the nature of reality and of the social context, and the extent to which culture and context can be seen as interchangeable terms. Just as common sense is a cultural construction, so reality is something which cannot be seen to have an objective existence that is completely unaffected by our interpretation of it. This is not to suggest that nothing exists outside language and interpretation; whilst I am happy to believe the quantum physicists when they suggest that our previous understanding of the laws of science has led to a too mechanistic understanding of the ways in which the world works, I would not argue that the table upon which my word-processor is resting whilst I type this chapter is only there because I have a view of reality which believes in its existence as a table. I assume that it will go on acting as a table regardless of my personal beliefs in the matter and regardless of my consciousness of its physical properties, and that there are some scientific principles that could objectively describe this phenomenon. Even in this example, however, I am conscious of the ways in which I am still reliant on my personal belief system to suggest a particular view of reality; when the reality being considered moves from the physical environment to social reality, it becomes still harder to separate the people in any context and the definition of that context. At the opposite end of my personal understanding of reality I know that I hold certain beliefs that cannot be objectively proved and which are not universal; even those who apparently share these beliefs may actually have a very different view of the assumed reality behind them.

Somewhere between my certainty in the objective reality that a solid and sufficiently strong horizontal object will support my computer and my much more subjective beliefs comes the greater part of my life experience in which I take as objective aspects of reality that I know are not what they seem. For example, I take as a working principle the reality of the value of our currency whilst at the same time holding at the back of my mind a suspicion that I would not really be able to take up the Chief Cashier of the Bank of England on his promise to pay me the value of a £5 note in gold. It is in this middle ground that culture has a role to play in creating some kind of shared context and understanding. For me, culture is much broader than some kind of aesthetic aspect of our lives. It is the shared reality we construct through our social encounters and which then acts as a medium through which we interpret these encounters. Our culture is not just the art forms and expressive aspects in our lives; it is every part of our daily interaction with other members of our society, from the choices we make about what to wear and have for breakfast, to the ways we behave with colleagues at work and with family and friends. As Geertz (1973) suggests, it is everything that makes us as humans different from other animals. In other words, I am taking an anthropological view of culture as the set of systems and patterns that distinguish any particular group of human beings and their way of life — 'whatever one has to know or believe in order to operate in a manner acceptable to [a society's] members' (Goodenough, cited in Bauman, 1973). This leads to a view of any culture as organic and flexible, in a dialectic relationship with the groups and individuals within it and thus with the language used by the members of the culture. This dialectic relationship will also lead to tensions between different cultural groups as they work out power relationships (Williams, 1958 and elsewhere; Freire 1972 and elsewhere).

Language and Thought

So far I have suggested there is an active relationship between language and culture in which each influences the other, but what of thought? Vygotsky (1962) has argued that it is not sufficient to see language either as a product of thought or as the origin of thought, but he has also hypothesized a clear and powerful relationship between the two. That thought has a separate existence which is not always directly dependent on language can be seen by Bruner's categorization of representation into enactive, ikonic and symbolic (Bruner, Oliver and Greenfield, 1966). The enactive category is used to describe those mental processes so deeply embedded in our consciousness that they seem automatic, such as changing gear for the experienced driver. However, since such thought processes have to be learned and since most are learned in a situation in which someone else is acting as instructor, language may well have played an indirect part in the establishment of such enactive thought patterns. In Bruner's category of the ikonic, a simple signifier acts to represent a single signified, such as the mental image of 'banana' or 'football match'. We may have a visual image of an ikon in our minds, or we may call to mind a sound or even a feeling or smell which represents the signified. Here, Bruner suggests a simple one-to-one correspondence between the ikon and the object, but in reality even ikonic thought would seem to involve cultural knowledge. Even bananas are not simply denotative but bring many connotations with them that trigger other images specific to one's culture and prior experience. In the case of such ikons as the face of a well-known public figure or the theme tune to a particular television series, these connotative meanings are potentially even more complex. Thus culture and thought seem inextricably linked in ikonic representation, but ikons will very often sit alongside knowledge of the verbal signifier. For almost all children, for example, ikonic thought will have been developed in an environment in which language is interwoven with everyday experience. Thus although Bruner's argument that there are ways of thinking which are less directly tied to language than symbolic thought (or in Vygotsky's terms, verbal thought) is to some extent convincing, it is also possible to see the difficulty of ever isolating our own experience from the language that has been associated with it, whether or not we see that language as having a role in shaping the experience.

What is important about Bruner's framework, though, is not so much the indirect ways in which language and culture may act on enactive and ikonic thought, but the way in which symbolic thought is totally dependent on its interaction with language, and thus with culture, for its development. Vygotsky (1962) has shown how we take on the ability to conceptualize as we grow up, and how we gradually develop verbal thought and inner speech as thought and language come together. When I invite students to attempt to sort out concept blocks by the use of nonsense syllables, as Vygotsky did in his own experiments, these mature adults rapidly look for some meaning in the apparently random signifiers, and they do this not only in terms of the cognitive but the cultural; they speculate as to what my intentions might be ('She wouldn't do that because it would be too easy', for example) in a way that draws directly on their cultural experience as students in my tutor group.

Language, Thought and Culture

All this supposes a link between language and thought that is embedded in culture. Volosinov (1973) contended that language is an inevitable part of culture, given its role as meaning-maker and its particular symbolic force, which by seeing language as being about meaning and symbol emphasizes this three-way dialectical relationship. Vygotsky (1962) argued for a model in which both language and thought exist independently of each other in the earliest stages of development but in which the greatest intellectual achievements rely on the interaction of thought and language to produce verbal thought and inner speech. However, he also argued that this interaction cannot be seen as narrowly confined in some individualist model of personal development but that what facilitates this development both ontogenetically and philogenetically is the location of mind in society. Through this, interaction language, thought and culture are inextricably connected and acting on each other so that we are shaped by our culture as we learn but also using our learning and language to reshape and redefine that same culture:

> ... [Vygotsky] gives language both a cultural past and a generative present, and assigns it a role as the nurse and tutor of thought ... And Vygotsky turns the cultural past into the generative present by which we reach toward the future: growth is reaching. (Bruner, 1986, p. 145)

Bruner has argued for a realignment of psychology that takes on the role of culture, drawing not just on Vygotsky but also on Geertz and the anthropological tradition to suggest that culture plays a key part in learning. Bruner cites Geertz's comparison between acting in a particular culture and interpreting a text (Bruner, 1986, p. 66) and this image has particular resonance as I argue for a model of reading which places every reading act in culture.

So far I have suggested ways in which language and thought are influenced by each other and by culture in a way that might suggest that culture determines language and thought. A crude Marxist interpretation would argue even more strongly for culture as a shaping force, seeing culture as the meaning-making force behind the social structure. This determinist view has echoes in the work of Sapir and Whorf, who between them developed the hypothesis that the language we speak determines our view of the world, within which they would combine culture and thought (Sapir, 1949; Whorf, 1956). However, it would be dangerous to see this as a simplistic one-way relationship, since Sapir also argued that every culture produces the language used within it, so that we have a dialectical relationship between language, thought and reality. Researchers developing this ethnolinguistic tradition have argued for the so-called weak form of the Sapir-Whorf hypothesis, namely that our view of the world is influenced rather than determined by the language we speak (see, for example, Mathiot, 1979), but since this form allows for this dialectical interaction between individual and society at the heart of Vygotsky's arguments, 'weak' seems a misnomer.

The ways in which culture, language and thought interact with each other would suggest that far from this being a straightforward relationship in which any one of the three can be seen to determine the development of the others, there is a much more complex and interdependent relationship in which each is influenced by and influences the other. Thus a child learning language does so in a cultural setting in which the language being learnt has already been shaped by the culture. As the child grows, the ways in which s/he and others use language for their own purposes will lead to a further change in the language. This in turn will have the potential to influence the culture. Similarly, as the child takes on symbolic thought, both the individual's thought processes and language uses will be affected by each other. The ways in which the child thinks of certain concepts will depend, too, not only on the language used to describe and define them but on that child's experiences of the concept in everyday life.

An example of all this would be the current move to use what has become known as 'politically correct' language. A child born as I was in the middle of this century would have been born into a world where in the English language the use of 'man' as a generic term was seen as unproblematic and generally accepted. As I grew up as a woman in society, I came into contact with feminist writings which argued that far from being acceptable, the generic use of 'man' was problematic in that it suggested a world where to be male was the norm and to be female was in some way less normal. I was able to set these arguments alongside my own experience and to change not just my beliefs but my own use of language to accommodate my acceptance of this view. However, whilst I may have done this, others may have either encountered these ideas and rejected them for a range of reasons or taken on the changes for more cynical reasons.

Here I would argue we can see that the cultural norms into which I was born, whilst shaping my early experience, have not constrained me from changing my stance and challenging those same norms. Nor has the language I was brought up to use determined my world view to the point where this can over-rule my own experience of being female. Both language and culture have influenced my thinking but I have also been able to reconsider my position and to change my thought. Similarly, though, my own experience cannot determine the culture or the language but it can influence both, as I and many others attempt to make more people reconsider the ways in which women are regarded in our society and the ways in which they are represented in our language. Even in my lifetime there are discernible, if small, changes in the cultural view of women and the uses of language. To give but one small example in terms of language use, it is now rare to find an official form which does not allow me the opportunity to put my title as Ms rather than Mrs or Miss, even though in practice many people still find this new form difficult to accept.

Some might suggest that such an example is loaded, in that it concerns an area of active intervention in culture and a self-conscious political relationship to language that could be seen as very different from everyday uses. However, I would argue that these examples are only different in that the change has been relatively rapid and visual and has come out of a contested area of social experience. In other words, they represent what is happening on a much smaller and more gradual scale with other aspects of language use but they are more apparent because they occur in this contested area and so we are explicitly aware of the change in our culture where other changes are less visible but still inevitable. Once we admit that language usage does change over time, then we have to acknowledge that the changes are brought about by action on the part of language users — a language in itself has no power to change organically without the intervention of those speaking and writing that language. The causes of change are sometimes due to less deliberate interventions, but they remain interventions even if accidental or based on misunderstanding rather than on political thought. In this way the visible and more rapid changes can give us insight into more general sites of intersection between language, thought and culture even while we remember the ways in which such visible changes are less typical.

These examples also emphasize the difference between official or generally accepted ideological stances and the positions of other groups or individuals within society. Culture is not homogeneous even within language groups or nationalities. Subcultures also use language as a defining tool, so that membership of the group may be confirmed or rejected on the basis of language use, whether this is in terms of Mitford's 'U' and 'Non-U' attempts to define social superiority or membership of more radical or subversive groups. Halliday (1979) has described how we use what he calls 'antilanguage' to separate ourselves into exclusive groups as well as using it to build bridges at other times. To recall Goodenough's definition of culture, what we need to know in terms of our membership of a subculture will be the particular language usages acceptable in that group as opposed to more general usage in the wider culture. At the same time our membership of the group confers on us the ability to influence the language usage by bringing our own idiolect into the group's language experience. Again a dialectical relationship can be seen, and this has wider implications than the purely linguistic, as Hewitt's study (1986) of interaction between London school students of different ethnic origins has shown.

So far I have argued that there is a complex interrelation between language, thought and culture. Not only can we trace dialectical relationships between language and thought, language and culture and thought and culture, but the effect of these three overlapping pairs is to produce an even more complex three-way relationship. To study any one of the three without looking at this interaction would lead only to a limited understanding. Were I to consider children's understandings and utterances without placing these in a cultural context I would be missing a vital aspect of their development. By identifying an area that can be seen as a specific site of intersection of language, thought and culture, I hope to hold this complex relationship together and thus to provide a more meaningful study of children's understandings. Narrative would appear to be just such a site of intersection.

The Crucial Role of Narrative

Narrative, as it brings together our use of language to create and contain meaning and to transmit and reshape culture, is particularly powerful both generally in children's development and specifically with regard to the ways in which we learn to make sense of print and television. Moreover, narrative's role can only be fully understood if we take a social view of narrative, so I shall attempt to consider what such a view might look like.

What is Narrative?

To do this, however, I need to start by considering what I would class as a narrative (and what I would see as non-narrative). I would suggest that any telling of events involving characters in one or more locations could be seen as a narrative. These events may or may not have happened; that is, we can have fictional narratives or ones that draw on real life. Even in those narratives that draw on actual events and people, there will be a greater or lesser distance between the told version and the original experience or person, but there is no requirement that a narrative must be completely created by the teller. The distinction drawn in public libraries between fiction and non-fiction does not result in a division of narrative and non-narrative texts. Fiction could, for example, also include non-narrative texts (lyric poetry or imaginary descriptions). Non-fiction relies heavily on narrative, particularly in the case of biographies, travel books and histories, and many other books not mainly written in a narrative discourse (such as instructional texts or arguments) will also make use of narrative at certain points. Similarly television programmes such as documentaries or news programmes, whilst generally seen as non-fiction, frequently involve narrative, and fictional programmes may involve non-narrative discourse, though this is less common and may involve some implicit narrative (for example, comedy shows that invent parodies of quiz shows or the weather forecast could actually be said to be telling the story of why such parodies are funny). Narrative and fiction, then, are not synonymous terms, and although the specific narratives used in my own research were all fictional, this was not a deciding factor in their choice.

If narrative and non-narrative cannot be aligned neatly with fiction and non-fiction respectively, we know more about what these terms do not imply but not much more about what they do imply. Identifying the constituent parts of a narrative may help to provide a more precise understanding, and as narratology has developed over the past century a plethora of terminology and definitions has arisen from the different schools. Many of these offer descriptions of the constituent elements of a narrative which are not mutually interchangeable. Although some rough parallels can be drawn between, for example, the Russian formalists' use of *fabula* and *sjuzhet*, Genette's *histoire, recit* and *narration* (Genette, 1980) and Rosen's story, narrative discourse and narrating (Rosen, n/d) as ways of dividing what has to be told from the manner of telling, each theoretical frame has its own different emphases so that the terms cannot be seen as mutually interchangeable. The term narrative is used in equally confusing ways. For some it is a kind of discourse and thus separate from the events being told; for others it acts as an overarching term bringing story and discourse together, as in Genette's *narration*. What is true, though, as Culler points out, is that for each school of thought 'there is always a basic distinction between a sequence of events and a discourse that orders and presents events' (1981, p. 70).

I need to be able to distinguish the difference that Culler has shown to be always necessary in narratology between the telling and the told, and so for my purposes I propose to follow Culler and refer to the told as story and the way of telling as discourse. (The term discourse has its own difficulties, of course, being used in a very broad sense by Foucault and a much narrower one by, for example, Culler.) Having said, then, that for me narrative consists of story and discourse, to arrive at a better understanding of the overarching term, each component part needs more consideration.

Story in some way implies more than a series of events. The events need in some way to impinge on each other through the actions of the characters, and so the characters too are a crucial element of story. Todorov talks of story in terms of the disruption and restoration of equilibrium (Culler, 1975), and this brings in the dimension of time. A story takes place within a certain time, whether this is a few minutes for the simplest story, such as 'The baby cried. The mommy picked it up,' (Sachs in Rosen, n/d) or over years for the more complex, such as *War and Peace*. There is always, though, the sense of a time beyond — a time before the story begins, and a time after it ends.

Stories are not all alike in complexity. At a minimal level, the example above consists of two actants, the baby and the mother, and two events, the crying which disrupts the equilibrium and the picking up of the child which seeks to restore it. (The setting here is not revealed although we can still assume that this happened in a particular place, be it real or fictive.) Most stories have many more events and they may be made up of a series of disruptions and resolutions, as in the case of episodic fiction such as *The Odyssey*, though all these minor disruptions are usually working towards the resolution of the major problem, in this case the return of Odysseus to his own kingdom.

In some extreme cases, the story may lie so far behind the discourse that we almost have to invent it for ourselves, as in the work of Robbe-Grillet, but such anti-narrative can only work by breaking the rules of narrative: as Culler stresses, such work relies on 'the assumption that narrative presents a series of events' (1981, p. 172). As it is, our experience of story either leads us to fill in what are admittedly bigger gaps than usual to supply a story which is at least personally satisfying or leads us to reject such work. Even here, we will (if we make the effort as readers) consider time, events, setting and character in creating the story.

For there to be a narrative, then, there must be a story, however far behind the discourse it is hidden. Ultimately what turns a series of events into a narrative is a process of selecting, ordering and recounting. The way the story is told will have an impact on each aspect of story considered above. The teller has control of the amount of information presented and the way it is presented. To take just one example, events can be reordered so that we begin at a later time looking back (*Wuthering Heights, The Wonder Years*). The time in which they are told will not necessarily be the time they took to happen; events can be condensed or expanded so that the telling is quicker or longer than the events themselves. Books and television have different methods at their disposal for this; a book may use a simple phrase such as 'Three years later' or a series of spaced out diary entries, whereas a television programme may use a subheading with the same information, a series of montages of stills or short clips, a calendar turning to suggest time passing, voice-over or other technical effects.

When the discourse and story come together, then we have a narrative; if for some reason the two elements do not come together, then we do not. This may help to provide a fuller answer to the question, 'What is narrative?' and its counterpart 'And what is not narrative?' For printed texts, there is a continuum from what is obviously narrative to what is not, with novels and short stories clearly at one end with both story and a narrative approach to discourse and telephone directories at the other with characters but no events or attempt at telling. For television, I would suggest that there are again some programmes (soap operas, dramas, detective stories) that are clearly at the narrative end of the continuum, but it is harder to place any programmes at the other end. The weather forecast is usually more of an account or description than a story, though at times of unusual climatic conditions (such as the great storm of 1987 in Britain) or where the forecast is embedded in another pro-gramme such as the local news shows, this distinction becomes less clearcut; some quiz shows, such as *Fifteen-to-One* or *Mastermind*, include very little beyond the asking and answering of questions and so would seem not to be narrative. In between these extremes in either medium the picture is less clear, with many texts including at least some narrative in the process of exposition, argument and instruction.

Fox has shown that young children telling stories draw on other discourses as appropriate, such as weather forecasts and reasoned argument, and embed these in their narratives. She suggests that maybe the hard and fast lines some might draw between discourses are less than helpful (Fox, 1989). Rosen has argued that in this middle ground we need to know more about the role of storytelling:

> There are stories wherever we turn. How do we understand foetal development
> except as a fundamental story in which sperm and ovum triumph at the denouement

of parturition? Every chemical reaction is a story compressed into the straitjacket of an equation . . . There are two sober questions we might well ask.

(i)   To what extent do scientists (amongst others) come to understand the principles and processes of their particular science through coming to master its particular set of current stories?

(ii)   To go further still, to what extent have the discoveries of science been made possible by the innovator constructing a plausible story?(Rosen, n/d, p. 16)

Bruner's claim that there are two modes of thought — the narrative and the paradigmatic or logico-scientific — concedes that story may be a step along the way to paradigmatic thought but argues that there is a distinction between the two:

[The narrative mode] deals in human or human-like intention and action and the vicissitudes and consequences that mark their course. It strives to put its timeless miracles into the particulars of experience, and to locate the experience in time and place. Joyce thought of the particularities of the story as epiphanies of the ordinary. The paradigmatic mode, by contrast, seeks to transcend the particular by higher and higher reaching for abstraction, and in the end disclaims in principle any explanatory value at all where the particular is concerned . . . Scientists, perhaps because they rely on familiar stories to fill the gaps of their knowledge, have a harder time in practice. But their salvation is to wash the stories away when causes can be substituted for them. (Bruner, 1986, p. 13)

Behind every scientific principle or cause, then, there may be a story waiting to be told. Perhaps the difference between narrative and non-narrative is nearer to that between narrative and the anti-narrative of Robbe-Grillet, referred to earlier; in non-narrative, the story may be implicit or hidden rather than explicit, the events and people submerged behind the abstraction. I will argue later in this chapter that in part the problems in definition stem from the way in which current theories of narrative are framed, and that it is only when a better social theory of narrative has been developed that we will begin to have a more satisfactory understanding of narrative as a concept. What is clear is that distinguishing between narrative and non-narrative is not an easy matter, and that each mode will in any case draw on the other as appropriate. What is also clear from these accounts is that however it is defined, narrative is an important feature in human lives, and I turn now to consider why this is so.

Why Narrative?

The *histoire* is the what
and the *discours* is the how
but what I want to know, Brigham,
is *le pourquoi.*
Why are we sitting here around the campfire?
(Le Guin, 1981, p. 188)

Particularly in terms of understanding narrative as a site of intersection of culture, language and thought, the 'why' of narrative seems fundamental. What is it that drives every society to tell stories?

In cultural terms, narratives have a part to play both in preserving and challenging the culture. The narratives told to the children of a culture explain the past, define the ways in which the culture is separate and unique and encourage the maintenance of the culture; the tales told by sub-cultures may challenge the mainstream values and support dissidence, but still they play a role in cultural transmission. This can be seen in the use of narrative to reinforce and extend knowledge of a group's history. For example, the *seder* meal eaten by Jewish families at Pesach is framed in a ritual retelling of the Exodus story. As Christians rediscover the Jewish origins of their faith, so this tradition has been woven into their commemoration of the Last Supper, linking this back to Pesach and thus to the Exodus. Thus narrative both maintains and reshapes cultural patterns.

This use of stories also happens on a smaller scale within families, where the sense of what it means to be a part of any family is shaped by the recollections that are handed down. Rosen describes the black trunk in which his mother stored all the family memorabilia, and the ways in which the stories of the contents were handed on to him and his sister:

> Every photo, every document, every object was inspected and for each one there was its proper story. There were relatives in Durban and Johannesburg, in Rochester and Philadelphia, in Strasbourg, and in Warsaw and Vienna. How did uncles, aunts, cousins, two brothers and a father come to be scattered over the face of the earth? Why were some of the men in uniform wearing the uniform of the wrong side? . . . Who married whom? Whose children were they? Who died young and how? Who lived in that house? What happened, what happened, what happened? A story for every item. We knew when she would cry and when she would laugh. We sat for hours and discovered who we were, the way of our world, motives, values, beginnings, endings, a kind of cohesion, sufficient stability in our terrifyingly unstable world. (Rosen, n/d, p. 8)

Narrative, then, is needed here to act as a way of transmitting and of adapting culture both on a societal scale and within the family. Here, there seems to be a clear link between language and culture in narrative, but what of thought?

As well as arguing that language and thought are mutually influencing and that such interaction can only be understood in culture, Vygotsky explored the ways in which actions aided children as they learned to separate objects for their meaning, and the role of play in such development. He argued that children learned in play to let one object represent another (a stick standing for a horse) just as they learned at the same time that a word could represent an object (Vygotsky, 1978). The child in play develops mental ability through the interaction of object and meaning. But we can draw a very close parallel between imaginative play and narrative, as Meek (1982) has shown. A narrative can be seen as play in the head, with words taking the place of objects in freeing our thinking to act beyond the here and now. This would suggest that storying has a large part to play in the development of thought, enabling us to move to abstraction. This argument has been supported by the empirical evidence of the Bristol Language Project (Wells, 1987), which found that those children who at the age of seven were most competent at subjects involving the use of symbolic thought were those who had the richest diet of stories read and told to them before starting school. This use of narrative as a step towards other forms of abstract thought echoes Bruner's arguments about story as a way to paradigmatic thought in scientists and could be seen to argue for a role for narrative not just in the developing thought processes of children but also more generally.

Narrative is thus bound up with culture and thought, and since most narratives in our culture are transmitted in language, this too can be seen to have a part to play. What I want to argue now, though, is that narrative is not just a site of intersection of language with culture and thought separately but that the interaction goes much deeper. Le Guin (1981) records the ways in which survivors of the concentration camps felt an existential need to survive to tell their stories; their whole awareness of who they were depended on their being able to share their experience. Such an existential need to tell and listen to stories goes beyond mere cultural transmission and suggests that yet again this is an area in which the way we make sense of the world is linked in a complex relationship with the social setting in which we live.

Not only do we use narrative to make our presence known to the world, but also to define ourselves to ourselves. Hardy has described narrative as a primary act of mind, which shapes our whole existence:

> For we dream in narrative, daydream in narrative, remember, anticipate, hope, despair, believe, doubt, plan, revise, criticize, construct, gossip, learn, hate and love by narrative. In order to live, we make up stories about ourselves and others, about the personal as well as the social past and future. (Hardy, 1977, p. 13)

In this interplay between the definition of self and of that self as a part of society are the seeds of the social theory of narrative for which I shall argue below. It has been argued (Sampson, 1989) that our Western concept of self as something created distinct from society is flawed, and needs to be replaced by an understanding of self as a social construct, in which we gradually create our own identity through our recognition of the difference and similarity between us and others. If this is so, then narrative, as a site of intersection between culture, thought and language, offers an important locus for the necessary interpenetration described above. As we tell each other stories, particularly stories drawn from our own life experience, we are defining ourselves to ourselves as well as to society and defining society to ourselves at the same time.

An example may help to explain this. We have a friend who is a garage mechanic in South London; my husband and I met him when we were all members of the same motorcycle club. He still enjoys riding his motorcycles on Rockers Reunion runs or at the Chelsea Cruise and listening to music from the 1950s and finds that this brings him in contact with a group of people who share his interests but not his life values. Every few months, he comes to see us and spends several hours telling us anecdotes about the lifestyles of the people he has met (most of whom we do not know) as though to check with us that we too find what he has to tell us outrageous or unacceptable. By doing this, I would argue that he is also defining his own values to himself; by telling us the stories he can confirm to himself that he does not fully identify with the group, and by our distance from the actual events and people he can also separate himself from us so that he feels clearer as to his own selfhood. He is both telling us who he is and telling himself at the same time.

This existential need for narrative as a way of defining ourselves and the world around us crystallizes the interaction between culture, thought and language that takes place when we tell stories. However, although the need to tell and be told stories appears to be existential and universal, that is not to deny the role of society in this telling. It is in our interactions with society that we can use story to create a clearer personal world view; it follows from this that the society or culture within which we tell and listen to the stories will influence the way of telling. Studies of storytelling in different cultures have shown that this is indeed the case. For example, when English-speaking students from California and Greek students from Athens were asked to retell a story they had been shown in a film about some stolen pears, there were clear cultural differences (Tannen, 1980); with the Greeks, for example, more were concerned to appear as good storytellers and with the Americans more were concerned to be accurate. Shirley Brice Heath's study discovered even in two small neighbouring communities widely divergent views of the value and role of storytelling (Heath, 1983).

Narrative, then, has a central role in our lives, but the shape of that role and the stories and ways of telling that will predominate will be influenced by our cultural and social context. Thus narrative is significant not just as a site for the interaction of language, culture and thought but as the means whereby this inter-section leads to our development as thinking individual members of society. If this is the case, then it is time to consider how best to explore the ways in which children might make sense of narratives in two media. To do this, before considering how we might read narrative, I need to pull together the various strands of argument above to suggest ways forward to construct a social theory of narrative that can frame my own research.

Narrative as a Social Act

If we work out through story who we are, and if we are not individual but social selves, then we need a theory of narrative as a social act to explain what is going on in this process, and that theory will need to be attuned to cultural difference rather than assuming an autonomous and universal model. Such a model will need to take into account those aspects of the reading process identified in the last chapter (reader, text and community) and to consider these in the particular experience of reading and telling narratives.

In terms of text, what will be needed is a model for considering texts which goes beyond structuralist analyses of textual patterns and features to consider which texts are the ones that any community of readers values and shares and which inter-textual patterns are most frequently resorted to both in telling and in retelling. Ultimately, if the way we consider texts is to help us understand their significance for those who read and produce them, we may need to identify from the community's own uses of narrative a canon of texts which that community tacitly or explicitly agrees have particular significance.

Consumers and producers of narrative will need to be considered in a way that examines the broad view taken of reading and narrative within the cultural group, so that individuals are considered neither in isolation nor as passively manipulated by societal forces but as active members of a community of readers with the power to influence and be influenced by the group. The expectations of narrative set up by individuals in this social context would act as a bridge between this broad cultural context and the particular situation of any specific encounter with narrative. Embedded in this view of readers as socially constructed individuals would need to be the view of text set out above, so that reader, text and community are brought together in a cohesive framework which considers all aspects of the reading process.

Much work has already been done in a wide range of traditions that would build into such a framework, in addition to that which has been considered above. Rosen has shown how in the specialized field of autobiographical narrative, the disciplines of literary theory, ethnography, psychology and cultural history are all exploring the role of narrative, though without researchers in each necessarily knowing what is being done in other disciplines:

> It's as though there is a treasure hoard stored in a huge chamber and those who would inspect it, analyse it and reveal its secrets enter the chamber by different doors. Those coming through one door are so intent on their business, they don't even notice others entering by other doors. (Rosen, 1994, p. 11)

This metaphor can be extended equally well to describe past work in the more general area of narrative; what is needed now is not a social theory that ignores all those coming through the different doors of structuralism, formalism, deconstruction, cultural studies and anthropology (not to mention such other doors as the theology of narrative) but one which draws on different disciplines to work towards a theory of narrative as a social act.

What Do We Have to Do to Read Narrative?

My research attempts to offer evidence which could be used to begin to construct such a theory. Before turning to my findings, though, it is important to add one last stage to this consideration of narrative. The last chapter asked how we read. Having shown how narrative acts as a site of intersection for culture, language and thought, I now ask how the concerns of each chapter come together by exploring some of the ways in which we have to behave to read narratives.

In suggesting strategies we use when reading narratives, I do not intend at this point to distinguish between media. This is not to deny that different media also require particular competencies which are not directly parallel. For example, at a fundamental level, if I wish to read a printed narrative alone I will need to be able to make sense of the print, and to know which direction this printed text runs in. If I wish to watch television, I will need to understand not just how to switch on but that the images are divided into programmes which are themselves subdivided into scenes, that when the camera focuses on something it is probably significant, that certain technical effects imply a dream or flashback and so on. The aim of this book, though, is not to explore these technical differences in a discussion of the kind already undertaken by Seymour Chatman and others (see, for example, Chatman, 1978), nor to pretend that there are no differences between the two media. I want to explore children's encounters with each of two media which offer many experiences of narrative, to see whether the broad strategies the children use in these encounters remain the same when the medium is different.

So how do we read narrative? Firstly, story, like play, involves moving beyond the here and now to act as if we were somewhere else. Britton draws our attention to Winnicott's description of play as taking place in a third area beyond both our experience of our own inner reality and the external realities of the rest of the world, and suggests that it is also in this third area that we read fiction (Britton, 1977). We have to suspend our disbelief and accept that what is happening on the page or screen is real and present, whilst at the same time acknowledging that it is not. We have to want to make this happen, which is why Coleridge talks of the 'willing suspension of disbelief'. In the case of written narratives, the pleasure we derive from the narrative which allows us to do this may not be immediately apparent, especially as we learn to read:

> The decision to read is rather closer to any decision which puts the self at risk — a first dive, for example, or a musical solo — but, unlike these, it leads to no more direct involvement with the world, no externally sanctioned release. What is new, then, is that the apprentice reader has to decide to withdraw attention from the external world (including the book as object) *and* from his own internal world as a preliminary to an experience which is unpredictable . . . The reader must agree to a surrender before fighting the battle. (Craig, 1976, pp. 17–18)

Although Craig argues that reading a book privately is different from seeing a play or being read to in that there are no intermediaries when reading silently, in the essentials our initial experience of many narratives in a whole range of media involves this surrender. Whether we sit down to watch a film or television programme, or go to the theatre, or listen to a story on the radio, we begin by moving into this same third area where we are prepared to let go of our everyday judgments and of the world around us but where we retain an initial uneasiness as we wait to become fully engaged with the narrative. Nor does this initial surrender lead to a later position where there is total control by the reader; when we read narrative, Barthes suggests, we need also to surrender to the pleasure of the text, whether it is the *plaisir* of the *lisible* or the *jouissance* of the *scriptible* (Barthes, 1973b).

This might suggest that I am arguing for a position in reading narrative in which the reader is relatively powerless, but this is not the case. As in any reading experience, there is still a very active role for the reader here in making meaning, albeit a different one from the roles we play in other situations. Britton has suggested that we can divide our experiences of language use into those where we are participants and those where we are spectators, and he would suggest that reading implies a spectator role (see, for example, Britton, 1972). We are outside the narrative, watching the events unfold, reflecting on the characters, predicting how they will react; even when we enter the third area we do not become a part of this other reality of the story. This spectator role is in no way passive; D. W. Harding suggests that it is a 'non-participant relation which yet includes an active evaluative attitude' which goes far beyond a simplistic identification with the characters (Harding, 1977, p. 59).

Reading fictional narrative in book form or watching it on television is a different experience from reading a non-fiction book or watching a documentary, since not only do we have to surrender to the power of the language and images but also to set aside our everyday knowledge of how the world works. In story, a different kind of logic holds sway. Even when someone tells me a story drawn from their own experience, I expect a different way of selecting and ordering events than I would if I simply asked them to recount their actions over the course of a certain period of time. In a story every event is expected to have some significance, to be there for a reason, whereas a description of a part of anyone's life would inevitably include a number of incidents which seemed unconnected. In the kinds of fictional narratives encountered in books or on television, this is even more the case. We come to accept that, in some stories at least, the reality being described is not that of everyday life (animals may talk, magic has real power and so on), but more than this, we learn to interpret actions according to a new logic. Culler (1981) points out how in a different discourse (say, in a court of law) the story of Oedipus could be seen as inconsistent and contains evidence to suggest that he is not the person who killed his father, but because for the narrative to succeed he must have committed patricide, we ignore the everyday logic and operate according to the internal logic of the tale. If we bring our everyday logic to bear on the story, it will collapse, but this is not a sign that the narrative is flawed, it is a reminder that in narrative a different set of principles operate. To criticize fiction on the grounds of its truthfulness is to ignore this different reality. This is not to say that stories never need to correspond to real-life principles, but to suggest that whether or not they do is not governed by our normal judgments but by our view of the modality of the story as well as its ability to display vraisemblance within the modal field it occupies. This will not be the same for a fairytale as for a spy story, and one of the things we have to do to read narrative is to make appropriate decisions about the reality principles we apply to each narrative we encounter.

I have already said that a story is a sequence of events in which there is an implied connection; it follows then that one thing we have to do when we read is to make those connections (this of course refers back to Iser and his suggestion that we read by filling the gaps in the text). We have to imply reasons for actions and seek to make sense of the pattern of the narrative so that seemingly irrelevant details are woven into the overall cohesion. To do this the reader will rely on presupposition and prediction, just as in the rest of life, but just as our judgments about reality will be different when we are asking not whether something in life is true but whether events in a story or the behaviour of a character are likely in that story, so the way we draw on our experiences of life will not be exactly the same when we are using these experiences to predict what might be the outcome of a narrative. Culler has pointed out that literary presuppositions are not at all the same as logical ones (1981, p. 115). Although the opening sentence of a fairytale (for example, 'Once upon a time there lived a poor woodcutter') may give little away in terms of events that have preceded this opening, it does bring to the minds of experienced readers a wealth of presupposition based on their prior experiences of this genre, which in turn will enable them to begin to predict what kind of narrative is likely to unfold. In other words, when we read narrative, we make predictions based on our interpretation of the situation so far, just as we do when reading a non-fiction book or when reading a football match, but these predictions, if they are to be helpful, will need to take into account our prior experiences not just of life but of narrative; this of course includes intertextual references.

Narrative — A Central Part of Human Experience

The triadic relationship of reader, text and community to the reading process, which I set out in Chapter 2, implies that each of these have a part to play in the reading process. The more complex and interactive relationship of language, thought and culture, however, cannot be regarded as slotting neatly onto the earlier triad. Rather, each of the earlier aspects is illuminated by a deeper understanding of the relationships mapped out in this chapter. The text has to be seen as a product not just of the author's intelligent use of language, but in the broader cultural context in which the individual writer's development of thought and language will have been developed, with all the interaction between the three of these concepts already implied. Similarly, just as the text is a cultural product which will in turn act as a potential agent of change in that culture, so each reader is an active participant in the dialectical relationship of mind and society and so will bring to the reading process not just their knowledge of language and their intellect but their cultural knowledge. The community, too, can be seen not as a passive social backdrop against which each individual develops but as an active partner in this development. Thus reader, text and community are all involved in the constant interplay between culture, language and thought.

Narrative is omnipresent in life, but in particular in reading and in watching television; it involves interpretation in a way which involves text, reader and community; and it acts as a key site of intersection of language, thought and culture. Since narrative is such a central part of our human experience, it is likely that there will be strategies even young children use to make sense of narrative which transcend the media in which the narratives are presented. Having seen what these strategies are with regard to data based on the two media of print and television, we may then be able to discern the ways in which children draw on more specific instances of narrative to develop their competencies in a way which also transcends media boundaries, and we may be able to suggest ways in which pedagogy could enhance the benefits of such transference so that children become better at reading narratives in any medium.

Chapter 4

Making Sense of the Text in the World

Having set out the theoretical frameworks behind my research, over the next five chapters I explore the data from my fieldwork and its relationship to the arguments I have presented so far, beginning with the broad social context and gradually focusing in on the children's responses to specific texts. (The detail of my fieldwork will become clear as this happens but at this point it may help the reader to know that it was carried out with a class of 8- and 9-year-olds in south-east England.)

When children read or watch television, they do so as members of society and their roles in the various groups in the society to which they belong inevitably have an impact on the ways in which they read the texts. The children in my study were no exception, and in this chapter I want to look at the impact their social context had on the ways in which they responded to television and to books. The questions I was asking, which produced the conversations I draw on in this chapter, were not originally designed to explore social context at all, but as is so often the case with research, the activities I had set up came alive as the children made them their own. From the children's responses and interactions I was able to see how significant was this area which I had until then overlooked.

Before exploring the insights into the role of the community, though, I need to start by explaining what the children were actually asked to do and how it led to the perspective offered in this chapter. I set the children in my main fieldwork group two tasks concerning scheduling and book choice. For the first task, the children were invited to work individually to construct an ideal evening's viewing for either themselves or for another group such as their family, which would last from the end of school to the family viewing time limit of 9pm (see Table 4.1). They were able to choose any current or past programming and to adjust programme length and decide broadcast time within the given period as desired. Apart from some help with spellings and timing calculations, the children worked alone and without adult assistance.

When the schedules were completed, we discussed the children's choices in two gender-based subgroups. During the discussions, I broadened the area of debate to include issues not arising from their written schedules — such as perceived gender differences in programme choice, parental prohibition and teacher attitude to television — as well as inviting comment about each other's choices and their appropriateness for the intended audience.

For the second task, all eight children were asked to choose the ten books they would choose to take to a desert island, and either ten books their teachers would choose, ten they would least want or ten for children of the opposite sex. These

Table 4.1: Children's viewing schedules

Programmes Chosen for Family Viewing

Kelly		Natalie		Sarah	
3.30	Freddy's Revenge	3.30	Land of the Giants	3.30	Playdays
4.00	The Two Of Us	4.00	Jaws	4.00	The Flintstones
4.30	Asterix & The Baby	6.00	Freddy's Revenge		Comedy Show
5.00	Gophers	7.00	Dallas	5.00	The Flying Doctors
5.29	Top of the Pops	8.00	The Two Of Us	5.30	Coronation Street
5.49	Wish Me Luck	8.30	Neighbours	6.00	Grease
6.29	Neighbours			7.00	Home and Away
6.59	Land of the Giants			7.30	Neighbours
7.59	The Bluffers			8.00	Stolen

Programmes Chosen as Personal Viewing

Alexis		Ashley		David	
3.30	Neighbours	3.30	Wildlife on One	3.30	Felix
5.00	Home and Away	4.05	Teenage Mutant Hero	3.50	Water Babies
6.00	Stolen		Turtles	3.55	Top of the Pops
7.00	Coronation Street	4.10	Knowhow	4.00	The Cosby Show
7.30	Freddy's Revenge	5.00	Superted	4.02	Tron
		5.05	Grange Hill	4.03	Roger Rabbit
		5.30	Sportsnight (Arsenal	5.03	The Two Of Us
			v. Spurs)	5.13	Neighbours
		7.30	World Cup Final	5.14	You Rang M'Lord
				5.19	Jaws

Programmes Originally Said to Be for Family then Changed to Personal Viewing

Neil	
3.00	Tummy Trouble
3.15	Blue Peter
4.00	Asterix & the Big Fight
5.00	Bullseye
5.30	Grand Prix
6.30	Short Circuit 2
6.15	Short Circuit 1
7.15	Honey I Shrunk The Kids
8.00	Oliver & Company
8.30	Top of the Pops
9.00	Karate Kid 3

categories did not exactly mirror the previous task, but came out of issues that had arisen during the discussions of the first task. Children were invited to work singly or in same-sex pairs to complete the task. Each child completed a list of favourite books and each pair or individual also completed at least two other lists. Again we held discussions, this time in two mixed groups, to consider the children's choices. One group spent about forty minutes discussing the task, the other about half an hour. In the discussions of both tasks, the children drew extensively on their everyday experiences and generalized from these; this led to a wide range of topics being raised, including sibling rivalry, parental inconsistency and the influence of television on reading choice.

Whilst the results of these activities were certainly interesting, the discussions were of far greater significance, since in explaining reasons for choices and speculating about others the children revealed a great deal about the ways in which television and reading featured in their everyday lives and about the ways in which the children were interacting with the social structures in which they lived. However, these discussions only make sense in the light of what actually happened in the tasks and so the first thing to do here is to say what this was.

Three of the children chose for themselves, three for their families and one, Neil, claimed to have chosen for the family but subsequently shifted his position to claim that his choices were in fact for himself. Among the personal choices (including Neil's) there was a marked difference between the one girl's schedule (Alexis) and the three completed by boys (Neil, David and Ashley). Fiske takes the view that gender is an influence on our viewing choices and that this influence is exploited or even created by television itself:

> Television's techniques for gendering its audience have grown more sophisticated, and nowhere more so than in its development of gender–specific forms. (Fiske, 1987, p. 179)

He distinguishes between feminine or 'feeling-centred' narratives (1987, p. 215) such as soap opera, which according to Fiske can be characterized by an emphasis on relationships, on inevitability of outcome and on multiple and oppositional meanings, and masculine or 'action-centred' narratives such as action series, which he claims tend to have greater narrative and ideological closure.

Alexis chose only five programmes for herself, all of them adult/family programming rather than children's programmes and all falling into the category of feeling-centred as defined by Fiske. Two of the programmes were made significantly longer by choice and the others ran for approximately their normal length. One choice, *Freddy's Revenge*, was a film only available in cinemas or by video rental. All the boys chose more programmes, and included a wider mix. All three had cartoons, two included documentary-style programmes, two included feature films and two included serial drama. All three had a mixture of children's television and mainstream programming. As can be seen from the completed schedules, the approach to programme duration is very varied and not entirely consistent, but all three have significantly shortened some programmes and lengthened others. Two of the boys' choices reflect their other interests (football and motor racing) and most of them could be described as action-centred.

The three girls who chose for their families (Sarah, Natalie and Kelly) have less of a range of programme type than the boys who chose for themselves, but a wider range than Alexis. They seem mainly to have chosen programmes which they themselves like but which would have been enjoyed by their families too. As the girls discussed their choices and compared notes on which things each family would enjoy, they displayed a fair appreciation of the difficulties of catering for the whole family with a range of programmes:

MR	How about Sarah's family list?
Alexis	Yeah, my family would all like that

MR   How about yours?
Natalie   They'd all like it but apart from, um, *Flying Doctors* and *Flintstone*
            Comedy Show
Alexis   And no, there's two, *Playdays* and *Flintstone Comedy Show* my mum
            and dad wouldn't watch
Sarah   But your brother would
Alexis   Yeah
            (Transcript 10, ll.27–35)

Two of the boys seem similarly aware of the differences between their personal preferences and those of their families when they challenge Neil's claim that his schedule is designed for the family:

MR   Do you think your whole family would enjoy this?
Ashley}   No!
David }   No!
MR   Why not?
David   Because they're all sort of kids, I don't . . .
MR   What kind of things, Ashley why don't you think your mum and dad
            wouldn't, as a family
Ashley   Well it's mainly things for . . .
David   . . . for children
Ashley   I can't see, I can't get all my family to like all those, all these different
            programmes, I couldn't get any, er, like all these about ten programmes
            in a row that are all my family'd appeal to
            (Transcript 9, ll.87–99)

Although Ashley's grammar leaves us in some confusion as to his precise meaning, it is clear that in some way he is aware of the problems of finding several successive programmes which will all appeal to a group of people with different tastes, and that families do not all like the same things as each other.

Individual differences of opinion are markedly stronger in the boys' comments than in the girls'; although there are some differences as seen above in the girls' opinions of their families' reactions to the proposed lists, and both Sarah and Natalie would happily watch Alexis' choices, with the exception of *Freddy's Revenge*, which Sarah feels may be too frightening for her. This may be because all of Alexis' choices are less tailored to her own individual interests than the boys' lists, or because these interests coincide more exactly with those of the other girls. The boys, though, take more diverse stands, as one might anticipate from the differences in their choices. Ashley is unenthusiastic about both of the other lists, and Neil dislikes David's. Even when David appeals to Ashley for a kinder reaction, Ashley is uncompromising:

MR   What do you reckon, Ashley, would you swap David's evening for yours?
Ashley   No
MR   Why not?
David   Do you like it though?

> *Ashley* I don't. the only one I should have put is . . . *Roger Rabbit*
> *David* Yeah, tough!
> *Ashley* That's the only one
> (Transcript 9, ll.70–7)

It may be that Ashley has other fish to fry here in terms of status and hierarchy; what is interesting is not so much whether or not he likes David's choices as the confidence with which he rejects them, compared to the striving for consensus amongst the girls. Buckingham (1993b) found similar tensions between the boys he interviewed. This may give some insight into the different social rules operating here in the two groups, and may also suggest that interpretive communities made up of single-sex groups function differently depending on whether they are male or female. This would support suggestions that boys and girls do operate differently in single-sex groups, as observed by Moss (1989) in her secondary school teaching experience:

> At form time I would watch what they did. Whilst the girls would sit in small groups of twos or threes — best friends, at least for the moment — the boys would sit round in much larger groups. These were much more public forums, with none of the quiet intimacy of the girls' conversations. With the noise level high, conversation raucous, they seemed to be spending most of the time trying to pick each other off by ganging up and making one of the group look foolish . . . the girls seemed much more tolerant of each other. (pp. 8–9)

If there are different ways of reacting to each other that are related to gender, then the ways in which girls and boys subconsciously relate their own experiences to those of the rest of the interpretive community to reach a new understanding of such concepts as literacy may well also be different. In Ang's exploration of this issue, she emphasizes the ways in which the work done by Morley and Brunsdon moves beyond an essentialist view of gender differences:

> . . . both Morley and Brunsdon start out to construct a tentative interpretation which does not take the difference between male and female relations to television as an empirical given. . . . In their interpretative work Morley and Brunsdon accentuate the structure of domestic power relations as constitutive for the differences concerned. (1989, p. 108)

However, even this attempt to take on the factors which might make the viewing experience different for men and for women and which may as a result lead to girls and boys taking on different understandings of television is problematic, in that it still seems to fail to take on the possibility that people have multiple concurrent membership of a whole range of communities, all of which operate to influence viewing behaviour in the home. What is clear, though, is that among the other influences on children as they make sense of television and of literacy in their world, gender differences are significant. This will also be discussed later in terms of the children's comments in their discussions.

Table 4.2: Categorization of choices

Book type	No. in this category
Fiction	119
Non-fiction	31
TV/pop star tie-in	50
Endorsed by teacher	44
Cartoon/comic	11
School books	14
Not actual titles	20

(Since some books come into several categories, totals add up to more than 200)

The group with which I was working had been carefully selected to include children who were all avid television viewers but with a range of reading ability. This obviously had an effect on the way they approached the second task, which most of them found much harder to complete. For the most fluent, enthusiastic readers, the problem came from narrowing down the choice to just ten books. Ashley in particular found it difficult to limit himself in this way. For several of the others, the difficulty was in thinking of ten books in the first place, let alone ten which they liked or thought others would like. This revealed itself not just in the length of time it took some of the children to complete this task but in the kinds of books chosen and the discussion of their choices.

In all, the children completed twenty sheets (200 titles) (see Table 4.2), although two of these were identical as Natalie and Kelly had worked together even on the first list and produced identical choices of favourites. Of those books which fell into the category of television tie-in, almost all were annuals based on soap operas or stars from these such as Jason Donovan and Kylie Minogue. The *Narnia* books, which were then being serialized on television, were also mentioned, although I cannot be sure whether the children had actually read these or just knew of them. By 'endorsed by teacher', I mean books read to the class by the teacher or by myself and other books by the teacher's favourite author, Roald Dahl. Only Natalie and Kelly failed to include any book in this category in their list of favourites, and only one appeared as an entry in a list of least liked books, this being *Going Solo*, Dahl's adult autobiography, included by Ashley. Again, with this category, I do not know how far the children had read these for themselves or were basing their choice on having had the book read to them.

In fact, I have little evidence that any of their choices were books they had read, except in the case of books I had seen them reading in school. Nor could I be sure how familiar the children were with some of their choices beyond their titles; it seems likely that Natalie and Kelly, neither enthusiastic readers, copied titles from the posters on the walls of the school library. However, certain factors, such as the influence of the school environment and the teacher and the role of television and other media, will merit further discussion later as I consider how the canon of approved works for any community is created; here it could be argued that social structures are acting to influence the children's choices in a very direct way.

The Social Context at Work

Within the Home; The Role of Power Relationships

The first context in which the children in my study had encountered television and reading was the home. When the children thought about programme choice, inevitably they also considered the real constraints on choices they had encountered at home. Television viewing in particular is a social act insofar as the television, or at least the main set, is usually in a family room which to some extent is neutral territory when compared to the set in a child's bedroom. Different members of the family will have more or less control over the programmes selected for communal viewing, and the power relationships within the family will have some bearing on these choices. Research carried out in this field is in some ways contradictory, but it does provide a useful backdrop to the views of the children in my study.

Morley's examination of family viewing concluded that:

> Masculine power is evident in a number of the families as the ultimate determinant on occasions of conflict over viewing choices . . . it is even more apparent in the case of those families who have an automatic control device. (Morley, 1986, p. 148)

Lull, though, reports the earlier work of Wand in 1968 in Canada, which suggested that this male dominance was more imagined than real:

> She found that mothers dominated fathers when they disagreed over what television show to watch, although fathers were generally perceived by family members as being in charge of the program selection process. (Lull, 1990, p. 87)

It could be that Morley's families were maintaining this false perception, or that the different contexts provoke different behaviours. Lull suggests that in fact parental control may be more complex than a direct power struggle. He suggests that at least four issues are involved in the choice. First, parents may sometimes choose what they wish the child to watch, selecting programmes that will reinforce their own beliefs or attitudes:

> . . . the value system of the parent is transmitted to the child and attitudes already in place are reinforced. (Katzman, 1972, cited in Lull, 1990, p. 41)

As an extension of this role, parents may use television to reinforce their own competence as authority figures within the family, and this may lead to the enforcement of prohibitions (Lull, 1990, p. 42). Intellectual competence may also be demonstrated, either by vocally challenging information imparted or opinions expressed by people on television, or by citing information given by the media as support for an argument (Lull 1990, pp. 42–3). Fourth, Lull believes that his research shows that:

> Men, women, boys and girls use television to communicate to each other attitudes toward the appropriateness of male and female behavior with respect to sex roles. (1990, p. 43)

Since my own research did not involve direct contact with the children's parents or any observation in the home situation, I cannot offer directly comparable evidence to the work discussed above. However, their work can act to suggest interpretations of the views expressed by my research group and possible sources of such views.

When asked about conflicts of taste within the home, at least one child was not initially prepared to admit these existed:

> David   If mum and dad don't like it then I don't like it either so I phone up and complain about it and say it should go off the air
> (Transcript 3, ll.33–5)

Although it seems unlikely that this was literally true, David's intonation at this point suggests that he wished us at least to believe that his taste coincided with that of his parents. Most of the children in my group, though, had encountered differences of opinion over preferred programmes, were beginning to move from a close identification with their parents' views towards an attempt to assert their own preferences, and had devised strategies for coping with this situation. Even David was prepared to acknowledge that he sometimes watched the small insert in the screen to see a different channel from that favoured by his parents. Ashley, too, used alternative technology:

> Ashley   I just go in my bedroom and record it 'cause there's normally about two programmes I want to watch, mum and dad have got a video and so have I
> (Transcript 3, ll.79–81)

Sarah claimed a more philosophical stance:

> Sarah   I just say, 'Oh, I'll miss it for one day, it won't hurt me' and I go and do something else
> (Transcript 5, ll.114–15)

There are suggestions here of Lull's ideas about parental control strategies, but there is also a clear awareness of the possibility of conflict and, in Ashley's case at least, an awareness that the conflict may not be just between one's own choice and that of another family member but between two or more conflicting personal preferences. Throughout these remarks runs an assurance and confidence about television. David knows that it is possible to phone up to complain, Ashley is at ease with the video recorder. These children already feel in control of the medium to a great extent.

So far the responses I have reported do not necessarily imply that the children's choices were disapproved of in any way by the parents, or that behaviour control was involved in the parents' overriding of children's choices. In the case of Kelly, however, there was clear evidence that she was conscious of television being used as a behaviour-modifying device. She reported arguments about the remote control, a prohibition on watching *Neighbours* because she gets too excited, and the use of other programmes as a reward for good behaviour:

> *Kelly* I can only watch *Watching* if I'm good
> (Transcript 6, l.22)

There were, however, other disputes about viewing that raised more generally issues of parental dominance and suitability of content, the main areas of tension being soap operas and adult films.

In the case of soaps, there was, in addition to the adult–child dimension, a complex gender issue. For the boys, adult soap opera scarcely featured in their schedules. Only David included any soap (*Neighbours*) and he only allocated one minute to this. However, when I asked them what they thought their parents would have chosen, soap figured high on the agenda, in a contradictory way:

> *MR*   What do you think, say instead of you choosing for yourselves, your
>   mums and dads had been choosing what was suitable for you, what would
>   they choose?
> *Ashley* Oh they would choose rubbish they would
> *Neil*   Yeah
> *Ashley* Like *Playbus*
> *Neil*   They would, *EastEnders* and *Coronation Street* and *Neighbours*
> *MR*   Would they choose that for you?
> *Ashley* If they chose what we wanted to watch, but I don't think she'd choose
>   anything I like to watch
>   (Transcript 9, ll.118–28)

Here the boys appear to have conflicting opinions. For Neil, soaps are equated with Ashley's 'rubbish', but Ashley himself seems to see soaps as desirable but disapproved of by his mother. Ashley expands this, though, to include, 'Things like *Science Starts Here, Really Wild Show*'. Ashley is the only member of the group known to have parents with strong views about television, and is not allowed to watch television for two nights each week, although on the other days he watches avidly, and he claims he has his own video in his room (see above). This may explain these differing views; Ashley has encountered more explicit parental criticism of television than the other two and is aware (as is revealed in many other places in his conversation) that soaps are often seen as poor quality viewing. The other boys may have mothers (and fathers) who enjoy soaps more than they themselves do, and so may have had to watch these rather than their preferred alternatives. The differences themselves suggest that each child is creating their own stance mediated by the experiences of others but not replicating any other person's view exactly.

When the girls discuss the same topic, a new dimension is added. My admittedly leading question, 'What do dads like?' provoked the following discussion:

> *All*   Football
> *Sarah*   *Wogan*, news sometimes

Natalie   My dad loves the news and football, he loves the news, every time my
mum tapes *Neighbours* while we're having our dinner
Alexis   We always have to watch football, always
(Laughter)
Natalie   My dad watches, my mum, we're having our dinner on the table because
sometimes we're not allowed but now we are, my mum tapes *Neighbours* and then when my dad sits down he goes, 'Right, turn the news
on, not having that rubbish on', and I said, 'Why?' and I said, 'I want
to watch *Neighbours*, Mum, tell him,' and he goes, 'No, I'm watching
the news' and I go, 'How boring' and I cover the telly up
Alexis   That's what my dad says but he only says it joking, he says, 'Come on,
turn it over, I'm not watching this rubbish'
MR   But he lets you
Alexis   Mmm
(Transcript 10, ll.50–72)

Here there is a clear divergence of views between Natalie and her father, yet there
is little sense of Natalie deferring to male power. Rather, she draws on the knowledge that for others *Neighbours* is seen as worthwhile viewing, and challenges her
father's stance with an appeal to her mother, whose willingness to record the show
is seen as tacit support of it. In this case, rather than parent imposing soap on child,
it is the adult who disapproves, in this case the father. However, Natalie's detailed
knowledge of this programme suggested that in this case the male adult is overruled
by the mother–daughter alliance. This echoes the findings about the ways in which
women watching *Crossroads* succeeded in doing so despite hostility (Hobson, 1982,
p. 110), or the ways in which the women in Radway's study defended their reading
space despite criticism from families (Radway, 1987, Chapter 3, passim).

It would seem from this that the girls' own preferences for feeling-centred programmes are shared by their mothers, and that the boys' leaning towards sport and
documentary is one shared by the girls' fathers at least. Since the girls generally
succeed in watching soaps, this may support Wand's findings rather than Morley's.
Furthermore, the issues of role-modelling raised here seem central to a discussion
of developing understandings about the nature of television within a social context,
implying that children are very likely to be more strongly influenced in their development of personal viewing choices by the parent of their own sex.

Other important parental prohibitions relate to violent or explicitly sexual
material. In the scheduling discussion the boys made no reference to any censorship
of this kind, but their schedules only included two programmes which might have
been controversial: *Jaws,* which has been on early evening television several times,
and *Karate Kid 3.* In the earlier discussions, both Ashley and David reported
prohibitions on horror movies, including *Jekyll and Hyde* and *Teenwolf,* and Ashley
also mentioned a further restriction:

Ashley   I'm not allowed to watch any of the Kung Fu films and I'm fairly into
Kung Fu
(Transcript 3, ll.89–90)

The girls seemed more aware of this issue. In answer to my question about what parents would choose, Natalie introduces *Freddy's Revenge*, a film that featured in three out of the four girls' lists:

Natalie	*Home and Away*, *Neighbours*, *Freddy's Revenge*, Mummy doesn't like that very much but . . .
MR	But they'd choose that for you to watch
Natalie	Yeah
Alexis	My dad's really fussy, he never lets me watch horror films or rude films
Natalie	No, nor does my dad
MR	So what would he choose?
Alexis	*Strike it Lucky, Wogan*, comedy shows, but my mum lets me watch all the horrors and rude films
Natalie	Rude films, yeah, remember that one where this man, right, this lady was on a tree right, and he got it out and he said, she went, 'That's a big one!'
(Laughter)	
MR	What was that?
Natalie	On this film, right, it was really rude, people getting in bed, it was horrible, I kept turning, my mummy kept turning it over every time there was a rude bit
MR	But they think *Neighbours* is okay for you
All	Yeah
MR	But you say your dad wouldn't approve
Alexis	No, but he lets me watch it anyhow
	(Transcript 10, ll.107–29)

Natalie and Alexis were certainly familiar with a number of films that have adult-only certification, as they were able to retell 'the best bits' in great detail. It appears that their fathers' views are overcome by mothers colluding with daughters; in other conversations, Alexis talked of waiting for her father to fall asleep or go out, at which point her mother would allow her to change channel. Here again Morley's image of the male-dominated family seems to lack support, and even Lull's description of parents working together to control children seems to falter. (This would seem to offer oblique support for Wand's findings; if mothers and daughters collude in this way, they may well also collude to encourage fathers to feel in control of the situation whilst unobtrusively subverting this control.)

My role in the above transcript extract is worth exploring. Natalie extends membership of this community of female viewers to include me by sharing specific details of one of the prohibited films, at the same time showing that this women's viewing is a complex and fragile bond — both she and her mother have at various times found this particular film too embarrassing and have turned over, both perhaps responding to lessons learnt in other contexts about what constitutes family viewing. At the same time as including me, however, Natalie's remarks can also be seen as a gentle testing of my own role: am I there as co-conspirator or will my teacher's instincts censor her remarks?

Even just in terms of parent–child relationships, the home viewing experience is complex. In addition to parents constraining children's choices, there are ways in which parent and child (here mother and daughter, but equally probably father–son, mother–son or father–daughter) challenge or ignore the view of the other parent, so that children see more than one view of television even within the adults in their family. This is even more likely to be the case within the extended family, and Natalie talked of her aunt allowing her to watch films disapproved of by her parents. It is again clear that the different families do have different, if overlapping, opinions here. Each child has encountered different views of television in the home and in sharing the differences and enjoying the similarities the children are moving from the home definitions to a moderated version of this which takes into account their own experiences and the views they encounter via their peers.

The question of power over viewing did not only arise in terms of parent–child interactions. Sibling relationships were also a significant element in the children's lives. Other research has suggested two social obstacles to viewing:

> The first was gaining permission to view from an adult, the second was negotiating with siblings or friends over what could be watched. (Palmer, 1986, p. 60)

In addition to negotiating with their parents about choices, several of my group certainly echoed Palmer's findings here, raising the sometimes conflicting demands of their siblings. Here again gender seemed to play a part. In my preliminary discussions with the class, Alexis and David described different experiences with their younger brothers:

> *Alexis* My brother loves it [*The Wombles*], we always have to watch what he wants to watch and I'm never allowed to watch what I want to watch
> *David* My brother has to watch what I want to watch
> (Transcript 3, ll.166–69)

What is significant here is not so much the accuracy of these observations, as the children's belief that this is the case and the way they represent this here. Alexis may or may not really feel as she does, but in this mixed group she says this is what happens, where David feels the need to stress his relative power in the viewing situation. This reflects their developing views both of television and power relationships in the family and of external expectations about these power relationships. Buckingham's study reported similar tensions, sometimes resolved through physical conflict (see, for example, Buckingham, 1993a, p. 112). For Alexis, the solution was to watch the television set in her bedroom. This might seem an equitable solution, but struggles over the choice of programme for the main television in the family living space are significant and for Alexis to have to retreat to her own space is a clear defeat in power terms:

> As long as there is a main set in the most comfortable room, the question of 'what to watch' will remain a subject fraught with conflict and requiring delicate negotiating skills on the part of different household members . . . (Morley, 1992, p. 215)

The girls in my group were not always defeated in these power struggles. Sarah, who has no brothers but a younger sister, has carefully evolved strategies to ensure success:

> *Sarah* If my sister likes something and I don't I tell her it's scary and then she
> doesn't want to watch it and I can put something else on
> (Transcript 5, ll.99–101)

Again this may not be an accurate reflection of what actually happens in Sarah's family. Sarah may or may not use this tactic and her sister may or may not give way if it is used; her comments elsewhere suggest an ambivalent attitude. However, the fact that Sarah chooses to represent her position in this way shows that she has clearly understood that this is about dominance as much as preference or appropriateness.

That the channel being watched is indeed as much a question of power within the family as choice of viewing in some cases became clearer still as Natalie described her experiences:

> *Natalie* My brother, right, when I was watching *Neighbours*, when I watch *Neigh-*
> *bours*, right, he keeps on turning the telly off all the time
> *MR* Is that because he doesn't like it or because he wants to irritate you?
> *Natalie* He wants to irritate me, my big brother is like that
> *Alexis* And my little brother
> *Natalie* My big brother, I go outside 'cause someone comes into my house right,
> and I go outside, and he turns the telly off quickly, and he goes upstairs
> and goes, 'Natalie, come and watch the telly then, come and watch
> *Neighbours*' and I went in there and tried to watch and he'd turned it off
> (Transcript 10, ll.130–40)

Even if she is not in the room, Natalie resents her brother's control of the set, and even though he does not want to watch an alternative programme, her brother interferes with Natalie's choice. This suggests far more at stake than preferences for watching or not watching *Neighbours*, and acts to strengthen the view of television as a factor in the power relationships of the home and in the developing understandings of the children about their position in the social context. The view of television that Natalie and the others are taking on here includes a dimension in which the actual television set constitutes an object over which power battles may be waged. This lesson seems more of an issue for the girls than for the boys, who reported far fewer anecdotes of power struggles; this may again be to do with lessons being learnt about gender roles, so that the girls already construe themselves as relatively powerless and so are more alert to power struggles which they tell themselves they expect to lose.

So far my consideration of my data in terms of power relationships has concentrated exclusively on television. When the children talked about television programme choice, these questions arose fairly spontaneously. When they talked about book choice, they said very little about conflicts of this kind. In fact, these discussions made hardly any reference to home life at all, and those that did were mainly to do with books owned or where they were kept. The children said they read mainly in bed:

David   At home I like to read under my bed
Neil   On my bed . . . everywhere really
Kelly   I make a camp with blankets and read
Katie   In my front room, outside
MR   What kind of a place does it need to be then?
David   A quiet place . . . in the front room it's too noisy
          (Transcript 2, ll.17–22)

If their reading mostly takes place in such private circumstances, there is less opportunity for social conflict.

Though there may be few conflicts at the moment of reading, one might expect to hear conflicts about the choice of reading as a preferred activity rather than some more practical involvement with the family such as domestic chores or entertaining younger siblings, or disagreements about the books or reading matter chosen. My own observations in children's bookshops or near the children's books in super-markets suggest that parents frequently intervene to override children's personal choices, possibly for the kinds of reasons suggested by Lull for intervention in programme choice. These children, however, did not mention any such conflicts. When asked where they got their books, they mentioned some home influences (Christmas and birthday presents, spending present money, jumble sales and public libraries) but none of the children mentioned any control over their choice or any related conflict.

I suspect that given the children's main sources of books (presents and books bought for them by relatives) they had little conception of the possibilities of choice in the way that they did with television. With television, all programmes obtainable on a set are potentially available to anyone in the household, and the choices are advertised through newspaper listings, listings magazines, teletext pages and through trailers and continuity announcements, so that children are aware of what is poten-tially available and what they are allowed to have. Given that there are at any time at least 30,000 children's books in print, it is not possible for these children to have any real conception of the full range of choice available. They would probably be unaware of the fact that each positive choice of a book title as a present was in effect a denial of access to many other possible titles. Thus the lack of comment in the children's discussions may not suggest so much an absence of parental control, but that this control is less visible and causes less immediate conflict. It may also be that in the context of the classroom, censorship of viewing was seen as more significant and worthy of comment.

Another issue here concerns the limitations of such a private role for reading and book choice in terms of the children's developing understandings of the nature of literacy in everyday life. There were few instances of children mentioning any reading which took place with parents except for having been read to or reading to parents when younger. Where this was mentioned, it was often in the context of learning to read:

> MR   What about when you were little, did you have books?
> *Natalie* I used to tear them up, my mum used to read to me and if I got a word
>   she'd clap
>   (Transcript 1, ll.58–60)

The only insight into parental views of reading also came from Natalie:

> *Natalie* My Nan buys them [books], my mum goes, 'Not more rubbish'
>   (Transcript 1, l.17)

Apart from this rather depressing comment, the children made no reference to reading as something which was discussed at home. During the discussions specifically devoted to the book choice task, this may be because of the nature of the books chosen and of my own interventions, but none of my other discussions with the children, even the most openly structured, produced any comment on this.

If children's views of television and of literacy are formed both from their own direct experience and from the way they compare that experience with the mediated experiences of other members of the communities to which they belong, then the invisibility of books and reading in the family lives of these children may be very significant to the view of literacy they develop. There is very little other research evidence into family attitudes to reading and into the ways in which books are talked about in families. Ingham's research into reading in Bradford found that typically avid readers had families where reading had a high profile in the home. Library membership was common, children had been read to regularly and in some cases, at least, children had explicit knowledge of the importance of literacy to their parents. The reluctant and infrequent readers had not had this family focus on literacy, a fact acknowledged by children and parents alike. Fry's account of the reading behaviours of six children gives some insight into the role of the home:

> Parents and teachers do much to encourage the readerly behaviour that accompanies reading and which helps young people to think of themselves as readers . . . I have written of the social transactions that surround reading, but I am aware also of the interactions between reading and feelings for other people, especially the family.
> (Fry, 1985, pp. 96–7)

He stresses the positive interactions and discussions about reading reported by the children in his study, who through these discussions begin to feel as though they are 'part of a community that reads' (p. 94).

Only two of the children in my study, Alexis and Ashley, could be described as avid readers, despite the classroom atmosphere being one which appeared to promote reading and despite the fact that even the poorest reader in my research group was not so weak a reader as to give cause for concern. This may be to do with the gap between the view of literacy encountered at home and that presented at school. Although there was also a divergence of views in the case of television, the children came to school with an enthusiasm for and competence in television viewing, and at least a developing understanding of the social nature of television and of the tensions and conflicts within the family as to the exact nature of television. This was sufficiently firmly established to prevent the invisibility of television in the classroom from disrupting the children's desire to watch, particularly since the official invisibility is coupled with a new range of views to be encountered within the peer group. It may be much harder for children coming to school with either little understanding of reading beyond the functional literacy of letters, birthday cards and environmental print or with a view of reading as something essentially private and rarely discussed, to take on the very public and social view of reading that prevails in primary schools.

School Experiences

At school, a complex network of relationships creates the broad context which could be seen to contain a range of interpretive communities created by the interactions in this network. Evidence of the influence of peers and of the children's limited perceptions of teachers emerged, as well as developing gender stereotypes. For Alexis, for example, there were the contrasting experiences gained with the other girls in the class, amongst whom she had no intellectual equal yet many shared experiences, and with Ashley, who in many ways was her best friend and intellectual peer, though with many widely differing tastes. She also had contacts with children from older and younger classes and with a range of adults including the class teacher and myself.

From these different groups comes the possibility of encountering a wide variety of views about books and about television. Children quickly discover that for many teachers, television is not seen as a relevant or legitimate topic of conversation within class time, leading to the official invisibility suggested above. One study of television and children found:

> . . . a number of instances of teachers excluding televisual experience either consciously and actively, or passively and unconsciously. Generally they did not seem to realize what they were doing. (Hodge and Tripp, 1986, p. 168)

This study gives the example of a child who included in his news something which he had seen on television, only to be told by his teacher that this was not really news:

> When Johnny was in school on Monday, television was said to be something which did not really happen to him on Sunday; it was rather something which the teacher would punish him for mentioning in class newstime. (p. 169)

This would suggest that the rules for reporting past experience are totally different in and out of school, given that many adults spend significant amounts of time discussing viewing experiences. Hodge and Tripp suggest that teachers are not really trained to cope with children's television experience, and that since it may be at least different from or possibly broader than the teacher's own experience, teachers may even feel threatened by their own lack of competence. For the children in my study, there was no conscious attempt by the class teacher to exclude television; however, as I shall discuss later, the television experience of their teacher was something about which the children had little knowledge.

For my group, as for Hodge and Tripp's children in Australia, there was a marked lack of interaction with teachers on the subject of television, but a great deal of lively interchange at peer-group level. One of the strongest themes revealed by the children's interactions with each other was their growing gender awareness and the ways this mediated their attitudes to books and television. In a task discussed in a later chapter, which involved sorting a pile of books into self-chosen categories, the girls had been keen to use the groupings 'Girls' Books' and 'Boys' Books' but had been unable to proceed. Although they were convinced of the existence in general terms of these categories, every time they tried to place a book, one of the group would object. If it was being suggested as a boys' book, one of the girls had always enjoyed it; if as a girls' book, then someone had disliked it. This paradox between the general schema of the world which seemed to exist in their heads and the actual way they operated in specific situations, which could again be seen as a focus of the tensions between the theoretical model offered to them by their culture and their individual experience, was also revealed by the tasks discussed here.

In each discussion I asked the children to imagine that the other gender group were coming to their houses and to suggest potential viewing for them. This led to much feigned horror and, in the case of the boys, blatant sexual innuendo, but when we had worked through this some interesting differences emerged. The boys' immediate (probably accurate) suggestions were the two early evening soaps:

> *Ashley* I'm not too sure about, I know it'd be that one, *Neighbours*, and they'd
> probably like something to do with Kylie Minogue and Jason Donovan,
> *Home and Away* and things like that
> (Transcript 9, ll.178–81)

Although there was some disagreement here and at other times among the boys about the merits of *Neighbours*, all of them watched most of the time, even those who were most critical. This may explain why they did not complain overmuch about the idea of watching these programmes with the girls. They grouped the girls together, but did also refer to specific girls in the class:

> *David* With Kelly or Vikki or someone like that it'd be adventure stories
> (Transcript 9, ll.207–8)

However, since the girls maintained a fairly united public front on matters of preference, this may not be a sign of over-generalization on the boys' part.

The girls both reacted much more strongly against the kinds of programmes that they felt the boys would choose and thought much more about the specific interests and enthusiasms of the boys concerned. They also had a very pessimistic view of their own prospects should the boys be choosing for them:

MR Say you'd got Ashley and Neil coming to tea
(Screams of horror)
Alexis Not going to watch the football no way!
MR What do you think they'd want to watch?
Alexis Ashley would want to watch the football and Neil would want to watch racing (others echo last bit)
Natalie Cars, he loves cars (imitates Neil)
MR What do you think they would choose for you?
Sarah They wouldn't, they wouldn't, they would just watch . . .
Alexis They wouldn't, they'd just say 'No, you're watching the, we're watching the football'
   (Transcript 10, ll.88–97)

This seems to imply that the children were aware of the social and personal relationships that operate around viewing situations. These two groups were developing different, if overlapping, stances, about the nature and purpose of television which were at least partly defined by their growing awareness of gender roles.

It is hard to make direct comparisons between the television-based and book-based tasks here, because for one the discussion was held in single-sex groupings and the other in mixed groups. One of my reasons for changing the grouping, though, was to see how this issue of gender-specific texts was discussed in these two different contexts. Being in a mixed group for the second discussion meant that the children had to confront the target audience of their choices where previously this had been mediated by me. There was a shift from an initial confrontational stance between the boys and girls in these mixed groups to a gradual admission of common interests and more thoughtful debate. To start with, for example, Ashley claimed provocatively to have chosen 'girly girly boring boring books' but by the middle of the discussion the group were able to concede that they had many overlapping choices. Later, they explored the stereotyping behind some choices:

MR So you tell me, did you notice anything about what the girls have chosen for you and what you've chosen for them and what you like yourself?
Ashley I don't reckon they, like, thought about the *Transformers* and stuff, we already said to them we hate *Transformers*
(unclear)
Alexis Well, we hate *Care Bears*
(?) Correct
Ashley They're typical boys' things, they think they're typical boys' things, *Transformers* and things like that

MR	What about *Care Bears*?
Ashley	Typical girls' stuff
MR	Do girls actually like that?
Alexis	No
Ashley	No, but if it was Kelly they do
MR	But do either of you like *Care Bears*, you don't?
Alexis}	No
Sarah}	No
MR	Did you ever like *Care Bears*?
Alexis	(very promptly) No — oh, I did when I was little
Sarah	I did
Alexis	I've still got the teddy my brother gave me for my birthday, I was always wishing that if I could have Care Bears teddies and I've got one from my brother
Ashley	And I've got the Transformers
	(Transcript 12, ll.119–42)

Ashley and Alexis begin by challenging each other's stereotypical stances but as they acknowledge their past likings for the programmes and related toys in question, they move into a much less confrontational discussion of shared memories.

Although here the children seem to have come close to acknowledging the limitations of gender stereotyping, Ashley is happy to answer the question as to what does make a typical boys' book. His answer, though, rather than being a generalizable principle, involves describing a book he has personally enjoyed, the argument seeming to be that since he is a boy and he enjoyed it that must be a typical boys' book:

MR	So what would be a typical boys' thing now then Ashley, what do you think?
Ashley	Me? Er, something like *Oliver Twist*, it's a really good, that's my favourite book at the moment, I've got all the, er, I've read *Journey to the Centre of the Earth* and that's quite good and I've got this big pack of books about this big all together and like er the last one I've read was *David Copperfield*, I read *Oliver Twist* before that, they're not that big, and it was really funny because like he went into this gang and he kept on stealing everything, it was like er if they knew (unclear) and he was a scruffbox
(Laughter from girls throughout)	
Neil	What did you say?
MR	Have you ever seen, have you ever seen the film of *Oliver*?
Ashley	No
Alexis	I have, I have, it's brilliant
Ashley	I'd like to see it
MR	So do you think that's a typical boys' thing?
Neil	Yes
Alexis	Not really
Sarah	I don't know
Alexis	It's about boys but it doesn't mean girls wouldn't like it
	(Transcript 12, ll.143–64)

Again, as with the television programmes, the children are still sure there are programmes designed for each sex, but they find it very difficult to say what these might be, to the point where their peers can see the weakness in the argument, as Alexis does here. The other group found it equally difficult to be clear:

MR   What about, what makes a good book for boys and a good book for girls then?

David   When they're for boys it's the, um, me, Rikky, Ashley, Matthew, and all the boys except Lee and Michael like adventure books don't we, like *The Hobbit* and *The Lord of the Rings, Going Solo,* I read that

MR   Are those books that only boys would like or would girls like them as well?

Kelly   Girls would like them
        (Transcript 11, ll.115–23)

This argument of David's is not only challenged by Kelly but weakened by the inclusion of *Going Solo*, which Ashley had included as a 'worst book', and by the Tolkien titles, which as David knew were enjoyed by boys and girls in the class. Again the need to stereotype appears to be stronger than the ability to do so in a way which moves beyond personal preference.

There was a fair degree of subversion apparent in this task which it is important to mention. Kelly and Natalie actually produced two lists of books for boys, one serious and one designed to provoke, made up of books they perceived to be for a much younger or predominantly female audience, including *Fireman Sam* and *Care Bears*. (Interestingly, this turned out to include one book actually fairly popular with all the boys, *Superted*, which the girls had seen as very babyish.) During the discussion, there were several occasions when Kelly was at least as provocative as Ashley had been with his 'girly girly' tag, yet the boys failed to notice (or at least to react to) this provocation. Certainly there was a high degree of gender awareness among all the groups, which led to a tension between girls and boys and a solidarity of approach from the girls. It would seem that children's experiences in the wider community are shaping their understandings of the relationships between gender and books much as they did over television.

Strong as the influence of the peer group may be, it might be imagined that the adults within the school would have a greater influence. However, in both tasks, as well as in earlier conversations, it became apparent that the children had what felt to me to be somewhat distorted views of their teachers' attitudes, and of their class teacher in particular. Although in the first task no-one had taken up my suggestion of planning an evening's viewing for the teacher, the teacher himself, intrigued by the task, had jotted down his own ideal evening's viewing. During the discussions I asked both groups to suggest what he might like. The children had a very limited view of what this would be. They felt that the topics currently being explored in class (birds and Egypt) would form the mainstay of the teacher's viewing for pleasure, though they did think that teachers probably liked *Grange Hill*. In fact, the teacher had chosen an evening of light entertainment and sitcom,

75

which had not surprised me at all. On reflection, I realized that although conversations about television were a regular part of staffroom talk, and of my own talk with the teacher, he rarely discussed this leisure viewing with the children; nor was there much overlap between his viewing and their own, which limited the possibilities for such talk. The only alternatives the children could offer to a chosen diet of wildlife and travelogues was some subversive speculation by the girls on the possibility of his watching 'rude films'.

The children's view of the teacher's taste in fiction was similarly out of kilter. They explained to me that the reason for having the class stories that they had was because the teacher found them personally satisfying:

> Kelly He's enjoying *Mrs Frisby and the Rats of NIMH*, and he thinks it's really
> exciting, and it's the same with *Matilda, The BFG*
> (Transcript 11, ll.183–5)

Although this was undoubtedly true at one level, the children seemed to imagine that his enjoyment mirrored their own, and seemed to have little idea that he might also read adult novels for his own pleasure.

When asked to speculate about the teacher's probable choice of television programmes for children, the groups were pessimistic, and seemed to have a one-dimensional view of teachers which precluded any desire to let children enjoy themselves. Both boys and girls had similarly gloomy views about the fate of television if teachers had more influence over schedules:

> MR How about, say teachers were in charge of television
> Ashley Oh no, all they would, all they would put is *Science Starts Here*
> David No, they might want to watch *Superted*
> Neil Or *Playdays*!
> MR Do you think children's television would be different if it was teachers running it?
> Ashley Definitely
> MR How?
> Ashley It'd just be *Science Starts Here*, it'd just be rubbish like that
> David *Grange Hill*'s okay
> Ashley *Grange Hill*, okay that'd be ...
> MR Do you think teachers like *Grange Hill*?
> All Yes
> Neil They'd probably put on Jason concerts or something (sings alternative version of *Tears On My Pillow*)
> David They probably don't want us to watch TV because they want us to learn
> MR You think you can't learn things from television?
> (unclear)
> Ashley They might even want us to, like, television programmes, tell us to tape it, like things like handwriting or something like that
> Neil Oh no!
> Ashley How to improve handwriting, how to improve history, things like that

David   I'd watch if it was to improve your handwriting because mine's rubbish
(Transcript 9, ll.213–39)

The girls' comments were very similar, with just one significant change of pronoun from Natalie:

Natalie   You wouldn't let us do anything, you would just say, 'Oh no you're not going to see rude things or horror films, the next day when you go to school you'll have nightmares or keep falling asleep'
(Transcript 10, ll.151–4)

In other words, teachers (including me, at least for Natalie, despite her earlier inclusion of me in the discussion of 'rude' films) are seen not as people who appreciate the range of potential of television to 'educate, instruct and entertain' but as regulators of behaviour with no interest in television beyond its educational value; the only alternative offered here is the subversive and facetious *Superted* or *Playdays*.

This is not so surprising, given the generally low profile television has been found to have in the classroom (see for instance Hodge and Tripp, 1986), but what was more of a revelation was the similarly limited idea the children had about the books that teachers would want to see being read. The class teacher is enthusiastic about literature and there were plenty of books in the classroom; the children were encouraged to read these and were read to regularly, although this was from a fairly limited range of texts, with a concentration on Roald Dahl. The children's own choices did reflect the teacher's choices, but when asked directly they felt he would see school textbooks as more important than fiction, with David singling out one novel some of the girls had chosen:

David   I don't think he would want us to take that [. . .] because it's really like a reading book, he would like us to take science books so we could learn
(Transcript 11, ll.174–7)

Overall, it was clear that the children had very one-dimensional views which were completely based on the professional side of teachers' lives. Even allowing for the lack of out-of-school contact with teachers, these children had a surprisingly narrow view.

The experience of the children in my research may not be typical but there is no reason to suppose that it is unique. This lack of opportunity to discuss books and television may have a deleterious effect. If we deny children information by not talking about our own positions, they will develop a view of the world based on the limited evidence they are given. To put this another way, if narrative is a site of interaction between culture and thought, we need access to the cultural if we are to develop the ability to use narrative to its full potential. The school as an agent of cultural transmission has a role here to widen the view children will have encountered through the necessarily more limited context of their immediate family.

Learning within Interpretive Communities

So far in this chapter I have argued that if we are to understand the ways in which children make sense of narrative, we need to look at the contexts in which they are learning to read and to watch television. I have suggested that we need to see this context as part of a creative and developing dialectic with the children. Through my analysis of the children's comments, I have shown how their understandings of power relationships and of gender roles are developing in the context of the conflicts and tensions they encounter within this dialectic. I have begun to suggest that there are implications here for teachers (an issue to which I shall return) in that if, as I have argued, narrative is a 'primary act of mind' (Hardy, 1977), and if it is a site of intersection between thought and culture, children need help to develop their ability to use and interpret narratives of all kinds. For this to happen, schools need to represent culture to the children, as well as to help the children recognize their own power within that culture as agents of change. They can do this partly by providing access to the texts of that culture but also by mediating personal and societal attitudes to those texts and helping children to know that they can challenge these attitudes.

One way to understand this is to return to Fish's notion of the interpretive community. I argued earlier that although Fish's model is seriously flawed, a redefinition of community which allows for a dialectic relationship between individual members and the community as a whole could be a useful way forward. If we see the children as members of a series of interrelated communities (home, school, friends) that are flexible and constantly changing but which are all subsets of Smith's 'literacy club' (Smith, 1988), then the complex interaction between children and the society in which they live may be easier to understand. Just as in any club, there will be a pre-existing culture and set of rules, however implicit these might be, which act to influence new members but which are also subject to challenge and change by members. The activities of the club (in the case of an interpretive community, the texts which are shared and the act of making and using meanings from these texts) will offer a site for growth and change for both individual members and the whole group. This takes my argument back to the creative tension between reader, text and community.

What I set out to do in this chapter was to examine the role of the wider social context and to describe the social context of the children involved in my research. I would argue that these children are trying to make sense of a whole range of possibly conflicting information. From home they encounter television within the power and gender relationships within the family and the conflicts and constraints on programme choice created by the social nature of the viewing experience. In contrast, these children have come to school with a view of reading as to a great extent removed from the social constraints evident in the case of television. At school they gain new information from peers and from encounters with teachers which to some extent conflicts with their earlier views, so that their own concepts are developed as they reconcile their own experiences with those of others. This process is also influenced by their growing contact with the wider world and the media play a not insignificant part both in providing a window on the world and by acting as secondary texts.

In other words, children are learning from their membership of interpretive communities not just how to read and watch television but how reading and television are seen in our society and how to act as readers and viewers by actively creating from their primary and secondary encounters a working understanding of these two key elements of twentieth-century life. What I turn to examine in the next chapter are the various expectations which these children bring to their encounters with television and print, particularly in terms of their understanding of narratives.

Chapter 5

The Expectations Children Have when Reading

In the last chapter we saw how, as children negotiate viewing within the family, they come to understand power relationships and to take on a view of the relative roles of television and reading; these understandings are then developed or challenged by the encounters the children have at school with peers and teachers. But between these broad understandings and the specific competencies children draw on to make sense of any particular narrative lie a set of orientations and expectations children bring to any viewing or reading situation. We need to ask how far children approach their own experiences of specific television programmes and books with prior ideas as to what these experiences will bring.

This chapter considers what kinds of expectations children appear to have and to consider where and how such expectations arise. First, though, we need to ask why our orientations towards texts are significant. Cognitive psychology suggests that we understand the world through internal networks of knowledge and understanding that we all build up through our life experiences; these act to offer us a framework with which to interpret each new situation we encounter. Smith (1978) talks of the model of the world we carry in our head as one which acts as a 'shield against bewilderment' (p. 57); we use this to anticipate and to predict, and when the model does not match what we find we either have to adjust our model to take into account the new information or reinterpret what we are seeing. In sociological terms, Giddens suggests that in any social encounter we rely on what he calls 'mutual knowledge' (Giddens, 1984, p. 4) which enables us to act appropriately in the encounter, but is not specific to a tightly defined set of situations.

Thus the world knowledge we have, whether described in psychological or sociological terms, will offer us a way of making meaning from our encounters with television. Our expectations of and orientations towards any text are just one part of the encounter; the text itself, through those involved in producing it, and the social system in which the text is encountered also bring their own expectations to the encounter. Thus all these expectations will interact with each other and change and be changed by each other. This mutual influence can be seen behind Neale's (1980) definition of genre, which he sees as a particularly significant factor in framing our preconceptions:

> . . . genres are not to be seen as forms of textual codifications, but as systems of orientations, expectations and conventions that circulate between industry, text and subject. (p. 19)

The key word here is 'circulate'; the expectations of all the partners are continually changing as this interaction takes place and the stock of mutual knowledge grows. Our interpretations of texts are influenced by this mutual knowledge so that as we read the texts, we are drawing on our expectations and adjusting these in a continual process which will largely be at the level of practical consciousness.

What I tried to do in my research was to create situations in which children's expectations were made explicit. I have divided these expectations into four broad categories. First, I revisit the notion of preference to emphasize the extent to which these children already have clearly defined tastes. Here I consider the ways in which books and television interact with each other in helping to establish these preferences. Next I explore the ways in which the children's expectations are affected by their perception of the target audience of any programme or book and its appropriateness for their own age group. Then I consider the extent to which modality influences the children's expectations before turning to a consideration of the role of genre in all this.

Making the Expectations Explicit — What We Did

Remarks made by the children in general conversations during the fieldwork and their discussions on reality during the scheduling activity offered some useful evidence, but in addition a specific activity was set up to explore the categorization systems employed by the children, based on the model used by Buckingham (1993a). This exercise was used initially during the pilot study to explore children's ways of sorting television programmes, and then refined and extended to include a book-based activity.

For the pilot, groups of children were given a selection of titles of television programmes written on cards and were asked to sort the cards out in any way that they liked. If this first sorting did not involve genre, the children were then asked to undertake a second sorting strategy in which the notion of genre (though not the term) was introduced, with a request that they should now sort by 'the kind of programmes'. Both during the activity and at its end, I took as limited a role as possible, but asked for explanations of certain decisions and acted as chair of the discussions where necessary. For the first two groups, the programmes given were drawn from the British Audience Research Bureau (BARB) ratings for the previous week; for later groups, the titles were drawn from programmes mentioned by the children in earlier conversations. Both of these ways of selecting programmes proved to have some drawbacks. The BARB titles, whilst including a good range of genres, included several programmes not seen by the children (nor always by the researcher) so that it was difficult sometimes to know whether children were basing their decisions on knowledge of the programme or guessing. The self-selected titles avoided this problem, but since they were drawn from children's discussions about favourite programmes, several genres did not feature at all. For the main fieldwork, the strengths of both were combined. The titles were drawn initially from those occurring most frequently in the viewing diaries of the children. This list was then adjusted to include a wider range of programmes and children were then asked how many of these they had seen before the final selection was made. To ensure a comparable pattern in terms of the book sorting exercise for the main fieldwork, the range of books in the classroom was increased from the start of the fieldwork by the introduction of some fifty extra books. The books for the activity were then selected from the enhanced class collection to represent a range of genres and children were asked at the beginning of the activity to reject any that they had not read.

For each sorting activity, children were in groups of three or four. For the pilot these were random groupings from the class as a whole (see Table 5.1); for the main fieldwork these were subdivisions of the selected group. For the television activity we worked in two mixed groups (see Table 5.2) and for the book activity in gender-distinct groups (see Table 5.3). This allowed some consideration of the social processes involved in such an activity in both mixed- and single-sex groupings.

After the completion of this activity, it became clear that certain issues would benefit from a supplementary task focused on audience and appropriateness. For this, working in single-sex groupings, the children were asked to complete a grid to show which television programmes and books they felt were appropriate for younger children, inappropriate for younger children but appropriate for themselves, and inappropriate for anyone except adults. Here the choice of title was left entirely open to the children and they were allowed to include video and film: this was to allow the inclusion of any material that might otherwise have been overlooked had I chosen the titles. Tables 5.1 to 5.3 set out the results of the sorting activities. Table 5.1 shows how the four pilot groups classified when asked to use genre. Table 5.2 shows all the strategies used by the main fieldwork group when sorting television programmes. Table 5.3 shows all the strategies used by the main fieldwork group when sorting books.

Preference

A dominant strategy for selecting any viewing or reading experience is that of preference. Even the youngest viewers of television programmes have their favourites; Jaglom and Gardner (1981) found that from the age of two, children exhibited clear preferences. Pre-school children who are read to also have a core of favourite books (Holdaway, 1979). When I have conducted categorization activities with adults in research seminars, there has been a tendency to talk in terms of preferred programmes even when genre has been the explicit frame in use. Similarly, the children in my study approached any viewing or reading situation with more or less strong expectations as to whether this will be pleasurable, and these are based on their prior experiences and on those of their interpretive community.

Throughout my discussions with the children, their own preferred viewing and reading formed a constant topic of conversation. The introductory discussions addressed this directly when I asked about favourite programmes and books. All the

Table 5.1: Pilot classification results

Group 1 (second strategy)
Quizzes
A Question of Sport
Fifteen-to-One

Animals
All Creatures Great and Small
The Natural World

Documentaries
First Born
Forty Minutes

Boring
The Money Programme
Pardon Us
Last Resort
Top Gear

Sort of quizzes
Bullseye
This Is Your Life
Blind Date

Children's things
Lost in Space
The Golden Girls
Annie's Coming Out

Comedies
Alexei Sayle's Stuff
Bread
Fawlty Towers
Colin's Sandwich

Guns and shooting
The Bill
Killer in the Mirror
Guns of Diablo
Mission Impossible
Boon

Families
Reaching for the Skies
Brookside
Emmerdale Farm
Coronation Street
Neighbours
Howards' Way
EastEnders

Group 2 (second strategy)
Stories
Guns of Diablo
The Last Resort
Pardon Us
Lost in Space
Mission Impossible
Killer in the Mirror
First Born
?The Bill

Everyday/People that know each other
Neighbours
Bread
Fawlty Towers
EastEnders
Brookside
All Creatures Great and Small
Howards' Way
The Golden Girls
Annie's Coming Out
Emmerdale Farm
Coronation Street
?The Bill

Quizzes
Forty Minutes
Fifteen-to-One
A Question of Sport
Bullseye

Sports
Top Gear
Reaching for the Skies

About the world
The Natural World

News
The Money Programme

Unnamed Category
Blind Date
This Is Your Life

Don't know
Alexei Sayle's Stuff
Colin's Sandwich
Boon

Group 3
Babyish things
Playschool
Rainbow

Talking about things
Wogan
Going Live
Wideawake
Blue Peter

Adventures
The Lion, the Witch and the Wardrobe
Knightmare

Monsters and weird things
The Munsters
The Wombles

Exciting
Beauty and the Beast
Neighbours
'Allo, 'Allo

Table 5.1: cont'd

School Simon and the Witch Grange Hill	*Soaps* EastEnders Neighbours
Sport Grandstand Snooker	*Serials* Dr Who The Lion, the Witch and the Wardrobe Grange Hill
Telling you things Newsround Record Breakers	Simon and the Witch First Born
Cartoons Stoppit and Tidyup Tom and Jerry	*Sport* Grandstand Snooker
Surprises Beadle's About Blind Date	Record Breakers *Facts — how to do things* Going Live
Life and death Wildlife on One Jimmy's	Wideawake Blue Peter
Science fiction Defenders of the Earth Dr Who	*Comedy* 'Allo, 'Allo Bread The Munsters
Not exactly comedy or serious EastEnders Bread First Born	Beadle's About *Quizzes* Blind Date Beadle's About
Group 4 *For very young children* Rainbow The Wombles Playschool	*Cartoons* Stoppit and Tidyup Tom and Jerry Defenders of the Earth
Factual Jimmy's Wildlife on One Newsround	*Each on their own* Beauty and the Beast Wogan Knightmare

children were able to discuss favourite programmes and most had some books they had particularly enjoyed. They were also clear about the programmes they least liked:

> MR   What's your least favourite programme then?
>
> Natalie The news, I wish they'd come off but they never would, they keep on talking about things and you can read it in the paper, and they repeat it three times
> (Transcript 4, ll.173–6)

The categorization task, with its open frame, added to the other evidence that the children were capable of expressing preference (such as their viewing schedules and lists of books). For several groups the initial strategy for sorting programmes was in terms of preference. Such preferences were not individually expressed in isolation from the group view, and much careful negotiation took place to ensure

Table 5.2:   Main fieldwork — classification of TV programmes

Group 1 (Alexis, Ashley, Neil, Sarah)
First strategy — Popularity in Group

Rank order for those liked by all

1. The Two of Us	9. The Flying Doctors
2. Top of the Pops	10. Blue Peter
3. Jim'll Fix It	11. The Cosby Show
4. The Bill	12. Home and Away
5. Playbus	13. Grange Hill
6. EastEnders	14. Neighbours
7. Rainbow	15. Count Duckula
8. Bergerac	16. 'Allo, 'Allo

Liked by three	*Liked by two*	*Liked by one*	*Not liked at all*
Blind Date	Coronation Street	The Real	Bravestarr
Doctor Who	Grandstand	Ghostbusters	Newsround
Survival	Holiday	You Rang, M'Lord	Record Breakers
			This Is Your Life
			WAC 90
			Wogan

Second strategy — Genre

Baby programmes	*Cartoons*	*Children's soaps*	*Comedy*
Playbus	Bravestarr	Blue Peter	'Allo,' 'Allo
Rainbow	Count Duckula	Doctor Who	The Cosby Show
	The Real Ghostbusters	WAC 90	The Two Of Us
	Record Breakers	Grange Hill	You Rang, M'Lord?*

Holidays	*Interviews*	*Music*	*Nature*
Holiday	Blind Date	Top of the Pops	Survival
	Jim'll Fix It	You Rang, M'Lord?*	
	This Is Your Life		
	Wogan		

News	*Soaps*	*Sport*
Newsround	Bergerac•	Grandstand
	The Bill•	
	Coronation Street#	
	EastEnders#	
	Flying Doctors	
	Home and Away∞	
	Neighbours∞	

(* moved from music to comedy in final check)
(•,#,∞ pairings of soaps)

Further programmes added by children in new categories

Children's books on TV	*Religion*
The Lion, the Witch and	Highway
the Wardrobe	Songs of Praise

Fairytales/pantomimes	*Children's Horrors*
Cinderella	ALF ('comedy')
Peter Pan	Dungeon Master
	Monster Squad

History	Labyrinth
'Things on Egypt or countries'	(Count Duckula — Ashley)
(no titles given)	(The Storyteller — Neil only)

Mysteries	*Horror*
Murder She Wrote	(rejected, on too late)

Table 5.2: cont'd

Group 2 (David, Kelly, Natalie, Rikky)
First strategy — Channel

BBC	*ITV*
Blue Peter	Count Duckula
Bravestarr	Rainbow
Grange Hill	The Real Ghostbusters
Newsround	WAC 90
Record Breakers	
(50/50 split of opinion over Playbus)	

Then divided into

Not Cartoon	*Cartoon*
Blue Peter	Bravestarr
Grange Hill	Count Duckula
Newsround	The Real Ghostbusters
Playbus	
Rainbow	
Record Breakers	
WAC 90	

Second strategy — Genre

Can't decide	*Children's programmes*	*Drama*	*Funny/comedy*
Holiday	Blue Peter	Bergerac	'Allo, 'Allo
This Is Your Life	Bravestarr	The Bill	The Cosby Show
	Count Duckula	Doctor Who	The Two of Us
	Newsround		You Rang, M'Lord?
	Playbus		
	Rainbow		
	The Real Ghostbusters		
	Record Breakers		
	WAC 90		

Hobbies	*Mysteries*	*Soap operas*
Grandstand	Blind Date	Coronation Street
Survival	Jim'll Fix It	EastEnders
Top of the Pops	Wogan	The Flying Doctors
		Grange Hill
		Home and Away
		Neighbours

Added themselves
Horror
Freddy's Revenge

---

a group decision for each placement, though within such negotiations it was clear that certain individuals had a tendency to hold a more dominant role than others, and that certain others were more isolated.

For example, the first main fieldwork group to sort out television programmes devised a complex system to ensure a fair result. Each programme was first assessed in terms of how many members of the group liked it. This gave subdivisions of programmes liked by all four, programmes liked by three, and so on down to programmes liked by none. Those in the first of these categories were then each paired with another to arrive at a rank order. Finally, the whole list was again read through to ensure that no-one felt anything was wrongly placed. The painstaking

Table 5.3: Classification of books

Group 1 — Boys (Ashley, David, Neil, Rikky)
First Strategy — Genre

Adventure
The Church Cat Abroad
Gorilla
Granpa
Mrs Frisby and the Rats of NIMH
The Perfect Hamburger
Rat Saturday
The Snowman
The Thief
The Worst Witch Strikes Again

Fairs
Fairground Family
Lost at the Fair

Fairytales
Book of British
  Fairytales
The Princess
  and the Pea

Funny
Breakfast Time, Ernest and Celestine
The Enormous Crocodile
Lovable Furry Old Grover's Resting
  Places
Prince Cinders

History
The Birth of Jesus
Brighton Between the Wars
Brighton in Colour
Early Egypt
Norah's Ark
The Romans
The Teacher

Horror stories
A Dark Dark Tale

Information
The Bicycle Book
The Guinness Book of Records
How We Used to Live

Sport
A Day with a Footballer
A Day with a Riding Instructor
Making Things Move

Science
Bringing the Rain to Kapiti Plain*

Wildlife
Barn Owl
The Beaver
How the Birds Changed Their Feathers
Life in the Wild
The Penguin
Sparrows
Tadpole Diary
Woodland Birds

(* Later the boys admitted none of them had read this.)

Group 2 — Girls (Alexis, Kelly, Natalie, Sarah)
First Conclusive Strategy — Genre
(Started with voting for most liked (same system as used for TV, i.e., all like, 3 like etc.)
but got bored. Then tried gender but not conclusive. Then genre:)

Animal stories
Bringing the Rain to Kapiti Plain
The Church Cat Abroad
The Enormous Crocodile
Gorilla
How the Birds Changed Their
  Feathers
Mrs Frisby and the Rats of NIMH
Norah's Ark

Cartoon/TV books
Granpa
Lovable Furry Old Grover's Resting Places
Rat Saturday
The Thief

Children's royal books
The Princess and the Pea
Prince Cinders

Christmas
The Birth of Jesus
The Snowman

Food
Breakfast Time, Ernest and Celestine
The Perfect Hamburger

Lost child
Lost at the Fair

Table 5.3: cont'd

Nature	*People and places*
Barn Owl	Brighton Between the Wars
The Beaver	Early Egypt
A Day with a Riding Instructress	
Life in the Wild	
The Penguin	
Sparrows	
Tadpole Diary	
Woodland Birds	
School	*Sport*
The Teacher	A Day with a Footballer
	The Guinness Book of Records
Tale	
A Dark Dark Tale	

nature of this reveals the importance of preference for these children as a prior expectation of any viewing experience, and since the two girls from this group then chose to repeat this in the girls' only group when sorting out books (and persuaded the other two in the group of its validity) it would seem that with books, too, this is an important factor.

In terms of the interrelationship of book and television experiences, preference seemed to be a strategy used in both situations; however, the connection goes deeper too, in that intermedia and intertextual connections helped to set up expectations of preference, on the very direct level of having enjoyed a film and therefore wanting to read the book and vice versa. Sometimes expectations set up in this way were not fulfilled:

> *Ashley* Reading's more exciting than TV 'cause you can picture it in your imagination and say in *The BFG* it's really different [the film] from what I thought it was going to be, it wasn't very good at all, they changed it a lot (Transcript 3, ll.48–51)

It seems clear, then, that when children sit down to watch a particular programme or read a particular book, preference will be playing a part in their understanding of what is to come. They may be watching or reading because they already expect to enjoy the experience or they may already feel some antipathy towards it. However, they also already know that these expected pleasures are not guaranteed and that they may be surprised or disappointed in spite of their prior expectations.

Audience

Another way in which the children in my study oriented themselves towards particular books or television programmes was in terms of prior views about what was appropriate for them to watch. These judgments about appropriateness were largely centred on two factors, namely age and gender. Both of these were present in the categorization strategies displayed by both pilot and main fieldwork groups. This echoes the findings of Buckingham's large-scale study into children and television which found: 'While gender was certainly a factor here, age was also important' (1993a, p. 55).

Two of my pilot groups used age as an initial strategy, with one group dividing all the programmes into the four categories of 'Children', 'Mixed' [i.e., suitable for children and adults], 'Adult' and 'Not Sure', and the other including audience alongside some genre groupings. Most frequent in later sortings was the creation of a category for programmes for younger children, used by three of the four groups, such as *Rainbow* and *Playbus*. Two of these three groups used a title that included the word 'baby' or 'babyish' which suggests a distancing from their own age group; the others settled for the emphasis in 'for **very** young children'. Three groups used categories of television programme labelled more generally as for children, and both of the main fieldwork groups either included a book category of this kind ('Children's royal books') or at least considered it initially:

David	That's good that is, it can go in the children's section
Ashley	But all of them are for children
Neil	Well that isn't for children
Rikky	Yes it is, children can read it
	(Transcript 16, ll.1–4)

What was noticeable, though, was that although these categories of 'adult' and 'children' might be seen as appropriate by adults too, the ways in which the children sorted the actual books and programmes was not necessarily so predictable, and seemed to isolate one aspect of a title at the expense of others. In the case of books, three different views emerged in as many lines. For David, above, the criteria was quality; for Rikky, accessibility seems to have been more important. For Ashley, the fact that all the books were from the classroom may have contributed to his view. (The book titles were of course more tightly controlled than the television programmes. Since the books themselves were to be in the classroom, it would have been inappropriate for me to include anything that might have been considered damaging by the teacher, school or parents. The television programmes were only represented by their titles and so a wider range was possible, particularly in the case of the groups using the programmes from the BARB ratings.)

In the case of television programmes, the children who used the 'adult' and 'children' categories seemed to be operating not so much on a decision about whom programme makers might see as a target audience but on the basis of their own experience. Thus, *The Golden Girls*, an American comedy series about a group of older women, was seen as a children's programme (despite the fact that at that point it was shown after 10pm) because the children concerned liked to watch it and their parents did not. This trend was also reported by Jaglom and Gardner:

Another complication is that children have their own definition of children's shows — namely, shows that they watch — and they adhere to this definition regardless of the age group for which a show is intended. (1981, pp. 17–18)

This was made even more explicit during the activity specifically designed to explore questions of appropriateness. The girls only came up with one programme that they felt was inappropriate for them (the film *Don't Look Now*) and included in their middle column ('Programmes Young Children Shouldn't Watch But Which We Can Watch') many films which were at that time only available on video and which are rated as only suitable for adult viewing. Again this seemed to be more to do with what they had actually seen than what they thought they ought to have seen:

Kelly	I tell you what is really scary, *Freddy's Revenge*
MR	But is it okay for children your age?
Kelly	Yeah
Natalie	Yeah
Alexis	Well it isn't really but . . .
Natalie	. . . but we want to watch it and *The Gate*, that's horrible
Alexis	. . . but my mum lets me watch it
	(Transcript 7, ll.29–35)

This ambivalence about appropriateness has already been seen in Chapter 4 in the discussion around ways in which mothers and daughters collude, and echoes the findings of Sarland (1991) into the reading habits of adolescents.

The boys' table made a more conventional separation between mainstream viewing such as the James Bond films and the more explicitly violent titles which they admitted they had watched but of which they knew adults did not necessarily approve:

MR	When you watch things like that . . .
Ashley	They're not suitable for us really
David	No, they're not really
MR	Why not?
David	*Lethal Weapon* my mum said 'No way Jose,' she said it's really bad, then when I went down to my uncle's he goes, 'Oh put the rude one on,' 'We're not allowed to watch that, its got rude bits on it,' 'Oh you don't want to (unclear) that, watch the violent one,' and so I watched *Lethal Weapon 1* and it was really nice
	(Transcript 8, ll.180–9)

This more circumspect approach by the boys contrasts with the attitudes expressed by some of the children in Buckingham's study (1993a) where the boys were the ones who were most challenging of adult attitudes.

Throughout this discussion both boys and girls were very clear that although they might be old enough not to be damaged by such viewing, younger children needed protection. When asked to explain why this might be, several interlocking preoccupations emerged, summed up by Natalie:

Natalie	I think, if there's snogging or rude things in it and they swear
	(Transcript 7, l.114)

One concern was to do with the risk that younger children might copy what they saw, with some comments about violence but with more concern about swearing:

> *David* They're going to start swearing, aren't they, they don't know what it means, they might think it's a nice word for somebody, they'll go, 'I like you, you overgrown beep'
> (Transcript 8, ll.214–7)

Coming out of this was a view that younger siblings might then act in socially inappropriate ways that could be embarrassing (and behind this concern is an underlying set of exnominated beliefs about the behaviour appropriate in any situation):

> *MR* So is it that little children don't like being frightened and you do? Is that something to do with it or not?
> *Alexis* My brother, he's really rude, and every time he sees like, someone naked, he says, 'Ooh, look!', and I say 'Oh, James, don't be rude,' especially when we've got guests it's so embarrassing, like last year my friend came round for Christmas dinner, and my mum was watching this film and we were behind still eating our dinner, and my brother said, 'Look, Nina, look at that,' and I go 'James don't be rude!'
> *Sarah* Yes, that's what I do to my sister, 'cause sometimes . . .
> *Alexis* It was so embarrassing
> (Transcript 7, ll.162–72)

There was also a concern about nightmares and being frightened:

> *Natalie* No, listen, 'cause once my friend got *Freddy's Revenge* and she's only a little girl and when she watched it, and her mum said 'If you have nightmares then you're never going to watch another film again' and she watched *Freddy's Revenge* and she nearly jumped out of the window
> (Transcript 7, ll.125–9)

However, the whole question of fear led to a more ambivalent position in that almost all the children in my research group (with the sole exception of Sarah, of whom more later) admitted that they were also frightened by these films and that they enjoyed being frightened:

> *MR* When you do watch things like that [*Lethal Weapon*], do you enjoy them?
> *David* Yes
> *Ashley* Yes, it's brilliant
> *Rikky* (unclear)
> *MR* Does it frighten you?
> (General yes)
> (Transcript 8, ll.190–5)

What they could not explain was why it might be that younger children would be less able to handle such fear, though both groups were able to assert that their own age was the threshold at which such films became appropriate:

MR How old do you have to be to watch these programmes, I mean you're all . . .
Natalie Eight or over
MR . . . Who's eight and who's nine?
Alexis I'm nine
MR Eight, eight, eight and nine, so you're all old enough . . . were you all old enough last year?
(General chorus of no)
Kelly No, because I watched this scary film, you know that *Thriller* video, well I watched that and I was really scared
Natalie Yeah
  (Transcript 7, ll.130–40)

Although these responses are very complex, as indeed are such concepts as fear and violence, there seems to be something at issue here about the need for these children to see themselves as autonomous and in control whilst displacing anxieties onto younger children in very much the way in which adults who are worried by television violence see themselves as in no danger but worry about the effect on others. Again, this echoes Buckingham's findings:

> Here again, the 'effects' of television were often displaced onto 'other people', notably children younger than themselves. (Buckingham, 1993a, p. 79)

These children seem well aware both of the broader view of society about appropriateness and their own experience as a reasonably reliable indicator of what they personally will find appropriate, with the boys in particular frequently referring to the ratings system currently in use for film and video.

These attitudes and concerns were not just expressed with regard to film and television. Though more ambivalent about the risk of books being too frightening or violent, again the children made similar points. They were also aware that books or computer games derived from films might have been changed, with David distinguishing between his computer game based on *Platoon* and the original film and describing the ways in which he felt books were changed:

MR Are there any books that you think are too frightening for little children?
David Yes, *Gremlins* . . . they're not written . . . they're not frightening . . . they are pretty frightening but they're not violent though because if children are going to read it they put, they put the first letter of it, f, and then they put dot dot dot dot dot and how much dots are in the . . .
Rikky And the f-u-c-k
(Laughter)
David Otherwise fuck
  (Transcript 8, ll.247–56)

The boys felt books were potentially as frightening as television, with Ashley suggesting that they might be more so, although at the same time showing an awareness of the role of the reader in all this:

Ashley   I reckon that you can put all those things in books in your imagination
           and you can make it six million billion trillion times as exciting and scary
MR   So if it's in a book it could be more frightening than on a film?
Ashley   Yeah, it could be more boring than a film if you don't read it the right
           way
           (Transcript 8, ll.340–5)

The girls were less prepared to admit to this but after an initial denial then spent
several minutes showing each other the frightening bits from certain books in a way
which suggested that their claims to enjoy being frightened were fairly genuine.
Both groups again stressed the need for younger children to be protected here.

Again, all these responses from the children raise questions about the ways in
which they have arrived at such positions. These will be considered at the end of
the chapter, where the particular case of Sarah, whose views were markedly different
from the others, will provide useful evidence about the social nature of expectations
about appropriateness.

The children found it relatively easy to agree about what was appropriate for
younger children (perhaps because there were no representatives from a younger
class to challenge this view in the same way?) but using gender was more problematic, just as it was in the scheduling task discussed in Chapter 4. The girls were
keen to sort books into 'Girls' Books' and 'Boys' Books' but when I asked them to
suggest books for the categories they had created, they quickly ran into trouble:

MR   Can you think of a book that is going to be for just girls or a book that
          is just for boys?
Alexis Um, for boys
MR   *A Day with a Footballer*
Sarah   Yes, that's for boys
MR   Anything else?
Alexis It wouldn't have to be for boys 'cause my mum plays, goes to football
MR   Maybe you need to think of a different way
Alexis My mum likes football
          (Transcript 17, ll.19–28)

This disagreement was within a same-sex group, whereas the similar disagreements
reported in Chapter 4 were in mixed groups. That this issue is contentious even
when discussed by a group of one gender helps to emphasize that this is a genuine
area of doubt and not just a way to challenge the opposite gender's position for
other reasons. Again, Buckingham (1993a) found a similar gap between generalized
positions over gender and actual viewing practice.

Modality, Reality and Realism

So far it could be suggested that, on the evidence discussed here, children come to
books and television programmes with expectations about whether they will like
the programme and about whether they ought to be watching it. However, these

fairly general expectations are only part of the pattern. Modality is also a key issue here, and from the data I have collected I will be suggesting that these children at least are still refining their judgments about the reality and realism of certain books and programmes, whilst being very clear about others.

Before considering the children's understandings, it is worth returning to the ideas explored in Chapter 3 and considering the question of reality and realism as it pertains to reading and television, particularly with regard to fiction. One study of children's judgments about reality suggests that there are at least three definitions of reality:

> At the most concrete definitional level, one may say that something on television is real and mean that it is exactly as it is without television . . . The other two definitions of *real* accept that programming is fabricated but do not use that as the basis for judging reality. Instead, reality means a fabricated experience in which characters, actions, messages, or themes somehow conform to real life . . . Two somewhat different meanings can be found within this second general definitional approach. In one, something is judged real if it is deemed possible. In the other, it is only judged real if it is deemed probable or representative. (Dorr, 1983, p. 202)

Dorr's research found that children in the second half of elementary school (i.e., the same age or just slightly older than those in my study) were operating with a definition of real as 'made up, but possible in real life' (1983, p. 205).

The Project Zero research found that pre-school children were still coming to terms with the differences between real life and television, typically moving from a view of television as so real that, for example, a drink spilled on television had to be mopped up in the living room, to an over-generalized view of television as totally constructed to the extent where children who saw themselves on television would deny their own reality, before beginning to move to a more conventional view (Jaglom and Gardner, 1981).

Hodge and Tripp (1986) found that one of the difficulties in exploring the relationship between fantasy and reality was that children had different under-standings of what was meant by reality and were operating on different criteria from the adults around them, so that they would base judgments as to whether people were more or less real on the frequency with which the children saw them; in this way 'some real-life people were seen as more real than others' (p. 121) even by 12-year-olds. This did not necessarily imply a lack of understanding in these children of the constructed nature of television, who could distinguish between actors and presenters. One 6-year-old in their study explained that his friend Shaun was more real than Yogi Bear 'because Yogi's a film and Shaun was born . . . God made him' (p. 123). Hodge and Tripp conclude:

> . . . children's modality systems are developing throughout childhood: their grasp of reality, the idea of reality, or the reality of television is not a simple matter. During this process of growth, children will often make modality 'mistakes', but it seems that their concepts of reality must sometimes be put at risk if they are to develop a complex and fruitful modality system, an elaborate hypotactic structure of the requisite scope, coherence and flexibility (1986, p. 130).

On this basis, I would expect to find some areas of uncertainty in the ways in which the children in my study use modality and distinguish between fiction and fact, not just on television but, as Hodge and Tripp suggest, in all semiotic forms.

Buckingham's study found little evidence of modality mistakes, but found that where these did occur, other children in the group would not let them pass:

> Overall, however, there was very little evidence in any of the age groups of confusion over the modality status of programmes, and where such confusions arose (mainly among the 8-year-olds), they were nearly always challenged. (1993a, p. 150)

This peer-group challenging may be one of the ways in which children adjust their own understandings of the world around them.

In terms of television programmes with low modality, the children in my own study had little difficulty in distinguishing between these and reality. Cartoon in particular was identified as different from other programmes by all the groups whose lists included cartoons. Three out of four included 'Cartoons' as a separate category in their final sorting, where the only difficulty it posed was that of overlap since the children set it alongside genre categories so that programmes had more than one logical location. For example, one group eventually decided to place *Defenders of the Earth* in 'Science Fiction' rather than with the other cartoons. The fourth group used it as an intermediate strategy before using genre, dividing all the children's programmes into 'Cartoon' and 'Not Cartoon' groupings.

It might be argued that an awareness of cartoon as different from other programmes does not necessarily imply a parallel awareness of cartoon's low modality status. However, one of the least televisually literate children in the class from which the main fieldwork group was drawn, who had grown up in Scandinavia and who still watched little British television because of his enthusiasm for playing ice hockey, was able to criticize one programme because of its apparent lack of understanding of the modality status of cartoon:

MR   Why is *Ghostbusters* called *The Real Ghostbusters* when it's on television?
Daniel   Yes, it's stupid, because it isn't real, it's a cartoon!
         (Transcript 1, ll.48–9)

The children also demonstrated an awareness of the difference between narrative and non-narrative, though this was less clearly established in their minds. When sorting the various nature books, the girls had originally grouped animal stories alongside information books, a juxtaposition which is hardly surprising given the tendency of writers and publishers to blur the edges of these two categories. Kelly, however, could feel the difference, although she found it hard to articulate, and eventually the other girls also saw what she meant and created two separate categories:

MR   Can you see any others now for nature?
Alexis   *Noah's Ark*
Natalie *Noah's Ark* because that's got all animals in

Kelly	Yeah but that doesn't mean to say it's to do with nature, does it?
Natalie	Yeah
Alexis	'Cause animals
Natalie	Kelly, Kelly it's animals
Kelly	But that doesn't mean to say it's all about nature . . . what I mean is nature is what they say like, um, they say something in it like um where birds live and that
Sarah	We could have an animal layer and . . .
Natalie	But it's not just birds Kelly
MR	I think Kelly's making an important point, what she's trying to say is some of these books tell you about the animals, yeah, like tell you what it is and . . .
Alexis	Tell you what, let's have story
Sarah	Animal story
Alexis	And nature study
	(Transcript 17, ll.34–52)

Ashley attempted to distinguish between fiction and non-fiction in the discussion of book choice:

MR	What about the things that happen in books? Are things that happen in books real?
Alexis	Sometimes, and some stories on telly are real, it depends
Ashley	If it's fiction, it isn't real
MR	So what things count as fiction? Look at your lists
Ashley	*Oliver Twist, Grange Hill, The Hobbit, David Copperfield, Mrs Frisby and the Rats of NIMH*
MR	And what's not fiction?
Ashley	*Arsenal Annual, Saint and Greavesy* . . . I'm not too sure about *Grange Hill*
	(Transcript 12, ll.418–27)

As can be seen here, the children's understanding was still developing in the area of what might be called 'realistic' fiction, which has a fairly high modality. Although aware in some ways that such television series as *Grange Hill* and *Neighbours* were constructed and involved actors who could also be seen on other programmes either giving interviews or taking on new parts, the children were still unhappy about seeing such programmes as not real:

MR	What about *Grange Hill*, is *Grange Hill* fiction or non-fiction?
Ashley	That's a hard one, a very hard one
MR	Why is it hard?
Ashley	Because it's (unclear)
MR	Can you explain that?
Ashley	Like, half of it could and half of it couldn't, it's really fiction and non-fiction
MR	Is that the difference then between fiction and non-fiction, fiction is things that could happen?

Ashley   Like, fiction is normally things that couldn't happen, like sometimes things have happened, like (unclear)

MR   Like in *Grange Hill* then, are those things that have really happened, are they real people or . . .

Ashley   Yeah they're real people but they're making that be their personality, like they make it look like real teenagers, I reckon they just leave them to wear what they want, just give them the lines, like it does look really good, like when you've been watching it for a couple of weeks you think, 'Oh, this is a really real school,' and it is actually a real school, but you think all of the pupils go to that school . . . like it doesn't actually happen but . . .

Neil   I'd just love it to be this school, *Grange Hill*

(Transcript 12, ll.428–45)

For Ashley, the difference between fiction and non-fiction is to do with possibility, as Dorr suggests, and for him at least *Grange Hill* is so strong in *vraisemblance* (Culler, 1981) that he has difficulty articulating what he knows about the actors and the constructed nature of television fiction. The same thing happens when these same children discuss *Neighbours*. They are quite clear later about the fact that it is constructed, though still reluctant to say without any hesitation that it is not true:

MR   What about *Neighbours*, is that true?

David   No

Kelly   Yes

David   It isn't true actually

Natalie   Some of it is, 'cause some of it, Daphne isn't dead really . . .

David   I know she isn't

Natalie   . . . and Helen isn't really even in hospital

Kelly   In a coma

Natalie   She doesn't want . . .

Kelly   It's only because she wants to get out of *Neighbours*

(Transcript 11, ll.320–29)

In both these extracts we can also see confusions about modality being challenged, as Buckingham (1993a) suggests.

The children also had at least some doubts about the reality of some of the books they were reading. Little research appears to have been carried out on children's understanding of the constructed nature of printed fiction, although there has been much debate about what happens when we read, and about children's general development in terms of distinguishing their own identity from that of others. Winnicott (1971) suggested that children learn through play to distinguish between their inner existence and their place in the external world, talking of play as an intermediate third area 'where we are more ourselves'. Britton, among others, has suggested that storying, and by development fiction, is a kind of deep play which we use in this way (Britton, 1977). Tolkien suggested that reading fiction entailed entering a 'Secondary World' (Tolkien, 1966, p. 37). Warlow reminds us of Coleridge's idea of the 'willing suspension of disbelief':

> Coleridge's analogy between literary illusion and dream takes us straight back to
> Freud, Winnicott and Britton. [. . .] And the importance of this insight, together
> with Tolkien's point about the spell being broken if disbelief arises, lies in the real-
> ization that there is an *all-or-nothing commitment by the reader*; either he is 'in'
> the Secondary World or 'out' of it. If the reader is 'in', then, as Coleridge said, the
> comparative powers of the mind are completely suspended. (Warlow, 1977, p. 94)

What research there is suggests that for younger children, there is a different
understanding of reality in books. Applebee (1977) found that among 5- , 6- and
7-year-olds, age was less reliable as an indicator of the understanding of fiction
than literary experience: some of the 5-year-olds were very sure that *Cinderella* was
just a story, while some of the 7-year-olds were sure she could be visited if only
they knew where she lived.

In terms of literary experience, Ashley and Alexis were by far the most widely
read of the children in my study, with Natalie (relatively able as a reader but
reluctant) and Rikky perhaps the least enthusiastic readers. Natalie was one of the
most sceptical about printed fiction in my study:

MR	So think about something like, I don't know, well maybe like *Gaffer Samson* . . .
David	Yeah!
MR	. . . is that something that has really happened?
David	Yes
MR	. . . is it somebody writing down something that's really happened?
David	Yes
MR	. . . or is it somebody making up a story?
Kelly	Making up a story because um . . .
[. . .]	
Natalie	I think that *Gaffer Samson* is just someone making it up
David	I don't
	(Transcript 11, ll.267–76; 281–2)

There is little in *Gaffer Samson's Luck* that could not really happen; other titles,
though, are less realistic. David was equally reluctant to believe that *Mrs Frisby
and the Rats of NIMH* might not be real, and again it is one of the least experienced
readers who challenges this view:

Rikky	No, it isn't true, because rats and mice can't speak
David	They do tests on rats and they might be able to let them go
[. . .]	
Rikky	But they don't make them talk though do they?
David	They can't talk, I said they can talk but not in our language
	(Transcript 11, ll.301–2; 312–13)

It is as though it is the more experienced readers who are more willing to play the
game and enter into the Secondary World, such as David who seems to want it to
be true that animals might learn to talk.

Although the least experienced readers here are reluctant to see fiction as real (maybe because their reading experiences have not been sufficiently satisfying to allow them to discover Tolkien's Secondary World), it is Ashley, the most experienced reader, who among other things has read *The Lord of the Rings*, who most firmly rejects that certain ideas from books might be possible in real life, despite his earlier doubts over *Grange Hill*:

> Ashley   I don't reckon though, television programmes, they're not very frightening, neither are books, like (unclear), like something it wouldn't happen, nothing, well, the only things, like, all the frightening ones couldn't happen (Transcript 8, ll.322–5)

What seems to be happening here is that Ashley is learning to distinguish between the fantasy that he encounters (in which category he seems to include the violent films the boys have been discussing in this conversation) and the more realistic texts such as *Grange Hill*, but that his ability to articulate the difference is still developing. Nevertheless, this comment, together with those quoted elsewhere in this section, shows that these children have a developing understanding of modality which they are able to bring with them to new viewing and reading situations.

This whole area, as discussed in Chapter 3, is complex; children are having to understand the difference between fiction and non-fiction, which are labels they will hear used to describe books, as well as the whole issue as to what we mean by such concepts as reality and truth anyway. These transcripts offer only a limited insight into the influences that have helped them to develop this view, although the comments above hint at the role of their own life experience. News items about *Neighbours* and other soaps may well be helping the children to distinguish between the lives and motivations of actors and the characters they play.

Genre

In terms of genre, the existing research is somewhat contradictory as to whether this is a significant feature of children's understanding. The Project Zero research suggested that children were aware of certain programme types very early on, with advertisements recognized by children during their fourth year, followed by cartoon (not strictly speaking a genre) and even news recognized before the fifth birthday (Jaglom and Gardner, 1981). Dorr (1983) also found that second- and third-graders regularly used genre as a cue to reality, which argues a recognition of genre itself as a differentiating feature between programmes. Eke and Kroll (1992), however, argue that such research is unreliable, and set against it their own work with 9- to 10-year-olds, which they claim shows genre to be an insignificant factor for children. Buckingham's much larger study (1993a) found that genre did form one of several ways children used to distinguish between programmes. His research design, as has already been stated, influenced my own approach, and both approaches avoided the weakness of earlier work criticized by Eke and Kroll in that the genre terms themselves were not used by the researchers. Nevertheless, both Buckingham and

I found not just implicit genre divisions which could be seen as paralleling those used by adults but also explicit use of such terms as soap opera and sport.

Again, the research in terms of children's categorization of the books that they read is limited. Much divides material into very crude categories. Whitehead's classic study (Whitehead, Capey and Maddren 1975) into children's reading habits divided fiction into adult and juvenile narrative, each then sub-divided into quality and non-quality, with fairytales, myths and legends separate. These categories were imposed rather than suggested by the children. A more recent attempt to study the reading behaviour of 13- to 15-year-olds showed more awareness both of the prob-lematic nature of dividing up fiction and more regard to the categories used by the children themselves, but again categories have been adjusted by the researchers and so give only limited evidence of the ways in which children categorize initially (Heather, 1981). Littlefair's exploration into children's awareness of register (1991) did involve some 9- and 10-year-olds. She asked children of this age and older to sort pages from books so that they were put with other pages which she initially signalled as different from each other. Littlefair's findings echo those of Applebee, suggesting that, 'pupils' awareness of register is related to their development as readers and not to their chronological age' (Littlefair, 1991, p. 60). However, since the original groupings were suggested by her and since only individual pages were considered, this has only limited parallels with my work.

My findings suggest that genre is a significant factor among others for the children in my study; the strategies used by the children in orienting themselves towards any reading or viewing experience revealed a clear awareness of genre. The problematic nature of adult genre definitions is well documented (see, for example, Neale, 1980), but it is worth reiterating the point here that the systems used by adults are far from providing a logical, neat series of sub-divisions of programmes and books which children simply have to adopt for a ready-made and coherent categorization system. Although I shall be considering the extent to which children seemed aware both of adult genre labels and of commonly used groupings in this section, this is not to imply that such awareness is necessarily better than the other more creative grouping strategies used by the children.

Genre and Television

Although not all groups used genre as an initial strategy in the television categor-ization exercise, it would be oversimplistic to assume that the children were less aware of this as a way of orienting their own expectations to any programme or book than of other approaches. Once children's attention was directed towards sorting by television programme type, they showed that their initial preference for other categorization systems did not stem from a lack of awareness of the differ-ences between programmes. In fact, many of the labels had come to the point where the children were using them very confidently, with little disagreement and an assumption of shared meanings.

As can be seen from Tables 5.1 and 5.2 (pp. 83–8), the children use several genre terms familiar to us as adults. These include sport and comedy, which were used by a majority of the groups, and were often among the first labels to be introduced. 'Sport' and 'cartoon' are labels frequently used by television itself both in programme names and by announcers, and this may be a reason for children's earlier use of the adult terminology. However, comedy is also clearly signalled by programme announcers and by the use of laughter tracks, yet the pilot group children at least were less confident in their use of these labels. Two groups used comedy as a category; one group, however, placed all the comedies together with soaps and did not use comedy as a label at all.

Other 'adult' labels used by the children included soap opera (although this was more contentious), serials, drama, nature, and horror. From the assured way in which most programmes were sorted into these categories, it would appear that children are not only using these adult labels but are well aware of the meanings, although there were also signs that some at least of these labels are still being used in not entirely conventional ways. In the pilot study, for example, one group extended their 'Sport' category to include the motoring programme *Top Gear* and *Reaching for the Skies*, a series about the history of aviation. Another group agonized over the notion of the quiz show before dividing the category into 'Quizzes' and 'Sort of quizzes', the first including *A Question of Sport* and *Fifteen-to-One* and the second *Bullseye, This is Your Life* and *Blind Date*. Even this hesitation, though, reveals an awareness of the discontinuities and similarities between these programmes.

Soap opera is a very difficult genre to define, as Allen (1985) has shown, and it is also a term avoided by television companies because of its pejorative overtones. Continuity announcements tend instead to use such expressions as 'and now it's time to pay another visit to Albert Square' and official representatives of the television companies refer to 'continuing drama series'. None of the pilot groups used the term 'soap opera' despite the high popularity of soaps with that class, but several grouped these programmes together (sometimes including situation comedy) under such headings as 'Everyday (people that know each other)' or 'Families'. Here it seems that children are actively drawing on their own knowledge and experience of such programmes to create logical groupings although they have not yet learned the adult nomenclature.

The main fieldwork groups did use this term more or less conventionally for adult soaps, though each had one programme in this group which might be questionable (*Bergerac* in one case and *Grange Hill* in the other). Alexis spent some time justifying the inclusion of *Bergerac* in a way that reveals what might be seen as an incomplete understanding of this category:

MR	Can we put all of them away except the soaps? What have they got that's the same and what's different?
Alexis	*Bergerac* is really a soap
MR	Yeah? Why?
Ashley	Yeah
Alexis	Yeah, 'cause it's got police in it and detectives and like in *Bergerac* there's um, and there's — oh no — there's another programme like *Bergerac*, something . . .
Ashley	*Inspector Morse*

> Alexis   Yeah, *Inspector Morse*
> MR   *Inspector Morse* would be the same?
> Alexis   Yeah, that'd be soap, and it'd be nearly exactly the same
>   (Transcript 13, ll.226–37)

Similarly, this same group had a category, 'Children's soaps', which was far from containing what might conventionally be seen as soaps, and again their discussion reveals the extent to which this genre label is still proving problematic:

> MR   What's in children's soaps?
> [Alexis reads out the numbers from the name cards]
> MR   What is a soap then? What kind of programme is a soap?
> Ashley   A film that's carried on over the weeks
> Sarah   Yeah
> Alexis   Every day
> MR   So you think they're all included in that category, yeah?
> Neil   Those don't carry on every day, nor does that, nor does that
> Ashley   Every week
> Neil   Those don't carry on every day!
> Alexis   Leave them there, leave them there!
> Neil   We shouldn't have children's soaps
> Alexis   Should
>   (Transcript 13, ll.179–91)

Here the salient feature identified is frequency, although, as Neil points out, not all those included meet the criterion. In the case of *Bergerac*, Alexis was using content; later, Sarah argues that *The Flying Doctors* cannot be a soap 'because it's got aeroplanes in it' and is therefore unlike the others, despite its continuing story. This is one genre that the children are still coming to understand, and the other group, whilst apparently using the label conventionally, also spent some considerable time debating it, with David, in particular, much more confident about the term than the others:

> David   Can I just say something, *EastEnders* is a soap opera
> MR   What's a soap opera?
> David   It's a thing like, it looks like real, and before you say it's not someone in the bath washing theirself with some, singing in the bath with some soap
>   (Transcript 14, ll.1–5)

For David, the term is something he is sufficiently sure of to joke about, whereas for the others it causes more debate. Later in the same discussion Rikky identifies yet another key feature, the cliffhanger ending:

> MR   Now Rikky what did you just say to me about *Neighbours* and *Home and Away*?
> Rikky   They always end at really exciting bits
> Natalie And we have to wait until the next day

Rikky	We have to wait till the next day
MR	Isn't that the same as what you're saying about these?
Natalie	Yeah, I think they should go there
David	Why don't we put that together then, because they're both soap operas?
Natalie	That's what I just said
David	Yeah, and you wouldn't listen to me when I said it
	(Transcript 14, ll.112–22)

In some ways one of the pilot groups, whilst not using the conventional label, displayed a surer sense of what these programmes might have in common:

MR	Can you think of anything else like it?
Sharon	That's 'Not really know' pile
Emma	Anything else that's a bit like it . . . probably go with *Emmerdale Farm* and *Brookside*
Katie	No way!
MR	Do you think it's the same kind of thing, a story that . . .
Katie	No, no, that's all about . . . *EastEnders* is all about a street or a . . .
Emma	Why don't we put all the ones about a street like *Coronation Street*, *Emmerdale Farm*, *Brookside*, *EastEnders*, that's all about streets on . . .
Sharon	Yeah
Katie	Emma!
Emma	That's about a certain street
Katie	Emma, Emma, look, *EastEnders* it's got lots, it's got about five families in it and that's got about . . .
Emma	*Howards' Way* has got . . .
Sharon	It's all about boats
Emma	Yeah, *Howards' Way* is about boats
Sharon	Boats
Emma	It's a boatyard
MR	Is it about boats or is it about people?
Sharon	About boats
Emma	It's about the people and the boatyard
Sharon	Put about boats here
Katie	No Sharon
Emma	I'd keep that with *EastEnders*
Katie	Yeah
MR	You're saying *Howards' Way* is a story about several families like *EastEnders*, yeah?
Katie	*EastEnders* has got several families, that's got several families, that's got several families . . .
MR	*Neighbours*
Katie	That's got several families . . .
MR	*Coronation Street*
Katie	That's got several families, and that's got several families
MR	*Brookside*
Emma	*Reaching for the Skies* has got about seven, six families

MR	So do you think it could go with those?
Emma	Yeah
Katie	Yeah
	(Transcript 15, ll.33–72)

Although Sharon, as in the case of Sarah and the aeroplanes, is distracted by the boats, the other two see through this and focus on the use of a small neighbourhood as location and the relationships between the families to build connections.

Several groups appeared that had contents that most adults would see as consistent genre groupings, but with the children's own labels. 'Guns and shooting' was one such. Into this went *The Bill, Killer in the Mirror, The Guns of Diablo, Mission Impossible* and *Boon*, which all have connections. Even *Boon*, which at that time contained little 'guns and shooting', is formally a crime series. Another group included *Wogan, Going Live, Blue Peter* and *Wideawake* in a category they called 'Talking about things'. Both of the main fieldwork groups put together *Blind Date, Jim'll Fix It* and *Wogan* (with one group adding *This Is Your Life*) but came up with different titles (the more conventional 'Interviews' and the more imaginative 'Mysteries').

There were some groupings which, whilst displaying a clear internal logic, had neither an adult label nor demonstrated a conventional grouping. This would seem to suggest that children are drawing on their own opinions and experience of programmes rather than content. For example, the 'Hobbies' category used by one of the main fieldwork groups brought together *Grandstand, Survival* and *Top of the Pops*. Other creative sets of groupings included 'Surprises' (*Beadle's About* and *Blind Date*), 'Monsters and weird things' (*The Munsters* and *The Wombles*) and 'Life and death' (*Wildlife on One* and *Jimmy's*). Here children seem to be striving to make sense of the content of programmes and to look for overlaps with no anxiety about the ways in which adults might make connections, although these groups also used a variety of conventional genre labels. What is clear is that children are not operating on some watered-down system picked up passively from parents, the press or from television itself, but that they are actively using information gained from all these sources and from their own experience to sort out for themselves the differences and similarities between the programmes they watch.

Genre and Books

It is clear that genre was a significant factor in terms of television programmes, but we also need to ask what happened when the children sorted books. Since the children were asked to sort books after they had sorted television programmes, perhaps inevitably they drew on this prior experience to complete the second task, with the boys' group going straight to a sorting system using genres and with the girls starting by using the voting system some of them had used for television. Despite this, the categories used bore little resemblance in name or content to those used for television, though, as I shall show, there were underlying similarities of approach not created by the closeness of the two activities but suggesting a deeper overlap of strategy.

For books, as Table 5.3 shows (see pp. 87–8), there are less clearly recognized categories and genre labels readily available to the children, yet the two groups who tackled this task identified several recognizable groupings, including 'Nature', 'Wild-life', 'People and places' and 'History'. In the latter, though, just as in the 'Sport' category discussed above, they took a broad view, including *Norah's Ark* (a story, possibly confused with Noah's Ark) and *The Birth of Jesus*. Other books were grouped thematically, with themes sometimes bringing together fiction and non-fiction, as in the case of the 'Christmas' category, which included *The Birth of Jesus* and *The Snowman*. This overlap is not necessarily part of the developing differentiation between fact and fiction discussed above. As has already been shown, the girls were at pains to differentiate 'Animal stories' from 'Nature'.

A thematic approach was used to sub-divide the fiction into smaller groups. The boys used 'Adventure', 'Funny books' and 'Fairytales', and the girls suggested 'Animal stories', 'Cartoon/TV books', 'Food' and 'Children's royal books', all with fairly predictable contents. The links in the 'Cartoon/TV' group were perhaps the most tenuous, with the inclusion of a story they had seen as a dramatized serial; one they said had been on *Jackanory*; the book that inspired the cartoon *Granpa* and which is itself drawn in a style very similar to the cartoon; and the almost uncategorizable *Lovable Furry Old Grover's Resting Places* (a *Muppet Show* spin-off drawn in cartoons which invites children to rest various parts of their anatomy on different pages).

A Common Strategy?

Although the actual categories used for television and books may at first seem very different, when considered in terms of the strategies used, a high degree of overlap is apparent. I do not believe this came from the proximity of the two tasks; rather, this suggests a deeper level at which the children's general ability to make con-nections and to identify differences in a range of situations helped to create more precise expectations of viewing and reading situations. These go wider than genre, and show the extent to which the four categories of preference, appropriateness, modality and genre work together to help children to orient themselves towards specific books and television programmes. These four areas are very close to those identified by Buckingham (1993a) as the most salient for the children involved in his research.

The children grouped both books and television programmes by intended audience and by predicted audience reaction. Modality was used for both books and television, both times to distinguish cartoon as a separate category. Non-fiction groupings showed a consistent use of content to create groups, but intention was also used, as in the case of the book group labelled 'Information' and the variations on 'Telling you things' used for television. The only strategy used for television and not for books in non-fiction was programme style ('Quizzes', 'Documentaries',

'Interviews'). For fiction, all the strategies showed an overlap. Where genre was the key categorization principle, the categories of 'Fairytales' and 'Adventures' were used for both television and books. Although other specific genre labels were used exclusively for television, the principle of dividing in such a way was common to both media. Similarly, the principle of classification by intended effect (such as 'Horror') and by content (e.g., 'School' and 'Christmas') was used for both media. This would suggest that the kinds of features of both television programmes and books, particularly in the case of narratives which are identified by children as particularly salient, are common. What is not clear from this is how far this is a categorization strategy learned in one medium and transferred to the other; it seems more likely that the strategy goes wider than either medium to operate in a much wider range of situations.

How Were They Able to Do It?

I have shown, then, that children have a range of expectations, but how have these developed? It is clear, for example, from the different ways in which the children talk about soap opera, that they are not all operating in the same way. In broad terms this would seem to support Giddens' model, in that if for each agent there is a genuinely dialectic relationship with the social structure they are in, then since each individual brings different experiences with them, the understanding developing out of the dialectic will indeed be different for each. This can perhaps be more clearly explained by considering Vygotsky's theory of conceptual development, which, like all his work, is also set into a framework of a dynamic relationship between mind and society (or thought and culture), as discussed above in Chapter 3. He distinguishes between the spontaneous acquisition of concepts, where children draw inferences about commonality and difference from a range of actual experiences of life, and the scientific or non-spontaneous, where the category is presented to the child first and the experiences help to give the category meaning. He suggests that in many cases both processes are going on simultaneously, and I would argue that this is certainly the case here.

On the one hand, then, the children are experiencing a whole range of encounters with books and television from which they are beginning to make generalizations. However, these experiences are not happening in a vacuum but in a social viewing and reading context, so that as the child has these firsthand experiences, messages about the existence of different ways of categorizing these experiences are simultaneously being given to the child. For Emma and Katie, their own experience of soap opera has enabled their spontaneous understanding to develop to a point where they are able to articulate some of the relevant properties of soap opera although they are not yet using this label. For Alexis and David, the label has been given and they are struggling to reconcile this top–down information with their own experience. The messages which offer the non-spontaneous concepts come from a variety of sources, some of which will be the same for all the children in my group and some of which will vary considerably.

Vygotsky also argues that children's ability to think in concepts develops only gradually, and that the last stage in this development before full conceptual understanding, which he calls the stage of pseudo-concepts (Vygotsky, 1962), is characterized by a tendency to rely too heavily on one attribute of a concept rather than being able to use several attributes at once. The children's discussions as presented in this chapter suggest that they are largely operating in this way (for example, the various discussions of soap opera often seemed to concentrate on one characteristic, as highlighted above). One factor, then, that will have influenced the responses of the children will have been their developmental stages — although Vygotsky does not suggest that these stages are arrived at independently, but that they are arrived at through the process of socialization as individual and society interact.

The Influence of Family and Peer Group

Although I have already explored in broad terms the ways in which parents, siblings and the extended family frame children's understandings of literacy, the data collected for this chapter can add more detail to this picture. In much of what the children say about violent or sexually explicit material, we can again see parental prohibitions and also ambivalence, and it is in this context that children are developing their own exnominated concepts of appropriateness and of what counts as rude, for example. The home, then, would seem to be one influence in children's developing ability to use such criteria as appropriateness.

A clearer picture of the different messages given by different families can be seen by comparing Sarah's views on violent films with those of her peers. Sarah was the only child in the group to come from the private housing estate on the other side of the main road from the school, and her dress, speech and manner were markedly different from the other girls. (Whilst a more ideological analysis would demand more precise details of Sarah's family background, I would argue that my knowledge of the area of the school and of Sarah's home, drawn both from my experiences during the time I spent with the class, from staffroom conversations and from my own experience of living very near Sarah, enables me to make this distinction, whilst acknowledging its subjective nature.) During the work on appropriateness, Sarah worked with Kelly, and this was not an easy collaboration. At several points during the discussion of the programmes on the finished charts it was clear that Sarah held very different views from the other girls and that she had seen far less of the adult material under discussion than they had. In broad terms, this was apparent from her opposite answers to general questions; more specifically it arose from her insistence that *After Henry,* stigmatized by Kelly as boring, was not suitable viewing for her 5-year-old sister, a position that left Alexis bewildered:

Alexis	Mrs Robinson, that doesn't make sense, on the second column it says 'programmes young children shouldn't watch which we can watch'
MR	Yes, so things that are okay for you but wouldn't be okay for younger children

> Kelly I know, but on, *After Henry* and that, I told her not to do that
> Sarah My sister isn't allowed to watch *After Henry*
> (Transcript 7, ll.88–94)

Again, when Sarah described her own sister's anti-social behaviour, her example is much less extreme than that of Alexis:

> Sarah It was really funny because my sister watched this programme and this man was fat and um, James came to watch, and she goes, 'James, you're like the person in this film,' and I go, 'Claire!'
> (Transcript 7, ll.176–9)

The other girls saw her experience as restricted, though softening this by focusing their comments on her sister rather than on her:

> Kelly   But *Mrs Frisby*, that's like a baby — sorry
> Alexis   That's like a children's programme, isn't it?
> MR   What do you think about *Mrs Frisby*?
> Kelly   It was her that wanted to write it
> Sarah   Yes, but there's mice in it
> Natalie But mice doesn't hurt children, does it?
> Sarah   But my sister isn't allowed to watch it
> Natalie Your sister isn't allowed to (see?) anything
> (Transcript 7, ll.95–102)

Since her school experience and contact with the media is very similar to that of the other girls, it seems likely that here Sarah is influenced by her home background on these questions, which would suggest that family and home play a large part in transmitting attitudes to appropriateness. Buckingham (1993a) found a similar example in the case of Ben, whose views on which programmes counted as adult stemmed from his home experience and were markedly different from those of other children. However, Sarah's views are now also being influenced by hearing the different attitudes of her peers, and the peer group is another important influence to be considered.

Throughout the exchanges detailed above, there is a clear sense of debate; the children extend, develop and challenge each other's ideas, a pattern of behaviour which is sufficiently clear for the role of the peer group to be said to be an influential one. The ways in which the children are explicitly teaching each other has been seen in David's attempts to insist on the others using such categories as drama and soap opera (see p. 103); what can also be seen from this is that there can be real resistance from peers to such peer pressure if it is seen as inappropriate or if it comes from someone with less power in the group. This resistance, of course, does not mean that the other children will not learn from David's information; just that they will be reluctant to let him see them doing so. There are in each transcript certain children who speak more than others and these children do seem to have more influence, or, as in David's case, to be striving to have more influence. This would suggest that within the community of the classroom, there are certain children who are more influential on their peers' development than others, just as we have already seen that Radway (1987) found certain adults to be more influential than others in the development of reading.

Messages from the Media and the Wider World

These children are undoubtedly influenced by home and by school contacts, but they are also encountering attitudes and information in the wider world. Attitudes about appropriateness may be influenced by the wider world as well as by family, through attitudes expressed in the media and also by such explicit labels as the film classification system, separate children's sections in bookshops and libraries, and 'adult' shelves in newsagents and videos. Much information about modality and genre is also passed on by the media. Both newspapers and television regularly pass on information about actors and about the making of various programmes that emphasize the constructed nature of television, and there are now more features on television about children's authors and about televised versions of children's books which again help to make explicit the modality status of fiction. However, the media can also present information that can confuse modality, when, for example, the cast of a programme such as *Casualty* appears in character on fund-raising programmes such as *Children in Need*, or when newspapers comment on the behaviour of characters in soaps and invite readers to offer their opinions in the same way that they invite comment on the behaviour of members of the royal family.

Both books and television often identify genres for readers and viewers. I have already mentioned the ways in which continuity announcers and programme names act as cues (as in 'time for sport' or *Sport on Four*). Television trailers also play a part here, particularly when they are for 'the new season's drama' or particular film series. The illustrations on some book covers also emphasize the genre, particularly in the case of what is called genre fiction; series of school stories or pony books will make this clear in the cover picture. (This is also true of adult books, such as the distinctive yellow covers of Crime Club novels.) Non-fiction books often come in series which make their genre explicit through the name of the series and which display this on the cover. Bookshops and libraries also help to stress genre categories — as do video shops — by grouping material generically and by labelling sections prominently. The influence of the children's school library in particular can be seen in such labels as 'People and Places' and 'History'.

A Developing Range of Strategies

In this chapter I have shown how the children in my research group come to each viewing or reading situation not just with broad understandings about television and literacy derived from their everyday experience as social beings, but that overlapping and extending these broad concepts are more specific strategies which orient and frame each individual encounter with text. These strategies include ideas about programmes and books which stem from understandings about personal preference, which for the girls are nearly exclusively drawn from narrative. They also provide views about appropriateness, which show an awareness but not necessarily acceptance of the views of adults and a distancing of the possibility of harm from them onto less powerful members of society. This is very similar to the distancing strategies seen in the critics of television discussed in Chapter 1.

More precisely, the children have developing concepts of modality and genre which show evidence both that they are drawing from prior viewing experiences and that external sources including parents and the media are providing complementary information. Thus, as children begin to read a book or watch a television programme, they already have a whole series of expectations as to whether they will like it, whether they are the intended audience, and what kind of text it will be. These strategies do not appear to be noticeably different for different media and draw on understandings used in many other situations.

The evidence offered by the data goes a long way towards confirming the theoretical models suggested above. In Chapter 3, I argued for a view of language, culture and thought as interrelated. In this chapter, I have suggested that one way to describe this interrelation is to draw on the model offered by Giddens, which in its turn echoes many of the ideas explored above of Volosinov and Bakhtin. Just as these children have been seen to be learning about broad issues to do with television and reading as social objects, so they are developing a range of strategies for approaching texts which acknowledge that every reading act takes place in a complex context of duality between what Giddens terms agents and structures. What remains to be seen is what the children do when reading particular texts.

Chapter 6

Personal Response to the Texts

I have suggested that to read narrative we need to do certain things: we need to interpret the text; to fill in the gaps left in the discourse; to predict; to empathize with the characters; and to become involved in the story as it unfolds. In this and the next two chapters, having shown how far the children in my study are reading in a cultural context and how they bring certain expectations to any reading situation, I look more closely at what the children did when we shared a range of printed and textual narratives. The next two chapters look at the ways the children drew on the textual evidence and at the evidence they drew from other sources. In this chapter, though, I set the scene by explaining what we actually did and by considering the children's personal responses to each of the texts. How far were they empathizing, hypothesizing, interpreting? And how did these competencies manifest themselves in different media and different genres?

What We Did

All the work described in this chapter was done with the core group of eight children in my main fieldwork, and for each of the six texts a similar approach was adopted. We watched or read the stories together and the children were encouraged to respond at any time as we did so; however, there were also moments when I stopped the narrative and asked for responses. The children were encouraged to predict what might happen in any particular situation and to comment freely on any aspect of the narratives. Many of their comments took the form of evaluative retellings, as will be seen below. All the sessions were taped and transcribed for analysis.

This joint emphasis on interpretation and prediction was not designed to check what the children said against some predetermined preferred reading; in fact, little of the analysis below is concerned with how far the children's predictions were borne out by subsequent events or with how far I might happen to agree with their readings. Rather, I encouraged such responses because I believed that this would necessitate active involvement in the texts by the children in a way that would allow me to look for commonalities and differences of strategies used on the texts, and the analysis below takes this approach.

The Narratives We Used

Altogether we explored six narratives, three televisual and three printed, but not all received the same degree of attention. The two central narratives I chose were the children's television serial *Grange Hill* and a children's book, *Gaffer Samson's Luck*, by Jill Paton Walsh. Although not immediately obvious, there were several parallels between these two which led me to this choice.

The television programme was chosen because it was apparent from the pilot that it would be valuable to look at an extended narrative, but if there were to be parallels with a printed text I felt this needed to be a programme which was extended into several episodes but which did not have the complete endlessness of a soap opera. *Grange Hill* seemed suitable on several counts: I was familiar with previous series; it was a text that had been created specifically for television; and a new series was being shown, so none of the children could have prior knowledge. A programme currently being shown on live television would also help to make the work as near to the children's usual viewing experience as possible. If the choice was to be appropriate in terms of the children's usual viewing, it also needed to be something which some at least would choose to watch.

To echo the experience of watching a bi-weekly serial, I chose to read a novel to the children and the choice of this was framed by the choice of *Grange Hill*. Here, again, it needed to be something new to the children but which built on their experience. *Gaffer Samson's Luck* offered the children the chance to use their own prior experience of schooling but asked them to deal with a less familiar rural setting. None of the children had read it and it had not been read to them or serialized on television; there was no copy in the school library. The length made it suitable for serialized reading in chunks of roughly the same duration as an episode of *Grange Hill*.

Of the children in my research group, four (two boys and two girls) were fairly regular viewers of *Grange Hill* and the other four had watched occasionally but did not watch regularly. This allowed some possibility of considering the advantages of regular viewing for prediction and so all the *Grange Hill* work was carried out in these two groups. To make things easier for the reader, Table 6.1 sets out membership of these groups:

Table 6.1: Membership of the groups

Regular Viewers	Less Frequent Viewers
Alexis	Natalie
Ashley	Neil
David	Rikky
Kelly	Sarah

The initial activity was carried out about a month after the children had been alerted to my interest in the programme and at a point slightly more than midway through the series. This involved using the title sequences of the previous series and the new series, considering some of the textual features of these and asking the children about why the titles might have been changed, but it also offered a way in to a more general discussion of the programme past and present. The following week the children were asked to agree not to watch the Tuesday episode on the understanding that I would video it for us to watch together in school. This then allowed the two groups to watch the episode, which I stopped at certain key points to ask what they thought might happen next and to allow some general discussion.

At the same time as the initial work on *Grange Hill*, I began to read the children the Paton Walsh book. I decided to read this aloud for a range of reasons. Firstly, I wanted to treat this as a shared experience because I wanted to encourage a situation in which it would seem natural to talk about the book even during the reading. If all the children had read the book for themselves, I would have had no access to their spontaneous reactions. As is the case in most primary schools, the children were used to being read to by their class teacher and so were relatively confident in the slightly new situation where interruptions and comments were permitted. Additionally, the group had been deliberately chosen to include children with a range of reading ability and for some the book would be very straightforward whilst others might struggle. Since my interest was — and is — in the ways in which children derive meaning rather than on their precise decoding skills, to ask the children to read the book for themselves would bring an unnecessary factor into play. The analysis I have undertaken does not focus either on the children's approach to decoding print or on their understanding of such technical aspects of television as camera angles or cutting and fading, and so it was far more appropriate to read aloud and ensure a common experience for all the children, with the advantages outlined above of a shared experience and immediacy of response, than to ask the children to read individually. Given the presence of reluctant readers in the group, and my own non-teaching role in the school, I could not have guaranteed that all the children would have completed any private reading I asked them to do. Thus both philosophical and practical considerations made reading aloud the best option for this situation.

Over the next four weeks I read to the children six times, and then we read the last thirty pages in one day with more specific pauses at key points in the narrative to ask for the children's predictions and reactions. The children worked as one group for this, although not all eight children were available on every occasion. This unavoidable change in group constitution lent itself to a genuine need to recap at the beginning of each reading session. After the final session children were given the chance to draw what they perceived as the most significant part of the book.

In addition to the work on *Grange Hill* and *Gaffer Samson's Luck*, I also worked with the children on the soap opera *Neighbours*. Although this is shown immediately after the end of children's programming on BBC 1, it is, strictly speaking, adult programming and so I had originally planned not to use this despite the great interest in the programme shown during the pilot. However, as I worked with the children they made many spontaneous references to *Neighbours* and it was clear that it was a significant part of their experience of narrative on television, so I repeated an activity from the pilot by recording the lunchtime broadcast of one day's episode and showing it to the children that afternoon. This enabled me to be absolutely sure that none of them could have seen this episode whereas for *Grange Hill* I had had to take this on trust. Again as we watched I stopped the tape to ask for predictions.

Neighbours, like *Grange Hill* and *Gaffer Samson's Luck*, is an extended (apparently unending) narrative and is, at least in theory, realist drama. As an extension of this work, I decided to consider some other narratives that were self-contained and which operated with a different view of reality. I have already discussed notions of reality and children's approaches to realist texts at some length above, but the distinction I make here between fantasy and reality needs explanation. The dividing line between fiction and non-fiction becomes blurred when narrative comes into play, in that whenever we tell a story of something which has happened to us, that story is not the same as the events, even if we are not deliberately or subconsciously exaggerating or misrepresenting the event; the telling by one person can only be that person's understanding of what has occurred and not the whole. Similarly, I have already argued that reality itself is an elusive concept and that different people have different understandings of reality, some of which may be more verifiable by research or experience than others, but all of which ultimately remain as working hypotheses.

The narratives I used with the children represent a range of views of reality, some of which are more firmly grounded in a world the children would recognize from their everyday experience than others. For ease of expression in this chapter, I describe three of the narratives as fantasy and three as realist, but, as will become apparent from the analysis below, what is really at stake here is the extent to which the children can draw on their everyday understanding of the world to interpret the stories as opposed to the extent to which literary rather than everyday experience is necessary. *Grange Hill*, *Gaffer Samson's Luck* and *Neighbours* are not identical in their closeness to the children's experience, but they do all have preferred readings which suggest that such things can and do happen in the world the children inhabit, and the children judge them in terms of their own perception of that world. The other narratives I used do not purport to belong to that same world, or where they do (as in the case of *Mr Magus is Waiting for You*) they suggest that the world is not as it seems by including experiences beyond the children's lives; in this case, magic and the secret of eternal youth. When I describe them as fantasy, or the other stories as realist, this is the distinction I am implying by these shorthand terms.

The choice of a fantasy television programme had to be of something available on video so that we could watch it together in one sitting. I wanted to avoid anything which might have been adapted from a book or which would be too familiar and so I chose a programme that had been made for educational television and which I knew had not been shown in the school. This was *Mr Magus is Waiting for You*, originally shown in three short parts but which we watched in one sitting. Although there was a book available, the book version had appeared simultaneously with the series (both screenplay and novel being by the same author, Gene Kemp) and was not in the school library. Although having an apparently everyday setting, the story included a magician and certain incidents which could be seen as magic. To set alongside this I chose two fantasy printed narratives, a version of a Russian folk tale called *Baba Yaga* and *Outside Over There*, a picture book by Maurice Sendak telling a story that owes a great deal to the folk tale tradition.

The activities based on these narratives were carried out in the summer term. Five of the original group were available for the work on *Mr Magus is Waiting for You*, which again we watched with pauses to discuss probable outcomes. The work on the books followed a similar pattern; again, only five of the children were there for all of this, though two others were there for part of the time.

The Children's Responses

Grange Hill

As the children watched and discussed *Grange Hill*, there was clear evidence that they were using what they had seen and heard but also what they already knew from their own experience both of life and other narratives, and including their developing understanding of modality. There was evidence that those who watched regularly did operate differently, but it was quickly apparent that the groupings I had created had rather more complex attributes than I had anticipated. Right from the beginning it was clear that even those who claimed to be infrequent viewers had views about the series and the characters, and that they were judging the programme as they watched. In fact, as the work progressed, it became clear that the children's view as to whether they were regular *Grange Hill* watchers came not so much from a direct relationship to the number of times they watched but some more complex identification with the programme. In the same way as I might describe myself as an *EastEnders* viewer because I try to watch when I can even though I often miss the programme for weeks on end, so some of the children saw themselves as *Grange Hill* viewers but then forgot to watch or were otherwise occupied, so that not all the group of regular viewers actually did watch regularly. Similarly those who said they did not usually watch often had quite a store of information; some had watched in the past but did not now either because they found this series less appealing or because of a clash with other programmes, others watched occasionally because there was nothing better on, and some had interest aroused by the extracts watched together and became more frequent viewers. I shall continue to describe the two groups as 'less frequent' or 'regular' viewers on the basis of this difference but behind this terminology lies the definition above rather than any simple quantitative one.

Despite this apparent overlapping of experience, those who had labelled themselves as regular viewers did respond differently. Although both groups had a good knowledge of the series, the regular viewers went beyond displaying this knowledge to use it to express more general opinions. They had the confidence to criticize unresolved or weak story lines and although they used less explicit references to visual cues, they drew on those they did use to make inferences in a way which the less frequent viewers did not. Not only did they incorporate more direct quotations in their retellings, but they used their knowledge to invent direct speech in these. They were more tolerant of change (as with the theme tune) and more likely to draw on their experience outside the texts, both of which show a more confident stance. When they had missed an episode they were anxious to fill the gaps in their knowledge, and they were more confident in their ability to understand and predict events. This confidence led them to be more critical of points at which they found the plot unsatisfactory; they tended to assume a weakness in the programme rather than thinking they had missed the point.

The less frequent viewers did have enough knowledge of previous series to identify characters and make value judgments about them. These judgments both identify certain behaviour as deviant ('he kept being naughty') and as entertaining. Natalie in particular describes Ronnie in both ways:

> MR   How about the people there, how many of those people did you recognize?
> Natalie Loads of them, quite a lot, Ronnie, Calley . . .
> MR   What things do you remember about them from other programmes that you've seen?
> Natalie They're not very good, well Ronnie wasn't, she nicked a jumper from a shop
> (Transcript 18, ll.146–52)

> MR   What are the bits from *Grange Hill* from the past that you do remember, that you enjoyed?
> Natalie I liked it when Ronnie nicked that jumper, I felt really excited then
> (Transcript 18, ll.213–15)

Here, Natalie makes it clear that although she can see the preferred reading that Ronnie's behaviour is wrong, she can also appreciate the dramatic value such incidents give to the programme; her first comment labels Ronnie's behaviour as 'not very good' where her second highlights her own response — 'I felt really excited'. Natalie's feelings about an incident in which two pupils are nearly caught using the photocopier are just as complex. While watching, she is so involved that (even though she has seen this bit before) she gasps, 'Oh no, they're going to get done' (transcript 18, ll.129–30) and yet later when describing this incident she describes it as:

> Natalie People being naughty and stuff like that . . . using the photocopier and we're not allowed so they shouldn't be . . .
> (Transcript 18 ll.182–3)

This reveals the complexity of the process of reading this text; Natalie is both caught up in the unfolding narrative to the extent where she vocalizes her concern almost involuntarily, and at the same time in spectator role (Britton, 1972) she is comparing the behaviour she sees with her own view of the world and passing judgment on the incident as 'people being naughty'. This later, more reflective pronouncement may also be her view of what she feels will be seen as an acceptable reaction in this school situation, but her reasoning (that is, if she is not allowed to behave in a certain way then neither should the *Grange Hill* pupils be allowed to) suggests at least some personal feeling that this behaviour is indeed inappropriate.

The regular viewers also make many comments which express their likes and dislikes of particular characters, but they go beyond this to express more general opinions which suggest that they are not just empathizing with certain characters but placing the whole series in a context alongside other experiences. In the course of the discussion about titles, for example, there are eight places in just under seventy lines of transcript where the view that the titles show typical school events is expressed by Ashley or David.

The children all attempt to fill gaps and resolve the implied narrative; the regular viewers are explicitly critical, though, of places where they feel they have been left to do too much of this, both with reference to the fire started by Matthew and the incident when the girls printing teeshirts were trapped in poisonous fumes:

Ashley   They never told us what happened though, like, they could have died but then they all came out but they could have died, they could have . . .

Kelly   They could have said when they, um, finished it, that they hadn't died or something
(Transcript 19, ll.221–5)

Although, in the case of Matthew's fire, the missing knowledge could be seen as relatively easy for a more experienced viewer to imply, the second example was genuinely unresolved and left up in the air in a way that I too had found surprising. What is clear, though, is that even when discussing very short extracts, such as the title sequence, the children have opinions to share that are triggered by this and that show that they are indeed interpreting and building meaning from what they have seen.

For both groups there was a sense of involvement when we watched together, with many gasps and advice offered to the characters (for example, when Tegs' father asks him to come and live with him, one of the less frequent viewers can be heard whispering, 'Say no!'). This involvement came through not only in the children's attention and commentary but in the ability they had to predict. Each time that I stopped the tape and asked the children what they thought would happen, they were able to respond with only one exception, and when they did respond, at least some of the responses suggested specific outcomes to the plot.

The actual predictions varied quite markedly between the two groups. This will be explored in greater detail as I begin to ask what strategies the children were using to make their predictions, but as a small example it is worth comparing the two groups' responses to the story about Neil Timpson's homework:

MR   So what things so far seem to be going on?
Natalie   Well Neil . . .
Neil   Huh?
Natalie   No, not you!
Sarah   Neil can't do his homework or something, he can't do it, he wasn't paying attention when the teacher told them
(Transcript 20, ll.17–22)

MR	What do you think is going to happen?
Ashley	I reckon his homework is going to reappear on that piece of paper and then it's going to disappear again
David	Yeah
Alexis	He's going to write it and then the other piece'll come up
MR	So there'll be two lots on top of each other?
Kelly	It's only a guess but I think somebody's swapped a book, same book round

(Transcript 21, ll.46–53)

In this second extract, the regular viewers, even those who have not seen the prior episode in which we were let in on the planned joke, offer a more detailed account of what is happening and will happen. Here the two versions offered as interpretations also highlight the effects of watching previously and of listening to the group discussion. Earlier David had reminded us of the plan to use invisible ink so that Ashley and Alexis (who had both missed the previous episode) come up with a plausible prediction whereas Kelly, who had watched the previous week (and in fact who seemed to have watched at least part of the episode they had been asked not to watch), has a less likely one. Even the less attentive Kelly, though, has a better understanding of what is likely to happen than the much vaguer interpretation by Sarah, who has even less to draw on.

The children's response to *Grange Hill* shows that they are actively interpreting what they see, making assumptions which will fill gaps in the text, predicting possible outcomes and identifying with the characters and situations in a way that suggests they are involved personally with the narrative. The ease with which they did this despite the constraints of working in unusual conditions (at school with me, in front of video and audio tape recorders) suggests that this behaviour is relatively normal for them. But what happens when children encounter narrative in printed form?

Gaffer Samson's Luck

When considering *Gaffer Samson's Luck*, I want to look at the same areas of potential support for interpretation as in the case of *Grange Hill*, that is, evidence of engagement with the text, of empathy with characters and of a spectator stance. First, though, it is important to consider how the two experiences differed.

Obviously reading *Gaffer Samson's Luck* was not a directly comparable experience to watching *Grange Hill*. In terms of the children's expectations, this was a very different situation in that I was now acting much more recognizably as a teacher by reading *to* them than I had been by watching television *with* them. Their class teacher regularly read to them, even if not in quite this way, and so almost certainly had every teacher they had encountered. This may have constrained the children so that, for example, they felt it less appropriate to criticize the text when I was so much more immediately the agent of production. These issues of the children's social expectations and of my own role have been discussed more extensively earlier, but they do need to be foregrounded here too.

As well as this change of approach, and in fact in part creating this, there was a change of medium, since this was what I was hoping to explore. This reduced considerably the amount of visual information (there are a few line drawings in the book, and a cover illustration) and removed the sound effects and music. This time the children all started with no prior knowledge of this particular text; there was a difference, though, in their reading experience and ability, and although the direct impact of this was removed by my reading the text aloud, the indirect implication was that some of the group had far more prior knowledge of how stories in books worked than others and had greater potential intertextual knowledge to draw on.

When we turn to consider how the children responded to this new text, there are some differences, but also some striking similarities. There is less hard evidence that the children are engaging with the characters and narrative, particularly in the earlier sessions, but given that they are starting from new with these characters this is not surprising. By the later sessions, there are several points at which the children do express opinions about particular characters. These are often negative comments about characters with whom the main character, James, has either a hostile or ambivalent relationship, and as such might be said to suggest that the children are adopting the preferred reading of this text, which is written from James's point of view. For example, when one character has an accident, there is little sympathy from Alexis, although the boys are less hard:

Alexis	I hope he's going to die
Kelly	Yeah
MR	You hope he's going to die?
Ashley	No
David	I wouldn't
Kelly	Unless his brain splinters up
Alexis	Oh God, Kelly! You're disgusting
Rikky	Yeah, why don't the baddies win for a change?

(Some others echo this, others make noises of disgust)
(Transcript 26, ll.245–53)

Particularly in the case of Angey, this tendency for the negative comments to be tempered with sympathy is strong, just as James finds himself being friendly towards her in spite of himself:

Natalie	I think James is going to tell Angey that . . .
Kelly	That she smells like a rubbish heap
MR	What did he say she smelt like?
Kelly	Cat food
MR	He said she smelt like earth
David	That's nice
Kelly	In a grocery store
MR	Yeah, under the potatoes, that kind of . . .
David	That's nice, I like it

(Transcript 23, ll.47–55)

Apart from Rikky's comment above, there is less comment on the morality of the action in this story, but there are fewer examples of admired characters acting in a way the children might see as wrong, so this may be to do with the texts. Although Rikky's comment is only a small sign, it does suggest that the idea of hero and villain is clearly established for him at least as relevant.

Although there are fewer signs in the transcript of active involvement by the children, there are still several points at which they do react. There are gasps of horror and disappointment, and there is laughter. There are also conversations in which children show that they have been sufficiently involved to draw on what has been said in previous sessions and to want to discuss their interpretations of what might happen:

MR	*... across half the hearth the tiles were solid, and the plant cover came clean away, like a heavy rug lifting, as he tugged and tore it from its entangled edges.*
MR	What do you think?
David	He's going to, um, the tiles ...
Rikky	Yesterday Kelly said that um, he might find the luck under the um, water, in the water
David	The, um tiles ...
Alexis?} Sarah?}	Yes
MR	It's a bit like that, but you were thinking of the river, weren't you, but it is under the water
David	The tiles are underneath a little bit of his house, it might not be a bit of his house, it might be the roof that came off in a storm
	(Transcript 26, ll.148–62)

David intervenes three times here to make the point he wants to, persisting despite the lack of explicit encouragement from me or the other children, and showing by his final comment that his involvement is at least partly intellectual as well as emotional.

Alexis in particular is sufficiently involved to be disappointed by the ending, not so much because the narrative is unsatisfying but because she wants more:

Alexis	Is that the end?
MR	Yes
Alexis	That's a bit ...
MR	Why are you cross?
Alexis	Because I liked that story
	(Transcript 26, ll.375–80)

As an avid reader myself I recognize this feeling of frustration that an enjoyable experience is over which can easily sit alongside a feeling of satisfaction in the resolution of the narrative.

There is a great deal of retelling and prediction here, more in proportion than for *Grange Hill*, and although some of this was invited, much of it (especially in the earlier tapes) was spontaneous, sparked off by a comment from one child and developed by the others into a conversation:

Kelly   Mrs Robinson, I think if, when he goes fishing he might find it under the sea somewhere
Alexis I thought he might fish it up
David   Gaffer Samson's bad luck
Kelly   Yeah, he might reel it up
Rikky   If he goes fishing the other kids'll catch him, 'cause they're fishing they are
          (Transcript 25, ll.42–9)

Even when I was stopping the story at set points in the final session, the children also spontaneously added their own predictions at other points.

Whereas in the case of *Grange Hill* the children showed their involvement as spectators by at times criticizing what they saw as weaknesses in the narrative, here there were no examples of this. Maybe the children were reluctant to criticize a book I was reading to them, but it seems more likely that this narrative structure had less of the same kinds of confusions and unresolved stories. One of the main differences between the kind of narrative in such television dramas as *Grange Hill* and the kind commonly found in children's literature is in the number of storylines. In *Grange Hill* there were different storylines running through for each group of characters, but in *Gaffer Samson's Luck* there is one main plot with a number of interrelated sub-plots. The complexity of continuing narratives often leads to certain storylines being left relatively unresolved, and so there may be more scope for children to comment on narrative uncertainties on television than in print.

Overall, the differences summarized here seem less significant than the overlaps. Even though it is less pronounced here than in the longer discussions about *Grange Hill*, the children did show signs of involvement and identification with characters in this new narrative, and this involvement increased as we got further through the book and the children felt more familiar with the characters. As I begin to discuss the other narratives that were considered, it will be important to think about whether medium is a more significant factor than length and familiarity.

Neighbours

In general, this experience confirmed the pattern shown by the children when responding to the earlier narratives. There was clear evidence of involvement and identification. The children's general enthusiasm for this programme was the reason for its inclusion. Their conversation frequently came round to *Neighbours* and even those who professed not to like the programme displayed a thorough knowledge of characters and plot. Their enthusiasm, however, was not uncritical, and their opinions were frank:

Ashley	I watch it but it's rubbish
MR	Why is it rubbish?
Ashley	Well, it's not rubbish some weeks, some weeks it is rubbish like when Des was having a kiss with this girl and his dad came in and she went (slapping noise), it was really funny
Alexis	That was stupid, really stupid
Neil	I like the one when they made . . .
Ashley	It didn't make sense 'cause he'd already seen them kissing and it wasn't Des's fault
Neil	I like the one when Des and his dad were having that argument and Mike goes, 'Right I'm going to bed now good night argue in the morning' (Laughter) (Transcript 12, ll.177–88)

The intensity of feeling about the programme made Alexis at least much less tolerant of talk as we watched:

David	What are they eating?
Alexis	Salad so shut up!
David	It's definitely not from Henry
Alexis	Be quiet! (Transcript 27, ll.71–4)

The children could recognize feelings and match them to their own response to situations:

MR	What about something that's happened that would happen?
Ashley	Like Todd running away
Sarah	That's what I was going to say, somebody could be horrible to you and they think they . . .
Alexis	That's what I feel like, when my mum tells me off
Sarah	And they could go to a burglar and they could go and grab that, those thieves
Neil	I sometimes get the feeling people are spying on me, like in *Neighbours* Todd and like my life (Transcript 12, ll.471–9)

There was a tendency to anticipate and predict even during extracts, as in this commentary on the closing moments of the episode:

Sarah	She's going to break it
David	Yeah, she's going to go . . . oh no . . .
MR	Is it going to work?
(General no)	
David	It's going to spring a leak
Alexis	All the water's going to go everywhere
David	Yeah, 'cause he's got some dishes in there (Transcript 27, ll.199–205)

This ability to predict was not confined to the more obvious situations but was also evident even in the more complex, adult-oriented storylines, such as the business problems of two regular characters:

MR	What do you think is going to happen about that, about Paul wanting to buy this other company?
David	It's going to happen and they're going to . . .
Natalie	Split up
David	. . . Get done, they're going to have to have, um . . .
MR	Did someone say they'll split up, why?
Alexis	'Cause Paul won't give up
David	And Gail will
Natalie	And Gail said she doesn't want to mortgage the house
Kelly	I think they'll have a row and they'll get divorced again like the other time, I think there's going to be a divorce this time
	(Transcript 27, ll.78–89)

Here the children all seem to have ideas about what will happen, despite the complexity of the issues, and these draw on past knowledge of the programme ('they'll get divorced *again like the other time*') as well as the events in this episode.

This question of the role of prior knowledge as a factor in personal response is foregrounded by the children's response to this text. The way in which the children use their prior knowledge of the series suggests that the lack or possession of prior knowledge is more important than the difference in media. *Neighbours* offers many more opportunities to children to increase their knowledge of it than either *Grange Hill* or *Gaffer Samson's Luck*. The latter, as has already been said, was completely new to the children, and no secondary texts in the form of prequels, sequels, television interviews with characters or author or speculation in the press about developments or the lives of the characters were available. *Grange Hill* has some of this; it has been running for the whole of these children's lives and does occasionally provoke news items or press or television coverage of actors or series. *Neighbours*, although more recent, is on twice a day all year and has generated tremendous media interest, with secondary texts including not only press features on the series and characters but appearances by the actors as pop stars and pantomime characters.

It is much easier, then, to have access to this prior knowledge in the case of *Neighbours*, but it is also more important within the peer group to have access to such knowledge. Similarly their use of generic knowledge and of the extra-textual information available about soaps emphasizes that the more information is available, the more children will use and the more confident they will be in coping with new sections of text. This may suggest a potential for difference between children's responses to written and televisual texts which is not inherent in the discursive differences but which stems from the context in which children encounter such texts. That is, there is generally less extra-textual information available for books, and often children have little prior experience to draw on when reading a written text. Where such extra-textual information is available, it may be that children will read with more confidence; this may go some way to explain the popularity of series such as Enid Blyton's *Famous Five* books or of books that have been serialized on television.

Mr Magus is Waiting for You

The first non-realist text I watched with the children was *Mr Magus is Waiting for You*, a three-part drama which we watched in one session with pauses at the end of each episode. The children had no prior knowledge of this at all, so that in this respect it was nearer to their experience of *Gaffer Samson's Luck* than of *Grange Hill*. At the same time, the story featured characters who were very much like the pupils in *Grange Hill*. The events of the story moved well beyond the realist drama of any of the texts previously studied, though, with a clearly magical theme introduced.

The children did respond to the characters, but did not empathize as strongly with them as with those in the more familiar television programmes previously considered. Their verbal responses were more those of the detached yet interested observer, whilst their behaviour often suggested intense concentration. Very early on, there is criticism of the characters' behaviour:

> *David* What's she doing? That's stupid
> *Neil*   Oh my God!
> (Transcript 28, ll.67–8)

Later, there is also some criticism of the actual discourse:

> *Kelly*   It shouldn't really start from where they're kicking the football 'cause we don't really know what's happening at the moment, because it should be . . .
> *Natalie* They should start . . .
> *Kelly*   . . . They're playing football and they accidentally kicked it
> (Transcript 28, ll.336–40)

Here there is a sense in which Kelly at least seems reluctant to fill in all the gaps and is critical of the amount of space given to the reader, even though she finds it hard to explain what she would have liked as the beginning.

However, the children do both spontaneously and at my request revisit the narrative to interpret what they have seen. There were many short comments to explain the action as we watched, which appeared not to be addressed to anyone in particular but to be a form of thinking out loud, or what Vygotsky (1962) might describe as inner speech, as when Sarah very early on says, 'The apple's got something to do with it'. At other times such comments would provoke a short exchange as children extended the comment:

> *David*   They've changed
> *Natalie* Just because she ate that apple she's changed
> *Sarah*   She ate the apples

(Sarah and Natalie look at each other and smile)
Natalie   The apples
            (Transcript 28, ll.99–103)

Sarah and Natalie acknowledge their shared perceptions not just by echoing each other's words but through their body language.

Sometimes the children challenged the offered interpretation:

Shot of clock, now at ten past three
David   Ten past three, that all took ten minutes
Kelly   No, that was years ago, they've been staying there for years
David   No
Kelly   Well how come the clock's all cobwebs?
          (Transcript 28, ll.281–6)

As the children come to terms with the time of the story (as opposed to the discourse) they have to resolve their experience of watching for about forty-five minutes with some ellipses, suggesting a story time longer than the discourse time, with the visual evidence of the clock. David and Kelly have different interpretations and challenge each other not just through contradiction but by drawing on the text.

There were also rather longer sections of dialogue where the children jointly recalled and interpreted what had been happening at my request. In these they often built on their earlier more spontaneous comments:

MR   And why did you think they were acting differently, you said they were
          acting differently
(Again same hands up — all girls and David)
Kelly   Because . . .
Natalie Because of the apples
Kelly   The apples
David   They must have had the magic in them
MR   What did the other two . . .
David   They didn't eat them
Natalie They walked off and so would I, they ate the apples and they're acting
          strangely and seeing things what aren't true
          (Transcript 28, ll.130–40)

Here there is also an element of empathy with the characters — as Natalie says, 'So would I'. Such involvement tended to be in this form of supporting or criticizing behaviour either by direct comment or by projecting themselves into the situation and saying how they would act:

David   I would ask him . . .
Natalie No, I would do what they do, shine the mirrors at him
Kelly   You wouldn't be able to do anything
Natalie You'd be going . . .
(Kelly and Natalie dance as Tracey and Jeff did)
          (Transcript 28, ll.292–6)

At other times, aspects of the story or characters were commented on as being desirable for the children:

Neil   I'd like him as a father
David He's trying to be kind
Kelly I'd like that for my little grandad
        (Transcript 28, ll.196–8)

David's comment here seems rather different from the other two, with more of a judgment about the character. However, all these comments show that the children are still taking an active stance towards the reading process, if a slightly more distanced one than previously seen.

Even though this text was completely new to the children, they still showed an ability and a willingness to predict, and, just as with their interpretation, the predictions were not only forthcoming when asked for directly but also happened spontaneously as the children watched. Not surprisingly, their early predictions tended to be inaccurate not just in terms of event but showed a limited judgment as to the genre:

Natalie That's going to fall in a minute
Neil   That's broken, that's broken
David   She's swinging
         (Transcript 28, ll.57–9)

As the children tuned in to the story, their ideas became far more appropriate for the story, if still sometimes inaccurate:

Sarah They're going to sort of change round and in the end Tracey's going to
        want to go home and that other girl's going to stay
        (Transcript 28, ll.160–1)

What is clear, however, is that the children are still confidently predicting and interpreting, and that they are taking on the story in a way that suggests involvement in a very similar vein to that demonstrated in the earlier transcripts.

This narrative differed from the first three in two ways; for these children it was a complete narrative seen in one sitting, with no prior knowledge, and it was a story that moved beyond the everyday to explore the possibilities of magic and rejuvenation. However, the children's ways of dealing with this story were not markedly different from their responses to the other texts considered so far. What differences there were, though, seem greater than the differences between the children's responses to *Gaffer Samson's Luck* and the previous two televisual narratives. This would seem to suggest that familiarity with the text and modality are more relevant as factors in determining which strategies the children used than any difference between the discourse of television and print. It remains to be seen how the children responded to the last two texts, both of which were printed, self-contained and in the folktale genre.

Outside Over There and *Baba Yaga*

The children worked on both of these in the course of one day; the session ran continuously from one text to the next. Both books were read to the children by me. In the case of *Baba Yaga*, I paused to show illustrations as we reached them; for *Outside Over There*, I read the text and showed the book to the children at the same time, since the illustrations are integral to the story. For this last one, then, for the first time in the research, all the children could see the printed words as I read them. This was also the only story where each one of them would have been able to read the print aloud by themselves with no difficulty.

As with *Mr Magus is Waiting for You*, these two stories moved beyond everyday reality although both were about ordinary people. Just as *Mr Magus is Waiting for You* had a wizard as well as humans, *Baba Yaga* includes a witch and *Outside Over There* some goblins. *Baba Yaga* also has an assortment of anthropomorphic characters ranging from a cat to a gate. These two stories are, though, more removed from the children's everyday experience than *Mr Magus is Waiting for You*, since they do not start in a recognizable twentieth-century Britain, and their modality status is lower because of this and because of their use of drawn rather than photographic images.

As with the other narratives, the children showed clear signs of personal involvement and active reading here, though there were some differences in the way this was manifested. There were conflicting messages in the children's body language and their actual comments at times. The children frequently raised their hands to respond, even though they had not been asked to do this, in a way which suggested an eagerness to comment.

At times, intense interest was shown through facial expression and interest in the illustrations:

MR   I wonder why she wants her clean
(Rikky comes to look at the picture — Ashley grins widely)
Ashley   She's going to eat her
         (Transcript 29, ll.144–7)

Here Ashley's grin suggests not just that he has understood the story and can provide the preferred prediction but that he is finding this pleasurable. For *Outside Over There*, there was also a great deal of joining in with the actual reading. All of this behaviour was in line with the ways in which the children had shown themselves to be involved in earlier sessions.

Their comments on *Baba Yaga* in particular, however, although showing that they were paying attention and ready and able to predict, displayed a strong sense of irony and subversion, notably but not exclusively, on the part of David:

MR   So Baba Yaga lives in the forest, and Marusia's stepmother has sent her
         into the forest to borrow needles and thread from her sister. What do you
         think is going to happen?

> *David*   She's going to crap herself
> (Transcript 29, ll.93–6)

> *MR*   Do you think she's going to find a needle and thread?
> (All say no)
> *David*   No, she's going to get a machine gun
> (Transcript 29, ll.135–7)

Although at times the others enjoy these oppositional readings and join in with it, they also act to distance themselves from it and to provide preferred readings to counteract David's versions:

> *David*   She's going to kick him
> *Kelly*   No she isn't, to stop it from barking at her she's going to tie it up
> *David*   Might pat it and go, 'Good doggie, good doggie'
> (Transcript 29, ll.112–5)

Here David is happy to fall in line and thus is able to show the others that he is providing an alternative not because he has not understood but to be subversive.

Some of this reluctance on David's part to provide straightforward responses can be explained by his need to distance himself from the genre, to which he is openly hostile at the beginning of the session:

> *Ashley*   It's too soppy, a bit soppy
> *Kelly*   And so are you
> *David*   Why can't it be about football or boxing?
> *Kelly*   Why can't it be like fairies, I like fairies
> (Transcript 29, l.17–21)

This feeling is first expressed by Ashley, but Ashley then accepts the situation and provides the preferred readings, perhaps because despite his expectations he becomes involved in the story or because of a desire to conform and please me. David, on the other hand, alternates between the subversion seen above and more straightforward responses.

Kelly, on the other hand, and the other girls, seem empowered by this genre, and Alexis in particular is far more vocal than in some of the other discussions. The girls take the lead in offering intertextual comments and are very quick to reject David's inappropriate use of *Cinderella*:

> *MR*   Why do you think it's like *Cinderella* David?
> *David*   Because she pricks herself
> *Natalie*}
> *Alexis* } No she doesn't
> *Kelly* }
> (Kelly's hand up — Alexis looking very alert)
> *Alexis*   That's *Sleeping Beauty*
> (Transcript 29, ll.54–61)

Although there were times in the other narratives where the majority would react scornfully to what they perceived to be inadequate or misinformed comments, nowhere was gender such a factor as here.

A common feature of the children's responses to both of these stories, which was rather different from earlier comments, was a lack of identification with or preference for character. This did not seem to prevent their active involvement, and seems likely to be a result of their unfamiliarity with the text (which we have already seen reducing such involvement in the case of *Mr Magus is Waiting for You*) coupled with the nature of the characters in these stories, who are all stereotypical folktale personae of the kind identified by Propp (1968). The few comments that the children do make emphasize their understanding of the roles that such characters have to play and the personal characteristics associated with these roles:

> *David*   No, she's been really kind, she's going to make ...
> *Alexis*   She's been so kind that she can (unclear)
> *David*   ... whatd'you m'call it ...
> *Kelly*   No, I get it, she, the witch is selfish and she's kind
> (Alexis leans forward with both arms outstretched)
> *Alexis*   Yes, she's going to make the witch kind ... no
>   (Transcript 29, ll.121–6)

> *Alexis*   It's got to be 'cause she's wicked and her stepmother's wicked
>   (Transcript 29, l.163)

Alexis here emphasizes the deterministic way these roles are viewed, first by her hesitation in speculating on the possibility of reforming the witch and later by using narrative logic to determine the relationship just as we have seen Culler shows is the case in *Oedipus Rex* (see Chapter 3, p. 53).

As with all the other narratives, the children show the ability to predict, to interpret and to make surmises about what they are hearing. They are able to try to work through the inconsistencies they perceive and to fill the gaps they see in the text:

> *MR*   It's got worse, what about the ship?
> *Ashley*   It's sunk
> *David*   That could be papa's
> *Rikky*   Papa's, no listen, he sent a letter to them 'cause he was dead
> (Ashley reads on, David turns back to check the storm)
> *David*   He could have wrote that letter and sent it before he was dead
> *Alexis*   How could the letter get there because he hasn't got a post office?
> *MR*   When they're in port
>   (Transcript 30, ll.79–89)

This extract also shows that, where these existed, the children were happy to use visual strategies with book illustrations just as they had with television. The possibility of re-reading to check might seem to indicate a difference between printed and televisual texts. However, these children are all used to watching not just live television but also video, where the rewind button is able to offer the same facility. When earlier we had watched and re-watched the two title sequences of *Grange Hill*, the children had shown their familiarity with this idea, and they also frequently asked to see snatches of the videotape of themselves working. Re-reading appears to feature more prominently in this session than earlier ones partly at my instigation, and partly because of the very short and self-contained nature of the second text.

As was the case with all the other texts, the children showed that they were actively involved in making meaning from these texts. Although their response to the characters was of a rather different kind, they still showed an engagement with the text and the ability to hypothesize and predict. For both these narratives they were able to use their prior knowledge of story to provide support for their interpretations and to recognize that their everyday experiences would be of less help here than with a realist text.

Active Meaning-making Across Media

For all the texts, there was a sense that the children were actively involved in making meaning, that they had a feeling of empathy for the characters and that they were indeed acting in the spectator role (Britton, 1977). Where the children had most empathy and involvement was with the two narratives with which they were most familiar (*Grange Hill* and *Neighbours*). This might seem to point to a difference in the ways in which the children responded to the different media, but again I would argue that this is more complex than it might at first sight appear. The way in which the children responded to *Gaffer Samson's Luck* developed as the story unfolded, with a correspondingly greater involvement in the characters and their difficulties. This was least evident in the three fantasy stories. What seems to be happening here is that the more the children have encountered characters, and the more these characters are operating in a relatively realist setting, the easier it is for children to take on an understanding of the way the characters act and to empathize with their predicaments. There may be some truth in the idea that televisual images help to create such realism, but this is not the only factor here, as is shown by the relatively limited engagement with the characters in *Mr Magus Is Waiting For You* compared with the three realist texts. In retrospect it would have been useful to talk to the children about any book series with recurring characters with which they were familiar (such as Enid Blyton's work) to test this pattern still further, but the evidence available so far suggests that this is not simply a difference caused by medium. But how were the children able to respond, to empathize and to predict? I turn now to consider the actual strategies used, firstly in terms of the information taken from the text.

Chapter 7

The Text as a Source of Meaning

In the previous chapter I have shown how the children in my study were able to offer personal responses to each of the texts we shared. But what evidence did they draw on to make these responses? The views of the reading process I presented earlier argue for the role of information in the text and in the reader's head, and both need consideration as we look to see which strategies these children are using. In this chapter, I examine the various kinds of textual information and consider how far the children seem to be using this in each text. I look to see how the children draw on the textual information provided through the words and pictures in the books and through the visual images, dialogue, sound effects and music in the television programmes. I shall refer to information provided in words, whether spoken or written, as verbal, and to illustrations and television pictures as visual. (This is not to deny that reading words involves a visual activity, but to distinguish between language as a symbol system and the kinds of information presented through illustration and picture in a way which highlights the main emphasis of each kind of information.) As I analyse the transcript evidence I shall look to see whether, and how, the children are using the cues offered by the text and whether there are parallels between their use of textual information across media. Rather than examining each text in turn, as in the previous chapter, here I consider each kind of information in turn and show how it was used in each text.

Visual Cues

In terms of specifically visual information, I looked for places where the children made particular reference to the way characters looked, to visual expression or to location, and for situations in which the inference drawn by the children was reliant on information presented in visual form.

When watching *Grange Hill*, both regular and less frequent viewers were able to use visual detail when they recalled events and both watched the title sequences with sufficient attention to be able to recall the images seen afterwards. Both groups were able to read the implications in a shot where two pupils who had been using the photocopier illegally went off leaving the lid up:

Natalie   That's where they get arrested, isn't it? Oh no, they're going to get done
(Gasps)
Natalie   They left the top open

Neil	And they left it on
Natalie	Told you, they left it on
	(Transcript 18, ll.129–34)

Kelly	They forget to do that thing, don't they?
David	What about the lid?
Kelly	She's got an ugly bum
(Gasps)	
Ashley	He'll find out because they've left it
	(Transcript 19, ll.244–8)

In both cases, here, however, some of the children are also drawing on prior experience and know what transpired, so it is too simplistic to see this as purely a use of visual information.

At other times, the regular viewers seemed more able to draw inferences from the visual images they had seen. Apart from the example above, the less frequent viewers' comments were limited to beginning to move towards interpretation built on visual cues:

MR	What do you think's going to happen?
Sarah	Well he looks very fierce and fat and sort of strong
Natalie	Probably go up to him and go like that and have a fight or something
Sarah	And then probably the headmaster's going to come in or something
Natalie	Yeah, or one of the teachers is going to come in and say, 'What's going on?'
	(Transcript 20, ll.78–85)

Here Sarah is identifying the relevant aspects of the character's appearance but does not explicitly use this in her prediction. By comparison, the more regular viewers are less explicit in their description of detail but use it to arrive at an interpretation:

David	That's bad
Alexis	He's in a temper
	(Transcript 21, ll.35–6)

Since the evidence for this comes from a scene in which hardly any words are spoken, the cues for this interpretation have come from the visual images of Mike and his father at breakfast (and the music, of which more below).

As the children re-tell, it is clear that some at least of each group are using the facial expressions of the characters and the direction in which they are looking as visual cues. Natalie describes Ronnie's shoplifting in a way that makes this very clear:

Neil	Why did she nick it though? Why did she steal it though?
Natalie	'Cause she looked at it and she looked around but the alarm went and

she didn't know there was an alarm and she looked all over the place to
see if anyone was looking at her and she just put it and put it in a bag
quickly and went up to and just went out of the shop quickly and then
the alarm went and she started running but the police got her
(Transcript 18, ll.218–24)

The repetition of 'look' here four times in three lines emphasizes the way she is
drawing on the visual information.

Several of the other group also use characters' expressions as cues:

Kelly   I think he will go innocent but I don't think Robbie will 'cause the look
on his face
(Transcript 21, ll.215–16)

Alexis   . . . he had that face like he is going to leave
(Transcript 21, l.357)

Kelly   You know those boys, I think they did it because they had a strange look
on their face
(Transcript 21, ll.362–3)

Again it could be argued that the more experienced viewers are more subtle in this,
but this might be overstating the case on this evidence. What is more important is
that all the children are using some of the visual features of the text to aid their
interpretation; how far they do so for other texts must now be considered.

As stated earlier, one of the differences between television and print, especially as experienced by the children in this situation, is the variation in amount of
visual and aural information. For *Grange Hill*, the children could draw on visual
images of the characters, location and action whereas for *Gaffer Samson's Luck* all
they had were the verbal descriptions in the text and the cover illustration (colour)
and ten line drawings (monochrome). Similarly for *Grange Hill,* as we shall see
below, there were sound effects and theme music as well as the voices of the
characters, whereas for the book all the children had was my reading voice and my
attempt to use Norfolk accents for Gaffer Samson and the village children. What
the children did have, though, for the book which they had not had for the television
narrative was an explicit narrative voice explaining the action, describing not just
events and location but also what characters were thinking and feeling. On this basis
we might expect that children would use a different range of textual cues when
interpreting a printed narrative, or even that they might find it harder to use textual
cues altogether without the iconic representation from screen and soundtrack.

Although there was so little possibility in *Gaffer Samson's Luck* for the children
to draw on visual cues, they did use the illustrations to check their understanding
and to compare with the information taken from the text:

Ashley   They're going to the dyke and it looks like water in there, there look
(sounds puzzled)

Kelly   Where's James?
MR   Guess, one of them's wearing a skirt
Natalie There's James, look!
Neil   The girl seems different in there [from cover picture]
MR   Maybe the pictures in the inside were done by somebody different from the pictures on the outside
David   She looks really thinner
            (Transcript 24, ll.37–46)

The pictures the children drew of the story after we had finished reading the book show some reliance on the illustrations in the book, but also suggest that some were using mental visualization based on the verbal information to help their interpretation. The picture by Alexis of the Rymers is very like one of the book illustrations; Kelly's is a more individual interpretation but still faithful to the detail given in the book.

When discussing *Mr Magus Is Waiting For You*, David uses *Neighbours* as an example to explain how he is able to predict. In doing so he highlights the role of visual information in the episode we watched together:

MR   Is it easier or harder to tell what's going to happen next on something like this or on something like *Neighbours*?
David   Harder
Ashley   On *Neighbours* you can tell because the music
Natalie Yeah, 'cause if you missed it, that's what my mum said, because it repeats itself over and over again, if you missed it for a year you'd still know what was going on
MR   Anything else?
David   It tells you it, like when the dishwasher came out with all the bubbles, you've got to notice it, Joe said but half a cup will do and Madge put a full cup
            (Transcript 28, ll.429–36)

This information had been conveyed at different points in the episode, with Joe's comments alerting the children to Madge's actions, shown in medium close-up, and the soap bubbles gradually claiming attention in the background of a medium shot of Harold, and then filling the screen in the closing minutes of the episode, still from a medium shot. David's comments here also emphasize the way in which different kinds of textual information work together, with Joe's speech working with the visual images; this use of several sources simultaneously is discussed below.

In the case of *Mr Magus Is Waiting For You*, visual information was again used to support speculation and interpretation and to interpret character and action. For example, at the first sight of Mr Magus, when he has yet to speak, Natalie spontaneously says, 'He's a wizard'. Later, when Mr Magus has begun to become younger, it is the visual change that David picks up, commenting '. . . he's in disguise, he had white hair'. At times they wonder aloud about the visual information:

Neil   What are they looking at? I wonder
Kelly   A garden of (unclear)
David   Looking at all candy trees
       (Transcript 28, ll.42–5)

Here the children are not only using what they can see in the set but also what the characters tell them by their facial expressions, a double layer of visual information.

At times the children focus in on details they believe will be significant. The cat in particular attracts frequent comment and although some of these comments are to do with discourse (see below) or interpretation of what has happened, even the cat's first appearance is noted as relevant by Natalie ('Look at that cat!'). Later on the cat's significance is emphasized not just by camera shots which focus on it but by the magician's comments to it, and even at this early appearance it does seem to be a visual cue which alerts Natalie.

There was also evidence here that the children were using visual cues not just to interpret the story but to help them understand the discourse. Their willingness to accept the reality of what they have seen is limited by the visual evidence of the transformed cat being a model:

David   Eurghh
Natalie   That's not a real one
Sarah   It's not real
Neil   Looks nothing like it! It's plastic rubbish
       (Transcript 28, ll.202–6)

The children know that the cat is not supposed to be ordinary but the unsatisfactory nature of the special effect leads them to challenge the discourse rather than the story. They were well aware of the reasons for using a model, but were still scornful of the result:

MR   Why were there two cats?
Ashley   They wouldn't be able to make a real cat go [imitates fierce cat], it was
       supposed to be all the same cat but it didn't look nothing like it
       (Transcript 28, ll.422–5)

This criticism of the discourse rather than the plot was not something previously noted in their conversations, particularly in terms of visual cues.

Neil used visual cues to create a deliberate and subversive misinterpretation:

The characters Jeff and Tracey go upstairs hand in hand
Neil   They're going to Frenchy, I know it
Natalie   Don't be so rude
       (Transcript 28, ll.207–9)

This comment came straight after the challenge to the cat model; it could be that it was sparked by this earlier criticism of the text. However, the others are not prepared to support this interpretation, as Natalie shows in no uncertain terms, and the focus turns back to the plot immediately afterwards, with all the children apparently concentrating hard on the screen.

One aspect highlighted by the use of video rather than audiotape to record this session was the way in which the children responded physically rather than verbally to certain visual cues. At times this was simply a mimicking of actions seen — as when Natalie and Kelly danced — and this had occurred earlier. Even this action replaces words, though, completing a sentence begun by Natalie. This use of action in place of language was also used by David:

> MR   Do you think Mr Magus knew they were coming?
> Natalie Yes
> David   He's got this . . .
> (David has hands rounded as though round crystal ball)
> Kelly   He's got this funny mind and he knows who's coming and who's going
> (Transcript 28, ll.182–7)

Here the impression is that David has seen the crystal ball on screen and has not gone from interpreting the visual representation to encoding this as a verbal sign but has to re-present the information more visually. In the past I have often observed similar physical interpretations from children listening to or retelling a story being read to a class; there would seem to be links here to Bruner's three modes of thought (see Chapter 3), with the enactive and ikonic here better developed than the symbolic, so that actions more readily come to mind to transmit meaning than the appropriate verbal symbol. Kelly does not respond to this physical sign and instead completes David's sentence for him, though giving a slightly different meaning in the process.

The higher number of illustrations in *Baba Yaga* and *Outside Over There*, and in particular the close tie between illustration and print in the Sendak book, made it possible to consider relationships between the children's strategies in television and print more directly, although there was still no soundtrack equivalent and only my voice for all the characters and narration. As in the case of *Mr Magus Is Waiting for You*, there was less information to draw on than for the first three narratives considered, since the texts were complete in themselves, unknown to the children and much shorter than any considered earlier.

In the children's comments on *Baba Yaga*, where the illustrations were few and acted as additional support to the printed text rather than as integral to our understanding of the story, the children made far more use of verbal cues than the visual ones. In the case of *Outside Over There*, where every page is illustrated and where the printed word alone would severely limit the listener's understanding of the story, the reverse was true. Far more use was made by the children of the pictures than of the print.

In *Baba Yaga*, there is only one comment that directly refers to the picture (where Alexis uses information from the picture to correct David), though there were other times when the children can be seen looking at the pictures. In *Outside*

Over There, on the other hand, there are not only far more individual references and moments when the children point at the pictures but also shared discussions about what might be happening.

At times the children's reactions are emotional responses to the characters and events:

Natalie   Look at that baby, he's really ugly
(Transcript 30, 1.9)

Here Natalie seems to be evoking support for her response from the others. At other times the children use the pictures to check their own interpretation:

David   A boat! That's . . .
Alexis   Papa's ship
(Transcript 30, 11.61–2)

This example is typical of several in which the children focus on the story suggested by the boats in the background of the illustrations. Many of these comments are very short, but at times there are also more complex comments:

Alexis   She's looking at the ship, and the baby's crying because of the goblins, and the goblins have got the ladder to climb up and get the baby
(Transcript 30, 11.68–70)

Alexis is not just focusing on a detail here, but working out the plot implications and retelling events; retelling, rather than predicting, because this is the second time the children have read the book.

This point may be one of the factors in the remarkable amount of comment on these pictures compared to those in the other printed narratives; by re-examining the book, I may have placed extra emphasis on the pictures. However, the way in which I showed illustrations in other printed texts also placed emphasis on them, since these showings stopped the flow of the narrative and placed the illustrations at centre stage. This would seem to suggest that my intervention was not so significant here. The fact that the children saw the pictures again and on this second viewing made so many comments may suggest that it was the repeated opportunity which was significant, and highlights one of the ways in which the common-sense view would say that books are different from television. I would argue that to see television images as more ephemeral than those in books is too simplistic a contrast. Certainly, many television images are seen once and no more, but these children were also frequently watching programmes more than once through videos and repeat showings. Within any one television programme, too, there is a certain redundancy in that even without significant images being shown in slow motion or normal speed re-run footage, backgrounds and settings remain the same and characters usually keep the same appearance, and so we do have time to review most images. Nor do children always have the opportunity to re-examine book illustrations, particularly in the case of texts read aloud by the teacher to which access may be limited. More significant in terms of the differences which I found would seem to be the children's assumptions about what needs attention.

Verbal Information

Whereas not all the texts had much visual information to offer, all had verbal information. The words heard by the children have a powerful influence on their retelling and prediction, as was apparent in their discussions of *Grange Hill*. Again there is a difference between the two groups in that the more regular viewers more often use direct quotation, but this is a feature of both groups. At times this direct quotation is to add detail to a retelling:

> *Natalie*   Yeah, 'cause I saw yesterday when um Calley, Ronnie and this other girl got arrested and Calley said 'I'm going to get done now, look, the police are coming' and she goes 'Do something' and she goes 'What can I do?'
> (Transcript 18, ll.142–5)

At other times it is used to give credence to a prediction:

> *Ashley*   Yeah, but I don't reckon he'll get in trouble 'cause er, the man said 'I've seen you somewhere, oh yeah it was at that fight in the pub' and he said 'No, you must have the wrong person'
> (Transcript 19, ll.395–7)

The children also create direct speech within their predictions, inventing conversations:

> *Kelly*   A battle, 'cause um if um somebody says, 'Oh, I'll tell them where I live blah blah blah' and then she goes, 'I prefer if you don't see them', he's got a real battle to go against, either face saying I have to go and see my dad or say um to his dad, 'Listen, I can't go, 'cause my mum said, my foster mum, my foster parent, because my mum said', I reckon it's going to be a battle between the mum and the dad
> (Transcript 21, ll.284–90)

Of particular impact are the sound bites that accompany dramatic or amusing scenes. These are often repeated in assumed voices as the children imitate the actors:

> *Ashley*   And she had to go to another modelling agency as well
> *Kelly*   And she went, she went like this, this is the lady, she went 'Hello, your name's thingamajig'
> *MR*   Georgina
> *Kelly*   'Georgina' and . . .
> *David*   'We haven't got time for you today'

Kelly   'We haven't got time for you today, better luck next time'
(Transcript 19, ll.406–12)

At times the children report direct speech but are unsure of its importance:

Sarah   And he's trying to give him something really expensive, and I think when
he get, he said, he'll, 'I'll get told off,' I don't know what he means by
that
(Transcript 20, ll.75–7)

At other times the use of what they see as taboo language fascinates them and is
incorporated into retellings:

Ashley   (unclear) . . . and there were five men and they said, 'I thought I saw a
Paki' and then she came out and then um there was a big patch of the
other fans and a big patch of the other fans and Robbie said 'Are you
going to the toilet?' and he said 'I thought I saw a Paki' and then he
kicked him in the ribs and they run and she had a big scratch across her
face and so er Aichaa and Robbie have broken up now
(Transcript 19, ll.379–85)

As is clear elsewhere, the children are unsure of the best way to describe non-white
people (of whom they have little real-life experience) but it is unlikely that Ashley
sees 'Paki' as an acceptable term. There is no evidence in these transcripts that
Ashley shares the attitude of the fans; in fact, given his empathy with Robbie, the
opposite is likely. Despite this, he enjoys repeating the term, which would suggest
that it is the very fact that he sees this word as unacceptable which leads to his use
of it here.

When drawing on verbal information, the children seemed to demonstrate a
very similar range of strategies when discussing *Gaffer Samson's Luck* and *Grange
Hill*, albeit with a different emphasis. Certainly the verbal cues are stronger in the
book, but again, even in the earliest transcripts, there is a good deal of direct
quotation and invented speech:

Ashley   In the shop, she went, 'Buy us a Mars bar'
Natalie   'Buy us a Mars bar'(laughs)
David   'Buy us a Mars bar'
(Transcript 22, ll.21–3)

As in the case of *Grange Hill*, this strategy is also used in prediction:

Kelly   No, I know, Angey tries to drive him out of the way, Angey's going to try
and get him out of the way like say, 'Oh why don't we go to the cinema?'
or something, and he goes, um, back and gets it
(Transcript 26, ll.83–6)

There is proportionately less quotation as a feature of the retelling and prediction in the *Gaffer Samson* transcripts, and there are no invented sound effects to echo those quoted in the *Grange Hill* discussions. There is an extra feature, though, in that some of the vocabulary from the book — which I would have said was not a part of the children's usual repertoire — is taken on, albeit inaccurately, and incorporated into their retelling even when they do not appear to be reporting direct speech. So David reports Angey's gran's comment, 'You don't want to believe all that twattle', (Paton Walsh, 1987, p. 70) as '. . . it might be just a load of twiddle about the gypsy' which would seem to be his attempt to take on a word he is unlikely to have met before.

Another feature that was more obvious in the children's response to the book was a fascination with and curiosity about the use of certain words and the printed word. The character Gaffer Samson repeatedly calls James 'bor' but does not explain that this is short for 'neighbour' until late on in the story. The children noticed this and asked its meaning, and also played with the possible meaning themselves:

> MR   *'And why do you keep calling me "bor"?' demanded James, exasperated*
> ?Kelly   'Cause he's a boring . . . (very quietly)
>   (Transcript 26, ll.43–5)

On another occasion Rikky picks up a certain word and asks its meaning in a way which shows how prior experience works with the textual information to produce an interpretation the reader finds acceptable:

> MR   *. . . so much sky made it dazzling*
> Rikky   Mrs Robinson, is 'dazzling' another name for Daz?
> MR   No, but I think it might be why they called Daz that, because dazzling means really brilliant white and they thought if they called their soap powder that people would think it would get their washing really brilliant white
> David   Yeah, because if it's really really dazzly it means to say it's really dazzling, it means it makes you dazzle
> MR   Yes, like you know sometimes you go down to the sea and it's really really sunny, it's very hard to look at, it's really bright down there, yeah?
> Alexis   When you look at the sun it makes you sneeze
>   (Transcript 25, ll.29–40)

This interest in particular words did not manifest itself during the work on *Grange Hill*.

Another feature of the work on *Gaffer Samson's Luck,* which is shown by this extract and which is not a feature of the *Grange Hill* transcripts, is the children's use of me as a source of clarification. They asked me about word meanings spontaneously as I read, but did not ask me to explain the television programme. This difference could be because, as already discussed, by reading to rather than watching with them I had placed myself in a different position, as one who was mediating the text. It could also be because the children were used to asking questions and commenting in this way when being read to, but were unused to doing so when watching television. It could be argued, though, that this suggests that the television was not so difficult for them to understand as the written text. However, there were times, as I have shown, when the children did have trouble understanding the television narrative, but their added confidence may have helped them feel they had understood. What they did do more while watching television was to ask for clarification from each other, so that I would suggest that it was my change of role that was the most probable cause of their changed behaviour here, rather than the change of medium itself.

I had to make the decision early on as to how to respond to the children's questions. It could be argued that the role of the researcher is not to offer added information; I felt that it was more natural to answer the questions, and that the children's usual experience of adults, particularly in school, was that questions were answered. I also felt that if the children were asking for clarification they needed to get this if they were to cope with the rest of the narrative. So, just as I did not attempt to stop them answering queries that arose more generally in the group, so I answered questions that were put to me and tried to take a role in the conversation that would be unexceptional to the children.

One feature worthy of examination is the power of the spoken word in *Neighbours*, for one child at least. At one point Natalie produced an unsolicited piece of writing about *Neighbours* approximately 650 words long. This was produced when she had been away and so could not undertake the task the group were working on. So that she did not feel excluded, I suggested that she might like to write about what might happen next in *Neighbours*. She said that she had already started a piece of work and then worked steadily to finish the piece, with no discussion with me or the other children, for a full hour.

The piece is not a prediction, but a retelling of a recent episode; what is remarkable about it, though, is that it is entirely written as dialogue. There is no intervening narration, nor even any attribution of speech to particular characters through such phrases as 'he said'. The piece is like a transcript of an episode, and at least in places is close to an exact record of the episode concerned. Nor does the way it is written make it particularly hard to follow; the characters explain the action through their speech, so that we are able to follow this relatively easily (for example, 'Jamie's getting really heavy arn't you Jamie go to nanny now thers a good boy' [sic]). It is possible that Natalie has seen this episode more than once, either by being off school and watching twice or by recording and reviewing, but even if this is the result of repeated viewing rather than a single viewing, it is an impressive feat of memory.

Although Natalie was very happy for me to read the end product, it had been started before I asked for it and she appeared to be writing for herself rather than for any other audience. Her concentration whilst doing this was considerably more intense than when completing other tasks either for me or for her class teacher. At the same time, the end product did not seem to be the point either, since Natalie was very happy for me to keep this and displayed no further interest in it. The process of recalling seemed to be what was significant, as though she was reassuring herself that she had held the episode in her memory accurately, and what she wanted to remember was just the actual dialogue, which might perhaps have served to recall all the accompanying information. The words seem almost to be acting as some kind of mantra or charm here. Their power seemed to be not so much in their meaning as in their retention; given the high significance placed by the children on knowledge of this programme, this may have been Natalie's way of reassuring herself that she had remembered as much as possible, with the dialogue as a shorthand frame for the whole. The power of the language of *Neighbours* seems to suggest that the differences noted above between the children's attention to the language of *Grange Hill* and *Gaffer Samson's Luck* are not so great as might be thought and are less dependent on the change of medium than on the actual language of any text and its impact on a particular reader. Again, this will need to be reconsidered in more depth below.

In the case of *Mr Magus Is Waiting For You*, the explicit comments which suggest how the children were making use of information from the text show some direct parallels with earlier texts but also some marked differences. It is worth reiterating some of the actual differences in the text here to act as a backdrop for the different responses by the children. First, this was a completely new text, whereas *Neighbours* and *Grange Hill* were already familiar and where the prediction activity for *Gaffer Samson's Luck* had come towards the end of several weeks of listening to the story. The relative brevity of the narrative also meant there was less text from which to take information. This time, too, the story was not a realist text. The main difference appears to be not so much between media as between all the earlier narratives and this one, and is not so much qualitative (though there are some variations of approach) as quantitative. There are far fewer examples here of the children drawing on verbal cues than in any of the other narratives so far considered, but when they do use these explicitly they display similar ways of doing so.

There is an interest in written text early on, with the children reading the credits as they appear. This had not happened in quite this way with earlier texts, although there had been an interest in printed language, as has been shown. Here the unfamiliarity of the programme may have accounted for this reading aloud. There are times when the children quote directly in their retelling. For example, both David and Natalie use quotations of direct speech to strengthen their interpretations:

> *David* I know, well um Tracey she's turned really really nice and she goes, 'Oh what a dear old man!'
> (Transcript 28, ll.155–6)

> *Natalie* Yeah, he belongs on the dark side, because that's why he said to Tracey, to Charlie, 'Your eyes are dull'
> (Transcript 28, ll.304–5)

This does not extend to inventing speech for the characters, though this may be because there are few points at which the children make sufficiently long predictions for this to be relevant. At one point, when suggesting a possible ending, David does use direct speech, but this is very probably an intertextual reference rather than a genuine attempt to anticipate dialogue of the kind we have seen earlier:

MR	How do you think it's going to end?
Kelly	Don't know
David	It's probably a *Beadle's About* gag-up
Kelly	When they find them, when the awful children come in it'll end probably when they see him as not a magician
David	'Surprise surprise!'
	(Transcript 28, ll.240–5)

This would seem to be a reference to the Cilla Black programme of this title which in some ways is similar in genre to *Beadle's About*.

The only example of a more genuine use of direct speech which is not a quotation comes when Ashley attempts to explain the difference between this and a more realist text:

MR	How is it different?
David	You only have three episodes for a start
Ashley	Like no-one could be like, they chuck the mirrors and they go, 'Oh, I'm turning to dust', you can't exactly see that on *Neighbours*
	(Transcript 28, ll. 356–60)

Even here there is little to suggest that he envisages this as a speech for any particular character to compare with the predictions made by the children in their discussions of other texts.

One notable use of text was a subversion of what was said which parallels Neil's attempt (p. xxx, Transcript, 28, ll.182–7) to subvert the image and to create a deliberately scurrilous reading:

Vince: 'You and your bloomin' ball'	
(All intent on screen)	
Kelly	Eurghh
Natalie	That's a bit rude!
David	How can it come off?
	(Transcript 28, ll.51–6)

Whereas Neil's attempt is rejected, this is a more general response. This may be because Neil is not an accepted leader of the group or because, by the point at which he made his comment, the children were more engrossed and less happy to be distracted, or it could just be that this double-entendre was more appealing to them than Neil's later reaction.

The children's use of verbal information in *Baba Yaga* and *Outside Over There* followed a similar pattern to that seen in other texts. They created direct speech in some of their predictions and also showed interest in the text for its own sake; they used generic knowledge and information drawn from the specific text under consideration. Much of the use they made of the language of these stories can more properly be considered in the light of what it shows us about their use of prior knowledge and experience, but it is worth focusing here on their invented dialogue. This was particularly noticeable in the work on *Baba Yaga*. Here the children made many specific predictions which gradually came to include more direct speech and a very close correlation to the language of the original. In the original text, the characters use a repeated syntactic pattern. The children's predictions move nearer to this with each incident:

MR	What will the dog say?
David	He'll say . . .
Kelly	He'll say . . .
Ashley	'She gave me some bread'
Kelly	He'll probably say, 'No, I wouldn't go for her because she gave me some bread and all you give me is a stinky smelly bone'
Alexis	And instead of biting her throat out he'll bite the witch's throat

(I read next two paragraphs to 'the servant-girl said to her':)

MR	What do you the servant-girl say to her?
Kelly } *Alexis*}	'She gave me a hanky'
MR	Will she say anything before that?
Ashley	'You never give me nothing but . . .'

(I read next sentence to 'the first time that she ever saw me':)

MR	What about the gate, what will the gate say?
Alexis	'She oiled me'
Kelly	'She gave me some oil to drink'

(Ashley puts his hand up)

Ashley	'You've never given me, all you've ever given me is a (unclear)'
Kelly	'All you ever give me is rusty hinges to eat'

(Transcript 30, ll.186–208)

Although these predictions are partly invited by my questions, the move to be nearer the syntax of the book cannot be said to be prompted in this way. Again the children are drawing on the information in the text to predict both outcome and actual dialogue, as has been seen in the discussions of other narratives.

It is apparent that verbal cues, as well as visual information, do have a significant impact on the ways in which the children identify with and interpret the narratives. The children use what they have heard not just to retell but to create satisfying predictions and to demonstrate pleasure, savouring the language patterns and the potential for exploring taboo areas. Buckingham (1993a), reporting similar behaviour patterns observed in his research on children and television, suggests that the exaggerated nature of the retellings and the acting out which he frequently observed acts not just as a pleasurable recall but can develop into a parody or mockery through which the children also distance themselves from the original and thus display their power over the medium. Although I rarely encountered acting out in the taped sessions, it was certainly a feature of more informal conversations in the class; even without this, the amount of gesture, sound effects noise and exaggerated intonation I did observe would support this interpretation.

Other Aural Information

One undoubted difference between televisual and printed texts is the extra aural information provided through the television soundtrack. Frequently, when the focus could in one way be said to have moved to the visual image in that there was no speech, music or some other sound accompanied the images. The children showed an awareness of the role of both music and other sounds in all the television texts we shared.

The theme tune for the new series of *Grange Hill* was one of the things that had changed and there was disagreement about the new tune. Of the less frequent viewers some preferred the old tune and some the new, but the regular viewers all preferred the new, which they sang every time they heard it:

MR   Yes, but I'm just thinking about the titles . . . how about the music?
(Instantly they sing the tune)
MR   What about the tune, did you like the old tune?
Ashley No
Kelly   No
Ashley It wasn't as good as this actual one now, I used to like it but I like the
          one now
Kelly   How does it go?
(David instantly sings the new tune)
          (Transcript 19, ll.31–40)

At one level the popularity of the theme tune may seem to have little to do with the children's ability to relate to the programme, but this desire to join in both suggests an identification and pleasure coming from the aural experience and signals the fact that the children are explicitly aware of the sound track.

Since the incidental music used the same tune as the theme tune, the children's familiarity with the theme may also have helped them to see the incidental music as important, at least implicitly. Some of the children were well aware of the role of incidental music. There were several points when children gasped as this was used to heighten tension, and Alexis at least was able to articulate this knowledge:

MR   You were saying you didn't like that music, why not?
Alexis It's scary
David   Spooky music
Alexis Something really bad's going to happen
David   Of course it is, he's that kind of man mate
          (Transcript 21, ll.118–22)

David, on the other hand, seems to be drawing the same inference from other information already obtained (and possibly at least partly visual) about the character involved, which reinforces my point about the different sources of information available working together.

After the episode of *Neighbours* we watched had ended, as the children discussed it, their awareness of the role of certain features of television became even clearer:

MR   How do we know what's going to happen next?

Rikky   Because I do

Sarah   You can always tell by the looks on their faces and if there's music you can tell by it

MR   Yeah, you, Alexis and Natalie, you reacted very strongly to some of that music, didn't you, why, what was it about the music

Natalie   Yeah, when there's the music, it means that something's going to happen wrong

David   Something's going to happen that's really funny, I like it when it goes 'de de de' (sings three rising notes, D, F#, A, with major 3rd and minor 3rd interval)

Alexis   Shush David, 'cause in the other ones and it had that music where it went 'de de de' (sings similar rising scale but Db, E, G, with two minor 3rd intervals) and everything goes wrong, and he goes 'Oh no' (Transcript 27, ll.272–87)

They are not just aware of the role of music but can recognize these quite subtle musical differences and attach a likely mood to each. The first set of three notes, starting on D natural, has a much more upbeat feel, and the major interval maintains this; in fact, what David sings is part of a phrase which usually goes on to rise to D before falling through B flat to A, a very common motif in comic silent films to induce mock fear or suspense. Alexis sings a phrase which, by starting on D flat and rising through two minor intervals, suggests much more serious tension of the kind found in thrillers or horror films.

Although there are several scenes in which the music is prominent in *Mr Magus Is Waiting For You*, including some in which there is no speech, the children made hardly any explicit references to the music in their comments. As I have shown above, they were aware of the impact of music in other series, and even refer to this explicitly here when comparing *Mr Magus Is Waiting For You* to *Neighbours* (see p. 134), so it may be fair to assume that they were aware of the music in this programme too. At one point, David does mention the music explicitly:

MR   You know there was a bit when he was walking down the road

David   With all rock music (Transcript 28, ll.400–2)

However, he does not build on this comment, nor do the other children, so it merely serves to show that he at least was aware of the music. What cannot be explained is why this music was not sufficiently important for the children to comment on it. This might be because of the relative unfamiliarity of the music, which they were hearing for the first time. The other music they had encountered when working with me had either been very familiar theme tunes or very familiar musical phrases used regularly on television to heighten tension, that is music linked to particular generic conventions. The music for this series was neither familiar nor so clichéd and so the children may not have seen its narrative significance because of unfamiliarity with a wider range of musical codes; alternatively, it could be that the music was less effective in creating mood or forwarding plot than the other music to which the children had earlier referred not because it was unfamiliar but because of some inadequacy in its composition or application.

What Else Do They Take from the Text?

So far each of my examples has been a particular strategy which can to some extent (though not entirely satisfactorily) be identified in isolation from others being used at the same time. However, by far the greatest proportion of the children's retellings and predictions are much more complex and involve an account of the events depicted, with some of the features above woven in at some times but at other times without any specific identifiable cues. Sometimes, where certain events are seen as worthy of recall, this takes the form of straightforward retelling:

> David   Yeah, he put, they just came up or something and he, he put invisible ink, and this boy, Locko, went into the cupboard to get an ounce of it, or a jar of it, and he goes, that brown boy, don't know what his name is . . . Aichaa's brother goes and puts it on his pen and he goes, and then he goes and does his homework and it doesn't work
> (Transcript 21, ll.57–62)

More frequently, however, the retellings are interspersed with speculation about the outcome illustrated by retelling to prove a point, of the kind seen above with retelling in direct speech, or with interpretations about cause and effect supplied by the children. The children seem to be using all the information available to hold a rounded memory of the events and their causes and effects which they then recall in the ways illustrated.

Certain events are picked out by the children for repeated retelling where other storylines are barely mentioned. The story about Mike and Robbie and the court case was relatively important in the series in my judgment in that it had a good deal of time devoted to it and was on several occasions used as a cliffhanger, so it may be that by focusing on this story the children are identifying the preferred reading in terms of kernels and satellites (Chatman, 1978). However, they also focused on other stories that were less significant in terms of screen time and narrative tension, such as the invisible ink joke and situations from past series involving what might be seen as behaviour which broke their conception of what is allowable in school:

Rikky	Um . . . there was one what I really liked when that kid with the ginger hair had some beer in school . . .
Sarah?	Oh yeah
Rikky	And he went down to the bridge near the school and these kids wanted it so he threw it in and they took all, he ran across the bridge and they caught him and they took all of his clothes off him and hung them up and they chained him up against the bridge and a little kid was going to help him but he left him there
	(Transcript 18, ll.232–40)

The focus on the ink story may have been brought about by my asking for a retelling of that particular episode (though there were other issues that they could have picked up) but what also happens is that the children set an agenda around their own interests.

As with the other televisual narratives, there are times when the children watching *Mr Magus Is Waiting For You* seem to be drawing on what they have noticed in the text but where it is not possible to say whether it is one specific aspect of the text they have used or a composite of verbal and visual cues working together. These comments usually refer to events that are being used to interpret what has happened and sometimes to predict what will happen. Natalie's reactions to the characters eating the apples, quoted above, illustrates this point. Here, although Natalie has seen this, it has also been commented on in the dialogue. The incident's significance for her is clear from the way she develops her point into a more general interpretation.

At other times, a more general comment summarizes a great deal of textual information:

Kelly	I know what's happened, they've changed their minds 'cause Tracey was acting like horrible to Jeffrey and then she started being kind like . . .
Natalie	Like giving him flowers and that
	(Transcript 28, ll.163–6)

Here Kelly is aided in this general comment by a specific incident offered by Natalie, but her own stance could be based on a whole range of textual cues that she does not make explicit.

Drawing on Existing Knowledge of the Text

One feature which is noteworthy, and which I have highlighted briefly in Chapter 6, is the way in which the children were able to draw on past storylines to interpret new developments. This was the case even with the plot development most outside the children's experience in life, namely the story evolving around Paul's ambitions to take over Lassiter's:

MR	And what did he say?
David	And guess who's the next one on her list . . . what's his name again?
Natalie	Derek Morris
MR	Who's Derek Morris?
David	It's this man, he goes, 'If you don't get off my premises you're dead meat'
Ashley	He fancies Jane, he fancies Jane
(General excitement)	
Alexis	Because Derek Morris is coming down . . .
David	There's going to be a fight
Alexis	. . . he's going to try and split Mark and Jane up
MR	If Derek Morris buys the company that owns Lassiter's, what do you think will happen to Gail and Paul?
Alexis	He'll sack them
MR	So what will they lose?
David	They're going to lose their house, they're going to lose their job, they're going to lose Lassiter's, they're going to lose everything
MR	What do you think Paul will do now he's found out about Derek Morris?
David	He's going to kick him in
Neil	They're going to (unclear) for that job instead
Alexis	He'll sue him
MR	Let's see then
Natalie	Mark's going to, what's his name? Derek Morris, he's going to sue Mark and Paul together because he loves Jane
Rikky	He'll get a machine gun and shoot her
David	Instead of Mad Max it's Mad Morris
	(Transcript 27, ll.165–93)

Although the children may not be clear about the actual details of the business deal or of the precise implications of suing someone, they are clear about the trouble ahead, and their interpretations are based not just on the reactions displayed by the characters in this episode but on past knowledge of the character not seen in this episode, Derek Morris. David even makes the intertextual link to the deputy head of *Grange Hill*, Mad Max, (and possibly to the film *Mad Max* from which the *Grange Hill* character may be thought to have acquired this nickname) to emphasize the villain's role for which Morris is destined.

Generic and Medium-specific Knowledge

The children also have a growing awareness of the contrived nature of the cliff-hanger ending and at least some awareness of the purpose of this:

David	It always stops at the exciting bit
MR	Why does it always stop at the exciting bit?
David	Because they're trying to wind you up to make you watch it next time
MR	They're trying to wind you up to make you watch it next time, Kelly,

	what were you trying to say? Why do they want you to watch it next time, why do they want you to watch it?
Alexis	To get more money
(Others echo this)	
Ashley	More money, get more dough
Natalie	To write in letters and say that it's good
MR	Sarah, you're waiting very patiently
Sarah	'Cause say if it's not on at the weekend, they could, people could think about it, and if they want people to watch it, they could um be more popular, and when people have accidents like Helen they um could show, how, what things . . .
David	How ill she is
Sarah	Yeah
	(Transcript 27, ll.306–23)

These comments are more explicit than those made about the other texts so far; it may be that the familiarity of *Neighbours* and the emphasis placed on such things as cliffhangers (by the practice the programme had at that time of repeating the last few minutes of each episode at the beginning of the next) work to help children have more explicit awareness. The vast amount of extra-textual information on soaps (in the press and on other television programmes, for example) may also have helped to raise the children's awareness, just as it has helped to develop their understanding of the genre in general (see Chapter 6).

Textual Cues Across Media

In terms of drawing information from the text, I have already argued that the relative balance between the use of verbal and visual information is more a by-product of the medium concerned than a separate non-transferable strategy. The ways in which textual cues were used (to predict, to retell, to confirm individual positions and to develop collaborative reconstructions) were very similar through-out the texts studied. There was some difference in terms of the amount of direct use of language patterns in inventing dialogue, but again the difference seemed to relate more to the length and familiarity of the text than to the medium. The only exception here might be seen to be *Baba Yaga*, but here the children's prior experi-ence of the genre may have encouraged them to use the language patterns to generate predicted utterances, as well as the very strong repetitive nature of this text. There did seem to be a tendency to use visual information more than verbal where it was available, but this may have more to do with quantity than preference. In the case of *Outside Over There*, the words offer very little since the written text is so short. More work on a wider range of texts would be necessary to establish the extent to which children do prefer to use visual information and to consider pedagogical implications. What is clear is that the children are happy to draw on a wide range of textual information and to use information of different kinds to arrive at their interpretation.

The television narratives had a great deal more to offer in the way of visual information, and they also had more complex aural information in that there were different voices, sound effects and music. The books had few illustrations and were communicated through my voice only. Not surprisingly, then, the children used more visual cues when dealing with the televisual narratives and more verbal information when dealing with print. The one exception to this pattern was *Outside Over There*, the picture storybook. Here, when the book form provided more visual than verbal information, the children again used the visual cues more. This would seem to suggest that the medium is not so significant as to cause a different approach but that the children in fact use visual information as well as verbal in proportion to the amount of each provided by any text.

Chapter 8

Using Information from Outside the Text

So far I have shown how the children in my research responded to the narratives we watched and I have explored the range of information from within the text that they drew on to interpret, empathize and predict. However, just to look at this textual information would ignore the active role which I have argued the reader has to play in drawing on prior knowledge, and so the use of such knowledge must also form a central element of my analysis. In this chapter I shall show how these children are using their experience of life to help them to interpret and predict. I shall look at that specialized area of life experience to do with their prior encounters with narrative, their use of intertextuality, and the ways in which this crosses or acknowledges media boundaries. The children's understanding of the ways in which televisual and printed narratives are constructed by other people and of the role of industry will also be considered. Their interest in and knowledge about language as a system will be another factor. Additionally, the extent to which they use all this information either as a set of individuals who happen to be working in a room with others or as a collaborative interpretive community will be an important element of the analysis. As in the case of the textual cue systems, the extent to which children's use of their prior experience either differs between or transcends media is a key element of my analysis. As in Chapter 7, I consider these issues here thematically rather than text by text.

Using Prior Life Experience

The views of the reading process considered in earlier chapters stress the role of non-visual cues, both semantic and syntactic. In this section I explore the extent to which the children can be seen to have used their knowledge of the world to interpret the texts they encountered with me. The biggest differences here came not between media but between the realist and fantasy texts, though familiarity with the text was also significant.

The less frequent viewers of *Grange Hill* made no explicit references to their own experience, but the regular viewers, and Ashley in particular, made three kinds of comment which could be seen as doing this. Firstly, there were times when the children would identify directly with a character's actions:

> *On screen, Robbie comes home, goes in, throws bag down*
> *Ashley* That's me, that's what I do
> (Transcript 21, ll.310–11)

This comment by Ashley was typical of instances of straightforward recognition of a match between the children's own behaviour and that shown on screen.

Occasionally the children would tell a personal anecdote which had a direct bearing on the discussion:

MR   Why do you think he wanted to go in the seats and not on the terraces?
Ashley Because he might . . . because in the terraces like there's more trouble because I've been to a football match and I saw a man being carried off on a stretcher and like in the stands, in the seats there's never any trouble and I've never been in the seats and it's boring and no-one sings the songs (Transcript 19, ll.371–7)

As a keen football fan, Ashley is able to compare what he has seen with his own experience of attending matches. Still there is a relatively direct connection between specific experiences Ashley has had and the incident on screen, but here he feels the need to support his claim by making this connection more explicit.

At other times the children confirm the *vraisemblance* of what they are seeing by more general comparisons to their own experience:

David   That is our school, people do go like that
Ashley It's like, exactly like when you start at junior school
(Transcript 19, ll.71–2)

This time the match is not directly with Ashley or David's own behaviour in isolation but to what 'people' do; Ashley marks this by a change from first to second person.

On one occasion Ashley makes a more oblique comment that challenges the narrative in a way which suggests that his criticism is based on the general beliefs about the world he has drawn up from previous experience:

Ashley Surely he must have found out, like, that all of this time, surely they must say who the witnesses are in the paper
(Transcript 21, ll.245–6)

Buckingham's study found similar generalizing behaviour:

Programmes were judged in terms of broad assertions about the world, often delivered without supporting evidence. (Buckingham, 1993a, p. 228)

Similarly here, rather than spelling out that he would be reading the paper in Robbie's situation or that he believes that crimes are reported in detail because he does read such stories, Ashley emphasizes what he sees as obvious by his repetition of 'surely'.

Although there are not many comments of this kind, those that there are make it clear that at least sometimes the regular viewers are making links to their own experience. What is more puzzling is that the other group do not; this may be because they are less confident and so do not feel able to voice comparisons, or because they are using their own experience more automatically and so do not feel the need to be explicit.

There are also times in the discussions of *Gaffer Samson's Luck* when the children use personal experience to confirm their comprehension of the plot. Alexis and Kelly both relate incidents from their past here to set alongside the accident in the book:

> *Alexis* Mrs Robinson, it reminds me of when my brother fell out of bed and cracked open his (unclear)
> *David* Ugh, you can see the bone
> *MR* Same kind of thing, isn't it? No, you can just see . . .
> *Kelly* My cousin, he was on the wall . . .
> *MR* . . . the children, the other boys coming in to rescue them, see?
> *Kelly* . . . my cousin was on the wall and it was the same as that, he tripped over, um, a stone and he . . .
> *David* Scarf is skinny
> *Kelly* . . . flew off the wall and cracked his head on the other wall and he had brain damage
> (Transcript 22, ll.266–76)

Though they do so in a way that apparently moves from the text to other experiences rather than from the experience to the text, it seems likely that the triggered memory is playing a part in bringing meaning to the text for them.

On occasion the children use more general prior knowledge to the same end, sometimes revealing gaps in their understanding in the process:

> *MR* How about the business about estate and village, did you understand that?
> *David* Yes, 'cause all the boys from the village are grotty
> *Ashley* The village are all scruffbags and all of the ones that come from the estate are 'OK yah man'
> (Transcript 22, ll.53–7)

Here Ashley's own experience of the word 'estate' leads him to draw particular conclusions about the difference being proposed by Paton Walsh. In his own experience of life, the word estate is used not to describe council or modern housing in a rural area but to describe areas of more expensive private housing near the council-built housing in which he lives and goes to school. These differentiations are to do with class and status rather than length of residence and he uses these to try to understand the book, creating an alternative to the preferred reading in the process.

Although these uses of personal experience do not exactly mirror the uses made in the discussions of *Grange Hill*, in the case of each narrative there are times when children explicitly refer to things that have happened to them or to prior knowledge as a way of interpreting the text. There were slightly fewer examples of this in the data relating to *Gaffer Samson's Luck*, particularly in the earlier transcripts. In both cases, though, the children showed the ability to use their experience of life and of other texts in their responses. The difference noted between regular and less regular viewers of *Grange Hill* (with regular viewers using more personal experience) could be seen to connect with the less extensive use of personal experience by all the children with the unknown printed text; here prior knowledge and the ensuing confidence may be more relevant than difference of medium.

In their work on *Mr Magus Is Waiting For You*, the children make far fewer direct references to their own experience, and those which do occur are early on in the transcript, as in this response to the appearance of the cat:

Kelly	It's the magician's garden
Natalie	Aaah!
Kelly	We're getting a cat like that
David	We've got a cat like that
Neil	I know, I've seen it haven't I?
	(Transcript 28, ll.37–41)

There are very few other references that draw parallels in this way; perhaps as the text itself moves beyond the realist events of *Grange Hill* or *Gaffer Samson's Luck*, the children are aware that it is less appropriate to make such comparisons.

However, the children do make other comments which suggest that they are very aware of their own experiences as they watch this story. Very early on, their own experiences of story serve to frame their viewing:

Ashley	It's a storybook made into a film
Natalie	Yeah, Ashley read this story in assembly
Neil	It starts off like your story doesn't it, sort of, 'I was eating my breakfast . . .'
	(Transcript 28, ll.14–17)

This comment from Ashley comes at a point when all that has been seen on the screen is the overall title *Middle English*, followed immediately by the opening shots of the story with first the title *Mr Magus Is Waiting For You* and then 'by Gene Kemp' superimposed; from this meagre information Ashley assumes this is a book, maybe because the author's name is so prominent, or maybe because the series name suggests this to him. Natalie and Neil seem to be identifying here more with the role of author/producer than with that of reader/consumer, seeing no distinction between Ashley's story and that of a professional writer. At the same time, Ashley's own comment seems to be more to do with positioning himself as an informed viewer.

The children are able to make joking references which draw on their own experience and show how they are aware of the different realities of the programme and their own lives:

> *Clock face shown set at 3 o'clock*
> *Natalie*   Time to go home then
> *Kelly*   It's not five past yet, we've got five minutes
>   (Transcript 28, ll.71–3)

This fascination with story time and real time echoes the comments discussed earlier to do with discourse time and story time (see p. 125).

Early on, before it becomes clear that the book is not a realist text, the children's predictions draw on their knowledge of the world around them, as in their mistaken prediction that the swing will break. There are no similar comments later on in the transcript, and all the comments that show an explicit connection between the children's own lives and this story are in the first quarter of the transcript. In this way there is a clear difference between the children's responses to this narrative and to the earlier ones; this difference is more particularly quantitative and again it seems to be more related to modality than to medium.

In the discussions of *Outside Over There* and *Baba Yaga*, there are places when the children use their prior life experiences, but these are far fewer than with the realist texts. This reduction in use of everyday knowledge is even more noticeable here than in the case of *Mr Magus Is Waiting For You*, which does have a more realist setting from which the fantasy develops. The children do use their knowledge of real life to try to untangle the extra storyline in the background of the illustrations to *Outside Over There*:

> *Alexis*   How could the letter get there because he hasn't got a post office
>   (Transcript 30, ll.87–8)

Here Alexis appears to be drawing a clear distinction between what happens in her own experience (we can send letters because we have a postal service) and what she is prepared to accept is possible in the context of this story. Because she cannot accept the possibility of a post office in the setting of the book, she is unhappy with the use of a letter within the story.

This distinction between the reality of everyday life and the world of the fairytale is also brought out in the children's attempt to explain this to me:

> *Alexis*   The shopkeeper wouldn't say to his helper 'Go and get some water ready
>   and some sticks', would he?
> *David*   Yeah, yeah
> *Kelly*   He'd probably say 'What kind, we've got large or medium or small'
> (All laugh)
> *David*   The one round the corner from me would probably say . . .
> *Ashley* The one round the corner from me is worse than Baba Yaga!
>   (Transcript 29, ll.264–71)

To make their point, the children turn to inventing direct speech appropriate for each setting to show the incongruity of the fairytale language in a realist setting. At the same time they can enjoy the potential for humour within this incongruity.

These examples serve to highlight the reasons why the children do not make more use of their own experience in these texts; they have already perceived that they are of limited usefulness. However, this does not mean that the children make less use of extra-textual information here to help their efforts to create meaning; rather, the kinds of extra-textual information are different.

Prior Knowledge about Language

The children's knowledge about language played some part in their discussions of each text, though the exact nature of their interest was different for each. They showed an interest in language patterns and in specific vocabulary, and showed pleasure in repeating certain phrases or words. Here there was at least as much difference between different texts in the same medium as there was across media, and so again it is hard to argue that the children are responding differently because of the medium rather than because of some other factor.

At times the children's prior language experience is used as a reference point. I have already discussed Rikky's interest in the word 'dazzling' and pointed out the role of his own experience; similarly David shows a fascination for checking his own expectations against the text:

David I was just looking over your shoulder and they spelt 'fro' there wrong, they just put f-r-o
MR 'To and fro', that's right
David What, f-r-o?
MR Mmm
 (Transcript 23, ll.22–6)

Again, here his assumption that the book has made a mistake is based on limited experience and so leads him astray, but his confidence in making the claim suggests a real sense of his own experience as being as reliable as the text.

At times the children built on a sense of the register of language appropriate to these stories; very early on in the *Baba Yaga* session, Ashley follows his comment about the genre by making a sing-song noise reminiscent of an adult reading to a child. Here the tune of the language as well as the specific words leads him to an appropriate genre label. Natalie uses her awareness of book language as she describes the typical outcome of fairytales:

Natalie You knew it was going to have a happy ending
MR How, why?
Alexis It always does
Natalie The monster's going to get killed and live happy ever after
 (Transcript 30, ll.114–17)

Here her inclusion in her prediction of the phrase 'happy ever after' draws on her knowledge of the language of this genre as well as of the typical plot resolutions.

In both of these cases the children are not just using the information in the text but drawing on their wider experience of language; the textual cues work with the knowledge they have about the prosody and vocabulary of fairytales.

At other times the children's interest in language focuses on particular words, as has been seen before. Again David picks up what he assumes is an error in the text:

> *David* 'Arbor', 'arbour, they can't talk proper
> (Transcript 30, 1.10)

He uses the information in the text together with his extra-textual knowledge and highlights the apparent mismatch he perceives.

Whereas at other times the children asked about unknown words, here my question about the meaning of 'pestle' reveals that they are happy to tolerate their lack of knowledge and to define this in a way which maintains meaning but not register:

> (I read on, next two paragraphs and to 'in a mortar which she drove along with the pestle':)
> *MR* Do you know what a pestle is?
> *Kelly* Yes, it's a motor
> *MR* David?
> *David* Like a car thing
> (Squabble between Kelly and David)
> *Kelly* A motorbike (does a motorbike impression)
> *David* A flying carpet
> (Transcript 29, 11.80–8)

Kelly has picked up 'drove' and 'mortar' and come up with a reasonable miscue of 'motor' which, as she and David add extra possibilities, linked each time to transport. With the suggestion of 'flying carpet', though, David appears to be moving back to a more appropriate choice for the situation.

Just as in the other narratives, the children here display a sense of enjoyment of language for its own sake as they play with the possibilities raised by the link made to the *Star Wars* character Jabba the Hutt:

> *MR* What were you saying before Rikky, about Baba Yaga, what should it have been instead?
> *Kelly* *Yogi Bear*
> *MR* That wasn't what he said was it, it was *Star Wars*
> *David* Baba Yaga more like Jabba the Hutt
> *Kelly* Jabba Cake
> *MR* What made you think of Jabba the Hutt?
> *David* Because he's really fat and really evil and he's got the eyes like it
> *Rikky* He eats frogs
> *Kelly* It's not a he it's a she

Rikky   What, Jabba the Hutt?
MR   No, Jabba the Hutt is male, Baba Yaga is female
David   They're mating right now
MR   What kind of children would you get then?
David   Babba Yagas
Kelly   Babby Yaga, Bogey Yogi
Rikky   No you'll get . . .
David   Bogey Fogey
Rikky   . . . loads of Jabba Hutts but really skinny
          (Transcript 29, ll.229–48)

Kelly's contribution, '*Yogi Bear*', also adds to the possibilities here. As well as the delight in language, this example allows the children to exploit the slightly subversive potential of this situation. The link between names is not just phonological; for David there is also a characterization parallel.

Intertextual Strategies

Both semantic and syntactic cue systems are being used by the children, but their use goes beyond their knowledge of the world round them. Two other factors can be shown to have some influence on the children's interpretations, namely their experience of other texts (intertextual influences) and their embryonic understanding of television as an industry.

    Sometimes the intertextual references are used as an attempt to prove a point:

MR   Why is it that you like *Grange Hill*, why is it that you watch it?
David   Because it's got, it's like *Neighbours*, it goes on, exciting
Ashley No, *Neighbours* isn't as good
Alexis No, it's not as good as *Neighbours*
MR   Why, Alexis?
Alexis *Neighbours* always ends at the exciting bit, it always ends at the exciting
          bit, but on *Grange Hill* it doesn't always end at the exciting bit
Kelly   Like when Charlene . . .
Alexis And *Grange Hill* is a ch . . . , not a children's programme, er
Ashley Teenagers' programme
Alexis A school programme, about school and *Neighbours* isn't, it's about a street
          (Transcript 19, ll.428–41)

The first intertextual reference is used as a comparison to answer my question, but this is then challenged by the others who are not prepared to see the comparison as valid. Here the awareness of cliff-hanger endings, which could be seen as an understanding of the generic conventions of television, illustrates the way in which very often the children's references to other texts and to the way television works are woven together. The children are beginning to know that the actors in programmes are in some way not the same as the characters:

> *Kelly*   I think, I've got a brilliant idea, he might jump on a London bus next to someone else
>
> (David makes scornful noise)
>
> *Kelly*   It's true, it's like *EastEnders,* isn't it, like Paul disappeared
>
> *David*   He ran away for a reason though, like he got fed up in *EastEnders* and he left
>
> (Transcript 21, ll.341–6)

Here Kelly's attempt to predict is based on another narrative, but her prediction is deemed invalid by David because of his extra knowledge; since there is no reason for him to suppose that the actor who plays Mike also wishes to leave the series, the comparison with *EastEnders* is not relevant for him.

Some references show a general developing understanding of the way things are in stories, as in Kelly's comments about the owl in the book being read to the class by their teacher at the time:

> *Kelly*   The owl in that story is really really kind in that story, I thought, 'Any minute now he's going to be killing her,' and then he goes, 'Come in, blah blah blah blah'
>
> (Transcript 25, ll.108–10)

Here Kelly's prior experience of owls in stories and in other texts such as nature documentaries leads her to predict a more realistic outcome. When this expectation is overturned by the narrative development, she remarks on the unusual behaviour then exhibited by the bird.

Some intertextual references are simply passing comparisons, as when Kelly reminded of another book she has read ('It looks like *Why the Whales Came*'). Others are brought in to add humour, as in David's references to the film *Jaws* and his humming of the theme music through the conversation about James crossing the flood water. At other times, however, the children's intertextual knowledge is brought together with their life experience to help them negotiate a shared understanding of a concept:

> *MR*   '. . . he has a haemorrhage that . . .'
>
> *Kelly*   What is that?
>
> *MR*   A haemorrhage is when you start bleeding inside you and it can't stop, yeah?
>
> *Kelly*   Is it like . . .
>
> *MR*   Like a nosebleed but it's inside you somewhere
>
> *Ashley* And unconscious
>
> *Alexis* I know!
>
> *Kelly*   . . . Like one of the moles on you and you pick it and it carries on bleeding till it stops?
>
> *Alexis* No . . .
>
> *MR*   Much much more than that
>
> *Alexis* Like say your bone's cracked
>
> *MR*   Yes but it's inside the skin, it's not outside and so there's a lot of pressure builds up and it can be very dangerous

David	I know what, er, what's it called again, er, unconscious is, it means he's asleep and he could die
Kelly	Helen's woken up
Sarah	From her coma
Alexis	Yeah I know, last night
Kelly	She was in a coma
	(Transcript 26, ll.278–98)

Here the children move from a shared attempt to understand what a haemorrhage is by comparison with their own experience to drawing on a recent event in *Neighbours* to deepen their understanding. This combination of approaches shows just how complex a process the children's reading of this narrative is. Just as with the television narrative, they bring together their past experience of life and of story in a range of media to interpret with the support of their peers the verbal and visual cues available. The possibility that the differences in the children's use of their own experience are due to the different modality is strengthened by the increased number of intertextual references in this transcript. These gradually become more frequent as the references to everyday life decrease, but they are present throughout.

Several of these references are to texts which in some way are seen by the children as similar. Other stories involving magic are mentioned and these references seem to act to help the children confirm the genre in which they have placed this story:

Natalie	He's a wizard
David	It's the man off *Mr Majeika* that plays God
Natalie	Look at that cat
Kelly	He comes out of *Puddle Lane*, the magician
Sarah	Yeah!
	(Transcript 28, ll.24–8)

David's very specific reference to the *Puddle Lane* series, which is a reading scheme with books about a magician and supporting television programmes, is echoed by Kelly's more general prediction:

Kelly	I think she's going to um, like, she turns into a fairy princess or a Care Bear . . .
	(Transcript 28, ll.116–17)

This would suggest a shared view that this story is not a realist text, a position confirmed later on when the children explain where their knowledge comes from:

MR	How do you know about magicians?
David	Because I read all the latest magician books
MR	What kind of books?
David	I read *Puddle Lane* books, I find them amusing, well funny, that little dragon

> *MR*   What about you Ashley, how do you think you know about magicians?
> *Ashley* Because of CS Lewis
>   (Transcript 28, ll.411–18)

Ashley's use of an author's name here is one of very few I encountered in the whole research project. This exchange, though, highlights not only Ashley's knowledge of authors but the cross-media nature of these references. Although, as I have said, there are *Puddle Lane* television programmes, here it is made clear that David at least is referring to print, just as Ashley is. In other words, what the children have read acts as a source of information and support when they tackle this television text. Whether Ashley's early comment that this is a television adaptation has encouraged this can only be speculated upon.

These comments all serve to locate the children in a particular genre, as I have said. Other intertextual references reaffirm this in a somewhat different fashion:

> *MR*   Ashley, what do you think?
> *Ashley* I reckon that old man's like *Freddy 4*
> (Ashley puts hands in Neil's hair in Freddy imitation)
> *David*   Yeah, Freddy
>   (Transcript 28, ll.173–6)

The reference to Freddy of the *Elm Street* films may be a recognition of the evil intent of the magician; it also has a certain potential for suggesting a subversion of the story, just as their references to game shows do. The children could be using the comparison to *Beadle's About* to emphasize the confidence they have in their decision about genre; they could, however, be covering an uncertainty about the probable outcome of the story by deliberately joking about this.

As well as being named directly, other texts act to support the children's comments by offering sources of appropriate language:

> *Ashley* If he sees himself like he'll be banished to a distant realm
>   (Transcript 28, l.254)

This is far from Ashley's normal speech pattern and is a clear case of his taking on an appropriate discourse for the genre.

In a slightly different vein, again with an element of subversion, Neil responds to the flashback sequence in the final part of the programme:

> *Second flashback of Mr Magus's past with rock music backing*
> *Neil* 'I'm James Bond, how do you do?'
>   (Transcript 28, ll.275–6)

The sequence has echoes of some of the James Bond films both in its visual and sound effects and in the appearance of the younger Mr Magus, which Neil is quick to pick up here.

Such intertextual references are not always recognized by all the group:

Kelly   It was, it was a magician who doesn't like mirrors so, like, because, is it because he wants to turn . . .

David   No, he belongs on the dark side

Sarah   He doesn't belong

Natalie   Yeah, he belongs on the dark side, because that's why he said to Tracey, to Charlie, 'Your eyes are dull'

Kelly   Probably it's because he's not on the sun side, he's on the rainy side, mirrors are part of the sun which you can reflect

Natalie   And everything's all misty

(Transcript 28, ll.300–8)

David's expression 'the dark side' can be seen as a reference to the *Star Wars* films, in which the forces of evil are referred to in this way, but the other children interpreted it slightly differently, with Natalie's comment being more ambiguous and Kelly's contrasting dark with sun rather than the 'light' of the films. (This acts to remind me that just as the children are using intertextuality, so my own intertextual knowledge may be encouraging me to interpret this phrase in a way David did not intend. That does not make the comparison with *Star Wars* invalid, but does emphasize the extent to which any interpretation of these transcribed conversations is created by the prior experience of the interpreter as well as the information in the text.)

A text that acts as an important point of reference is *Neighbours*. I have already referred to some of the ways in which the children use this programme, but there are broader intertextual issues not raised by my earlier comments. At times, events are compared as a way for the children to emphasize modality differences, as has been shown above. Another comparison is made as Natalie argues for a longer version of *Mr Magus Is Waiting For You*:

Natalie   No, like, this is what I mean, you know when *Neighbours* is on it's ages, every single day

David   Oh yeah half an hour, that's really ages

MR   No, you mean like every day for weeks and weeks

Natalie   Yeah that's what I meant, 'cause this isn't, *Mr Magus*

David   That's because it's a book

MR   So should it go on for longer or not?

Natalie   Yeah, because it's good

David   No, otherwise the book's going to be that thick and the story's over an hour

(David holds arms about half a metre apart)

Sarah   It couldn't be published in a book

(Transcript 28, ll.379–90)

Here Natalie's awareness of the different possible structures for television narratives leads on to comments about the implications for book length, which again suggest that the children are drawing on their knowledge of both media.

This example can also be seen as showing the children's use of their knowledge about the structures of television, in that they are clearly aware here of the constructed nature of these programmes and of the possibility of producing a sequel to almost any story. Similarly, their criticism of the realism of the cat model coupled with an awareness of the limitations of cats as actors emphasize their awareness of television as a created product. The children also display an understanding of the purpose of providing a review of one episode at the beginning of the next, a technique with which they were familiar from *Neighbours*:

> MR   What was all that about in that episode where they showed you the beginning again, what was that for?
> David   Um, they was telling you what they did
> Kelly   Just telling you, a reminder of what they did
> David   No
> Kelly   And to tell you what they did
> MR   What, for us?
> David   No, for them
> (Transcript 28, ll.317–24)

David's final comment seems to indicate some confusion about this, but could also be read ironically; his tone of voice does not make this clear.

As the use of direct personal experience decreased in the discussions of these two texts, so the number of intertextual references increased dramatically. Whereas with *Mr Magus Is Waiting For You* these references appeared gradually to increase as the story developed, for *Baba Yaga* and *Outside Over There* the children began to make these connections almost immediately and continued to do so throughout the discussions.

As before, many of these references simply name other stories, but here the purpose of naming is more clearly to do with locating the story in a given genre and then using their wider experience of the genre to interpret and predict. To begin with, the children tried to match this story to a specific known tale:

> Alexis This is like, this is like, *Snow White and the Seven Dwarves*
> David   Yeah, I thought that
> (I read next sentence to '*she soon grew to hate Marusia*')
> (Kelly points at me)
> Kelly   Oh, I know this story! *The Storyteller*, it was on *The Storyteller*, wasn't it?
> (I read on to end of next paragraph, '*from my sister who lives in the forest*')
> Kelly   Unless it's spinning wheel thing
> David   She pricks herself
> Kelly   Eurgh
> (David's hand goes up)
> David   Um, um, it's between the *Snow White* and . . .
> Kelly   It's between *Snow White* and *Storyteller*
> (Transcript 29, ll.34–47)

Here each of the features revealed as I read the story is built into this attempt, leading to later comparisons to *Hansel and Gretel* as the children discover that Marusia is sent into the forest.

Once the children have begun to make comparisons to other stories, they then use the events of these other stories to predict what is likely to happen here:

> *MR* How do you think, now she's been sent off into the forest?
> (Ashley has his hand up — David sings 'Hi ho, hi ho, it's off to work we go')
> *Kelly* I know, I know
> *Alexis* They find a little cottage
> (Ashley shakes his head)
> *Kelly* Unless she's got three brothers or something 'cause that's what it did on
> *Storyteller* and then they . . .
> *MR* Are forests good places to be in fairytales?
> *All* No, no
> (Transcript 29, ll.65–74)

Kelly is explicit about her strategy but it seems very likely that Alexis is also drawing on past story experience in her prediction here.

This explicitness as to how they are able to predict is addressed by the children later on:

> *Ashley* Because it was a fairytale and it seemed so obvious
> *MR* What about fairytales?
> *Ashley* Like, because, the beginning, it seemed, so obvious, once upon a time, and then
> *MR* What's obvious about that?
> *Ashley* And then you could tell it was going to be a combination of stories, 'cause really it was *Hansel and Gretel*
> *MR* Which bits were like *Hansel and Gretel*?
> *Ashley* When they were sent to the forest
> *David* When she was going to eat them, she wanted to fatten them up
> *Alexis* And the bit in the forest was like *Snow White and the Seven Dwarves*
> *Ashley* And *Hansel and Gretel*
> *Rikky* I thought it was going to be the *Little Match Girl* 'cause her mum died
> (Transcript 29, ll.293–308)

Although they express a rather crude version of the idea that story motifs in folktales tend to recur, they have a clear view that this is the case and are able to make specific points about the features they have observed in other stories.

One particularly notable feature of these intertextual references is the extent to which they cross media boundaries. Above, the references to other fairytales include several to the television series *The Storyteller*. In the discussion of *Outside Over There*, the children refer to two films:

> *Alexis* Oh, I can't remember what it's called but one day I watched this video and it was like this, but it had a squeaky voice

> *David* Oh I know what it was, it was *Star Wars*
> (I read '*the goblins came*')
> (Chorus of 'eurgh' at pictures)
> *Alexis* What's it called, *Labyrinth!*
> *David* Yeah, *Labyrinth*
> (Transcript 30, ll.15–21)

David picks up the *Star Wars* analogy again later when talking about the way the goblins are drawn, comparing them to characters in the first *Star Wars* film. For the children, the media boundary is less significant than the story, and so similar stories are used to explain the new one without any reference to the difference of medium.

It seems clear here, as in the case of *Mr Magus Is Waiting For You*, that the children are able to discern which prior experiences will be most helpful in understanding a new story. When considering realist texts, as I have shown, there is a greater reliance on everyday experience. In dealing with fantasy, prior story experience is more important. When the story begins by appearing to be realist and then moves away from this tradition, the children also begin by using lived experience and move away as they locate the story more firmly in its genre. In all of this, the kind of story seems far more significant than its medium.

Other Influences on Interpretation

There were other influences from beyond the text which seemed to play a part in the children's search for meaning. There were times when they showed some understanding of the role of media industries, particularly in relation to modality:

> *Kelly* Right, and she said when they scratch, you can get a lot of chemicals and that in you and you can die, but I don't know how they could get the monkeys to scratch, I don't really think they did, I think they had something like a banana or something or anything like that and they just scraped it and then she just scratched herself when she had long nails
> *Alexis* How could a banana scratch?
> *MR* You mean the stem bit on the end of it?
> *Kelly* Yeah
> *Alexis* Yeah
> *Kelly* Yeah, the stem bit, it looks like brown, the monkeys are brown, it looks like brown and when they scrape it . . .
> (Transcript 19, ll.301–12)

As Kelly tries to understand how a monkey could be trained to scratch the girl, she hypothesizes a special effect answer which, although crude, shows some understanding that what we see on the screen is constructed. Both Hodge and Tripp (1986) and Buckingham found children to be 'extremely inventive' (Buckingham, 1993a, p. 225) in offering explanations of special effects very much like Kelly's account here.

At times it is clear that such realist television texts as *Grange Hill* and soap operas stretch the children's grasp of modality and that they are still uncertain as to how far the series is a fiction and how far it is real. The following conversation is typical in the way in which the children say things, initially indicating a firm understanding which is gradually revealed to be rather less sure:

MR	Say somebody gets hurt on the news, yeah, you see a film of someone getting hurt in the news, and somebody gets hurt in something like *Grange Hill* or *Neighbours*, is that the same? How's it different?
Natalie	Say when Danny died in *Grange Hill*, he might not die but someone else might in true life
Sarah	Yes
Natalie	Like Eileen is or Daphne in *Neighbours* but it's really . . .
Sarah	Eileen has died in real life but Daphne hasn't
MR	But Eileen's not dead in *Neighbours*, is she, she's just supposed to be away
Natalie	Yeah
Sarah	And Daphne's dead in *Neighbours* but she's not really in real life
MR	So what is it that's different?
Sarah	Don't know really
Natalie	In *Grange Hill* I think it's the same 'cause when someone dies in *Grange Hill* um, it's just the same, someone else is dead or sometimes they're not

(Transcript 20, ll.319–37)

Here Natalie in particular has trouble explaining where Sarah is more confident; Sarah's final reluctance to attempt an explanation may suggest that she too is less certain than her earlier comments might suggest. However, although this may be a developing understanding, the children have already identified that this is not a straightforward business. They are not happy with a direct correlation between these narratives and those included in news programmes even though they cannot yet articulate the difference clearly enough to be sure that they have a firm grasp of this.

In the discussions on *Grange Hill* there were moments when the children showed a developing awareness of the roles of actors and producers and of modality. For *Gaffer Samson's Luck*, neither of these factors appeared. The children neither discussed the reality nor made comments about the role of either author or publishers and booksellers. I do not believe that these two omissions are related to each other; in a later activity, the children had no hesitation in describing the book as fiction and were already much clearer about the modal status of realist fiction. The gap between print and mental image is perhaps a clearer modality indicator than the more complex move from fictional character portrayed by live actor to mental image. As a result, the children probably saw the modality of this story as needing no comment, whereas their less assured grasp of the modality of *Grange Hill* led to the responses seen above.

In terms of industry awareness, though, I would argue that the lack of comment sprang not from a confidence about such issues but from a limited awareness of them. Whereas television is now relatively transparent in its exploration of agency and industry — with features on such programmes as *Blue Peter* about the making of programmes and films popular with children — the business of book production is still rarely discussed either in everyday life or in classrooms. Personal appearances by actors on chat shows and children's programmes may heighten the children's awareness of television as a construct whilst blurring modality boundaries; the rarer appearances by children's authors do not seem to have helped these children to focus on the role of the author.

Collaborative Strategies

The most significant strategy, and one to which I shall return when considering the pedagogical implications, was the collaboration in which the children engaged. This happened with every text and showed a consistency of style and approach which was very striking. The children showed the ability to engage each other in drawing out their understanding, in resolving uncertainty and in developing interpretations and predictions through their interactions with each other. The only significant factor here causing some slight differences appeared to be the relationships within the group and their attitude to each other. In this case in particular the medium appeared to be of no relevance to the children's ability or desire to collaborate.

In the discussions on *Grange Hill*, collaborative retelling was a central feature. The regular viewers in particular used a shared model of telling in which the children together constructed a shared version of what they had seen, or of what they thought would happen. By this I do not mean just a point at which different children in turn provided answers to one of my questions, but something much more collaborative where children even finished each other's sentences and there was a genuine attempt to arrive at a communal view of either past or possible future. This is described by some researchers as collective remembering (Middleton and Edwards, 1990) and is considered in Chapter 3.

At times this is a straightforward (yet evaluative) retelling:

Ashley   I reckon when Danny Kendall died, that was . . .
David   He was knocked unconscious
Ashley   . . . he was taking drugs I reckon . . .
Kelly   He was laying in Mr someone's car
Ashley   Mr Bronson's car, 'cause he hated him 'cause Mr Bronson was always moaning on at him about because he was like . . .
David   I remember 'cause he used . . .
Ashley   He never liked Danny Kendall's idea and he always thought there was something wrong with him and so like, er, Danny Kendall started like, taking drugs and then he was found dead in Mr Bronson's car
         (Transcript 19, ll.157–67)

After Ashley has begun the topic, the others quickly interrupt and the next three lines all add information in a similar syntactic pattern. Ashley then picks up again as Kelly fails to remember the teacher's name and adds the reason for Danny's choice; he is in turn supported by David before continuing and concluding the anecdote.

At other times there is a negotiated prediction which, in the case of the less frequent viewers, can be a tentative and circuitous process. This is frequently an extended business and the example here is by no means unusual in its length and sustained development:

Sarah	Oh, I know, that man, um . . .
Neil	He probably kills him
Sarah	He sort of, he sort of like, 'cause he said, 'Do you want a game of cards?', he's probably playing cards
Natalie	Getting money, to get money
Sarah	He's, and he won, and they're playing for money and he wants his money, and the man hasn't got money 'cause he's poor and . . .
Natalie	No he isn't poor
Sarah	No he isn't poor, but he hasn't got the money
Natalie	He hasn't got the money
Sarah	And he's trying to give him something really expensive, and I think when he get, he said, he'll, 'I'll get told off,' I don't know what he means by that
MR	What do you think's going to happen?
Sarah	Well he looks very fierce and fat and sort of strong
Natalie	Probably go up to him and go like that and have a fight or something
Sarah	And then probably the headmaster's going to come in or something
Natalie	Yeah, or one of the teachers is going to come in and say, 'What's going on?'

(Transcript 20, ll.64–85)

Again here the children expand and complete each other's utterances, add justifications and qualifications and use each other's syntactic patterns as they move to an agreed position. The correction of each other that is evident here (see Natalie and Sarah above) is also very important, with a great emphasis on getting it right, another feature also observed by Buckingham (1993a).

As can be seen in the above extract, when there is dissent this is often resolved in the process of the shared retelling. So powerful is this collective action, too, that at times I became involved in it myself, as in this short extract from a much longer exchange:

Ashley	He didn't set his flat on fire, he just sounded the alarm didn't he?
David	No . . . we didn't see him do that though did we?
MR	No but we saw him with the matches
David	Yes, he goes (match noise) while his mum was getting some food, his dad . . .
Kelly	Why did he do that?
David	Who's that brown man?
Kelly	Why did he do it, that's what I want to know
Alexis	Because he didn't like the flat or . . .

> *Ashley*   He thought they'd get a house because like, I was getting frightened because it was all rough and I thought his mum was going to get murdered or something
> *Alexis*   But he didn't have to burn the house though . . . oh yes he did, didn't he?
> (Transcript 19, ll.314–28; exchange actually continues to l.362)

My own comment here serves to challenge Ashley's statement and to develop David's point further, so that David takes this up and develops it. This extract also shows how questioning is part of the negotiation, as Kelly and David ask for clarification from the group.

This process is not entirely smooth. At times, certain children are scornful of others' lack of understanding. Here to start with the group are prepared to tolerate Neil's lack of knowledge about Ronnie's past but there comes a point when this tolerance goes:

> *Neil*   Is she in prison now?
> (Noises of disgust at this idea)
> *Sarah*   You just saw her
> *Rikky*   She wouldn't be at school otherwise would she?
> *Natalie*   Well she wouldn't be doing that thing would she?
> (Transcript 18, ll.225–9)

Although Neil's questions are answered, just as Kelly's and David's were, the noises of disgust and the patronizing emphasis created by the tag questions show a lack of sympathy with the question not evident in the other extract.

This negotiated approach, although used by both groups, is the most notable feature of the regular viewers' conversations, and it raises questions about the difference between the two groups which go beyond simplistic answers. Confidence in personal knowledge may make the regular viewers more comfortable with this shared thinking aloud. It may be that simply because the regular viewers have more knowledge they retell in all ways more extensively and so this is not proportionately unexpected. Certainly each transcript of the regular viewers is longer than the corresponding transcript of the other group, but even allowing for this there is a much higher proportion of shared retelling in the former group's discussion. Individual differences created by the children's different backgrounds and prior experiences may also be significant here, as may friendship patterns and previous social interactions in the groups. If so, then similar differences between the children's responses may emerge as significant factors in the discussions on other narratives.

The children frequently collaborated to retell and to predict when working on *Gaffer Samson's Luck*. This happened from the second episode on, becoming more detailed and sustained as the story developed. Even on the first occasion on which the children retell, they collaborate to do so:

> *David*   He met this man . . .
> *Ashley*   . . . A man called Gaffer
> *MR*   Gaffer Samson who lives next door, yeah?

David	I know, he had this little garden and . . .
Natalie	And he saw a girl called Angey
MR	Can you remember who Angey was?
Natalie	She was a traveller
David	She was a (unclear)
Natalie	And she was poor
Kelly	She was all mucky
Natalie	And she was poor
Kelly	And they wouldn't let her . . .
Ashley	. . . In the shop, she went, 'Buy us a Mars bar'
Natalie	'Buy us a Mars bar' (laughs)
David	'Buy us a Mars bar'
	(Transcript 22, ll.9–23)

Already the children are finishing each other's sentences and echoing each other in the repetition of enjoyed lines. Ashley expands David's opening comment, and David in turn adds more detail before Natalie adds a new point, which in turn is expanded with David and Kelly's assistance before Kelly moves the story on again.

By the final episode, the retelling is much longer, more complex and involves more negotiation:

David	They were looking for . . .
Kelly	Gaffer Samson's luck
David	. . . Gaffer Samson's luck and um . . .
Kelly	He said um . . .
MR	David?
David	. . . Terry's gang was chasing after them and . . .
MR	How did they get out of the way?
David	They dived into the . . .
Kelly	They dived into the weeds and . . .
MR	That's right and, Alexis . . .
Alexis	And James's father brought a map home
MR	That's right
Kelly	About, showing this thing and um . . .
David	They should have taken it with him, though, because he might have forgotten what it looked like
Kelly	. . . And his, granny . . .
Sarah	They did
Kelly	. . . went to Mr . . .
David	Mr Gaffer
MR	Gaffer Samson
Kelly	And er, started um saying something about these gypsies . . .
David	Yeah, they were hard to him
Kelly	Yeah, and saying something about these gypsies that perhaps they keep on telling lies about the stuff
David	They were arguing, they keeped on going
Kelly	They weren't
David	They were arguing

MR	And she was saying, 'Don't take any notice of what they told you, don't worry about it'
David	'Don't take any notice of them, gypsies are just twerps'
Kelly	No
Alexis	You're just saying that Kelly
	(Transcript 26, ll.9–40)

Again the children recall what has happened and negotiate a shared version of this, but this time the children mention seven stages in the episode under recall as opposed to three above (and yet each section of the book was of similar length). There is also a development into evaluative comment within the retelling and points at which one individual's view is confirmed by others or challenged. Again the power of this activity can be seen by the way my own comments turn from those which could be seen as in some sense chairing the discussion to a more active involvement in the construction of a shared meaning.

As in the case of *Grange Hill*, the collaboration went beyond retelling to the production of negotiated predictions:

MR	*'He sat . . . on the attic floor, and thought about the weir.'*
MR	What do you think he's going to do?
David	He's going to make a bridge
Kelly	He's going to make a sort of bridge there
MR	But what's he going to try and do, he's going to?
David	He's going to try and do it
Alexis	He's going to try and do it because he's sort of, because he's made Terry do it . . .
Sarah	He could pretend he's done it
Alexis	. . . He's feeling sorry for Terry
David	If he did it then he's going to do it and he feels sorry
	(Transcript 26, ll.305–15)

Even David's first comment here seems to take for granted the answer to my question (i.e., James is going to cross the Rymers) and to jump to how he will do this. The children have a shared understanding of what they are thinking and find it hard to see the need to be as explicit as I am asking them to be. They assume that my question is not about what James will do, but why, and their answers show a shared view of his motives. Possibly their experience as children of the codes and rules concerning dares is more immediate than mine and so they rapidly move to a consideration of motive and method where I am still asking about intended action in a more general sense.

This negotiated, collaborative approach is a feature that the children's approach to each text has in common, whereas their use of personal experience was different in degree and detail, though broadly comparable. The only difference is that here there are no instances of the children pouring scorn on questions from any member of the group, possibly because all are on an equal footing in terms of prior knowledge.

Just as in the other texts so far considered, the children engage in a great deal of collaborative retelling and interpretation about *Mr Magus Is Waiting For You*. Several instances of this have already been quoted above in other contexts, such as the discussion about the dark side. Very often these seem to be straightforward examples of collaboration to arrive at an agreed position, as we have seen before in other narratives, and some of the examples here are retellings not of the programme under discussion but of *Neighbours*, again something which has been shown before.

As before, there are times when this collaboration is not totally inclusive and where it leads to a certain scorn for those who do not take a similar view or join in:

Natalie The apples
Neil What's wrong with an apple, it's red, it's green, you can get any colour
(Sarah looks at Neil in disbelief)
Kelly Because it's the magician's garden he's put a load of power and magic into it
(Transcript 28, ll.103–8)

Sarah and Natalie have come to a shared understanding very early on, and they find it hard to believe that Neil is not sure of their meaning. The importance of non-verbal signals between the children in this collaboration is shown here by the way in which Sarah and Natalie support each other and Sarah distances herself from Neil by their looks. This response to Neil was also noted in the discussion of *Grange Hill*, but not of *Gaffer Samson's Luck*, and earlier I suggested that it might be to do with prior knowledge. Here, though, there is no prior knowledge outside the actual viewing situation. Since each time the target of scorn is Neil, this may be more a question of group dynamics than of textual or media difference; this attitude to Neil was not confined to the research situation but was also observed in everyday classroom life.

When Kelly ties herself in knots trying to find an acceptable way of describing the black character in the story, there is a different kind of collective action:

Kelly I think she's going to um, like, she turns into a fairy princess or a Care Bear, I think the black boy . . . I mean the whatever colour boy . . .
David Jeffrey
Neil The whatever colour boy? The yellow boy!
Kelly Jeffrey, oh the brown, oh! Jeffrey and . . .
David Caroline
Kelly No!
Natalie } Tracey
David }
(Transcript 28, ll.116–21)

David and Natalie help by offering her the names of characters, where Neil this time is the person to react more scornfully. These examples show yet again the extent to which collective retelling is dependent on the willing participation of each member of the group, and emphasize the ways in which such collaboration can be divisive as well as cohesive, depending on the prior tensions and current relationships within the group.

Collective retelling and prediction was also a significant factor in the case of *Baba Yaga*. The children's use of this strategy followed a very similar pattern to that described for the other texts above and thus a long analysis would lead to repetition. The children still build on each other's ideas, expand and support meanings and complete each other's utterances.

It is worth focusing, though, on the way in which the children bring prior knowledge to bear on the negotiations:

Kelly   It might not be her aunty
Alexis Mrs Robinson, isn't that her aunty, 'cause it's her sister's her stepmother
David   It's her stepmother
Kelly   It isn't, it's pretending 'cause you can't get an aunt . . .
Alexis It's got to be 'cause she's wicked and her stepmother's wicked
          (Transcript 29, ll.158–63)

Here, as already mentioned, Alexis is operating as much on narrative logic as on her understanding of family connections and feels the need for the story's sake for the relationship to imply wickedness. It is interesting that while arguments to do with real life knowledge are contested, the final comment by Alexis, which relies on this narrative logic, wins the day and the conversation then moves on.

Using the Most Relevant Prior Experiences

In Chapter 3, I suggested that our understanding of reality is social and that we need a social view of narrative to help us understand how we read narratives and why they play such a significant part in our lives. The evidence in this chapter shows that these children are both drawing on the view of reality they have developed from their social context and working socially to interpret the new narratives they are encountering; moreover, this study shows clearly that they are doing this with both television and printed narratives. Through their negotiations they are able to help each other in building a shared understanding of each text, drawing on relevant prior life and literary experience. Rather than the medium of any narrative being the key factor in the ways in which children approach it, their social context, prior expectations and collective negotiations appear to be most significant.

Whilst it would be too strong to argue here that there is no connection between the medium of the story and the strategies used by the children, what is clear is that the children do show the ability to transfer the competencies they have between media and that other factors such as the nature of the text and its modality, and the makeup of the group, are as relevant as the medium if not more so. The children's own intertextual comments were often cross-media; they often referred to a television narrative which offered a parallel to what was happening in a printed text, and vice versa. All this would seem to argue that the strategies the children are learning when they learn to watch narratives on television have the potential to aid them as they take on printed narratives. Although learning to read will involve using a different symbolic system, the ways we interpret the meanings contained in that system are, on the evidence presented here, very similar to the ways we make sense of televisual narratives.

In terms of their use of their own prior life experience, the children used this most in situations where the narratives being discussed were realist in nature. This was true of all the realist narratives in both media, though the children's still developing understanding of the modality of such programmes as *Grange Hill* and *Neighbours* may bring about a greater use of life experience when considering these texts as opposed to *Gaffer Samson's Luck*, which they had clearly seen as fictional. Whereas at the point at which I had only presented the information on this drawn from *Grange Hill* and *Gaffer Samson's Luck*, it seemed possible that television did make a difference here, the limited use of own experience by the children for all the fantasy texts compared to all the realist texts would suggest that the use of prior life experience is much more related to modality than medium. The extra confidence shown by the regular *Grange Hill* viewers, and the increased responsiveness to *Gaffer Samson's Luck* as the story developed, suggests that a secondary factor here is familiarity with the actual text; however, the children also showed the ability to compensate for a lack of prior knowledge of specific texts where generic knowledge could act as a substitute, as in the case of *Baba Yaga*.

Intertextual information and prior knowledge of story were more commonly used by the children when discussing the less realist texts. Although there were intertextual references throughout, just as in each case there was some use of personal experience, the children seemed to know that the less realist the text, the more useful they would find it to refer to other stories and the less helpful would be their everyday experience. What this suggests is that children are making judgments about the most helpful prior experiences to draw on along some kind of continuum from their own everyday experiences, through generalized world and life knowledge, to story experiences and their understanding of literary logic, which as we have seen was at times taken as having an overriding authority. Their choice of a position on this continuum was not related directly to the medium of the text, though since there was a slight bias towards the realist in my choice of televisual texts, there was some increased use of life experience when discussing these.

Chapter 9

Children Reading Print and Television

I began this book by arguing that our everyday attitudes are based on what is presented as common sense, but that these are better understood as a series of cultural assumptions. In their comparison of television and reading, these assumptions use a set of oppositions which suggest that reading is a linear mental process involving a staged series of verbal exercises to arrive at a previously determined meaning, whereas television is portrayed as play rather than work and as an undemanding visual activity. These positions ignore similarly polarized debates about the nature of television and about reading pedagogy which are also part of everyday discourses, and all these discourses ignore the central role of narrative.

I went on to suggest that reading any narrative is a rather more complex process than has been suggested by these everyday discourses. In pedagogic debates about literacy, in literary theory and in media studies, similar avenues are being explored, and these seem most fruitful when attempting to take a view of the interaction between reader, text and community. I argued that key questions here were the role of the interpretive community and the relationship between the canon of texts, the reader and the community. Underlying all this is the relationship between language, thought and culture, with narrative as a key site of intersection of these three. I suggested that in order to develop an increased awareness of the ways in which children actually deal with texts in different media, an exploration which used narrative as a central feature was necessary. Furthermore, such an exploration needed to take into account the idea that narrative is a central part of human experience and as such needs to be considered as essentially social.

From this I hypothesized that if we knew more about the specific ways in which children make sense of narrative (including the ways in which they use their understanding of the different realities present in different narratives) then we might be able to frame a more coherent set of pedagogic practices than has so far been possible. I suggested that what was needed was a thick description of the ways in which children actually engage with narrative in both media that considered the respective role of reader, text and community across television and reading and that this could lead to an improved understanding of the ways forward for pedagogy.

The fieldwork reported in the second half of this book set out to provide this thick description, but what has it actually shown? Before setting out a possible way forward for teachers, I need to summarize the findings of this work as a backdrop to my suggestions.

The Role of the Reader

For this group of children, the role of the reader is crucial in reading texts from both media. In each case, the children are actively engaging with the text as they decide which information is relevant to their interpretation, both in terms of what they take from the text and in what they bring to it from prior experiences of life, language and narrative. There is clear evidence of the orchestration described by Bussis et al. (1985) as the children bring together the different sources of information at their disposal.

There are several important differences of approach here which need considering. Firstly, not all the children are engaging with the text in the same way all the time. However, the differences of approach are not clearly identifiable with either of the two variables considered when forming the groups, namely gender and reading ability and experience. Moreover, all the children do show evidence of this engagement at some point for both printed and television narratives, and this is more significant here than the variation, which often seems more related to motivation and interest in the task and to internal group relationships than to any intrinsic difference caused by prior experience of print or television or by gender.

Secondly, the children are actively varying their approach as they take account of the relative value of prior life experiences and of their understanding of narrative as derived from prior reading experiences. Their use of life experience analogies decreases as their intertextual references increase, and this change is directly related to the modality of the story. In other words, as the children recognize the place within the modality continuum of any text, they are actively discriminating between the various kinds of knowledge they have and choosing the most appropriate information. As Alexis points out, information about local shopkeepers is not much use when predicting the outcome of a fairytale; far more helpful are related incidents from other tales in the same genre.

This active selection of appropriate information also strengthens my argument that even where the children might seem to be using medium-specific approaches, they are not doing so in an exclusive way. If there is visual information, they will use it; if not, they will rely on the information they do have. If there is written information, they will use that too, whether it comes in a print narrative or in subtitles or captions on a screen. What might appear to be a medium-specific difference is in fact evidence that whatever the medium, the children are actively orchestrating all the available information in their search for meaning.

The role of the reader is not confined, though, to orchestration of textual and extra-textual information in a vacuum. There is also interaction with the community around the reader. That adult or peer attitudes are not passively absorbed at the expense of the reader's own position is shown by the ways in which the children subvert adult prohibitions on certain texts, by their challenges to adults and to each other over what counts as an appropriate text, and in particular by the collaboration into which they enter. In their attempts to retell or interpret collaboratively, there are many instances of individuals challenging the group as well as working with it. Sometimes these challenges end with the individual shifting ground but at other times the group position is adjusted to take account of the new information offered. Again this happens for both media.

As they read narratives in print and in television, these children are actively engaged in resolving a dialectic tension between their existing knowledge and expectations and the new information they are taking from the new text and the particular reading situation. But what part does the text play in this process?

The Role of the Text

In terms of the role of the text in the reading process, this study gives two kinds of insight. Firstly, in terms of the specific texts used, certain features of the texts are significant in the children's interpretations. The children are drawing on the text and it is in part helping them to predict and interpret the narrative. This is something that happens in both media.

Particularly worthy of attention here is the way in which each individual text teaches the children how it works as it develops. As the children become more familiar with the text, they are thus more able to notice textual cues. There are differences in the research reported here between the children's responses to familiar, ongoing narratives and those which were new and self-contained. The children were partly so confident in their predictions and interpretations of *Neighbours* because of the degree of prior textual knowledge brought by these habitual viewers; similarly, as already seen, the more regular viewers of *Grange Hill* were more confident in their responses to that text. Since many books are self-contained, complete narratives this could be taken as an indication that television is different in this respect. However, the children also encounter self-contained narratives on television, particularly films, and there are ways in which print narratives make themselves familiar. As the children listened to more of *Gaffer Samson's Luck*, the book's style and characters became more familiar and so became easier. The evidence of this study would suggest that the relevant feature that helped the text to teach the children was familiarity, and that the link to the medium is indirect rather than causal.

This study also begins to show how children's repertoires of familiar narratives are implicated in the reading process. In all the narratives used in this study, and in the other more general discussions, both the names and particular features of a wide range of texts form a significant proportion of the discussion. These prior texts have helped to teach the children how to read new narratives, as is shown so clearly by the children's response to *Baba Yaga*. Here again this study shows that there is no sharp division between media. Not only do children use intertextual references in dealing with both print and television, but these references themselves cross media boundaries, so that televisual narratives the children have seen are drawn on to explain print narratives and vice versa.

There are some important differences here which emphasize the need to set the role of the text alongside the parts played by reader and community. The more experienced print readers such as Ashley and Alexis are actively looking for new authors to read and thus are extending their repertoire of intertextual understanding;

all the children have a wider repertoire than is drawn on in any one transcript, so that clearly they are actively selecting relevant intertextual cues. But they are not doing this in a vacuum; the wider community is significant here.

At the most immediate level, family, peer group and teachers will introduce new texts in both media; many children (and adults) begin watching *Neighbours* because their friends are talking about it, or read books which have been read to them by teachers, for example. There are also wider influences which come largely from television's capacity to advertise itself. As the children watch established favourites, they will also encounter trailers for and features about other programmes which helps to extend their repertoire; newspapers and listings magazines also play a part here. Although to a limited extent television also introduces children to print narratives, through televised versions and through occasional programmes focusing on books, there is a definite imbalance here for the children in my study which has the potential to limit the role of text in the reading process; this will be considered as I suggest possible teaching strategies.

The Role of the Community

As I have discussed the relative role of reader and text, it has become clear that the community is a significant force. The children in this study are situated in a real social context which has a powerful influence on their reading practices; in the explicit debate around power and control which goes on at home; in the importance attached to reading in the classroom; in the implicit messages derived from the relative invisibility of reading as a social practice in their homes; and from the almost total invisibility of television at school. As is already clear, though, this is not a case of a one-way influence, and I have already highlighted the way in which this study increases our understanding of the interplay of reader, text and community as children make sense of narrative in both media.

What I wish to amplify here is the evidence provided by this study for the interactive model of interpretive community which I set out in Chapter 2. It is clear from the children's approach to collaborative interpretation that they neither control nor are controlled by the group; also, as they change group membership, they bring experience from other situations into the new group, and thus this suggests a picture of a fluid network of social interaction around reading practices rather than the rigid set of deterministic communities argued for by Fish (1980).

What this research shows is the fallacy of earlier oppositions of the social and the private in terms of reading. Rather than a simplistic contrast between private reading or viewing and group encounters, a more complex interactional model is emerging in which individual encounters with text are both informed by and inform both group viewing and reading situations and other more indirect literacy and viewing practices such as informal discussions or the more structured debates reported here. This has important implications for the classroom, but is also one step further along the way in the search for a theory of narrative which will take on the dialectic relationship between thought and culture. I turn now to look more closely at the ways in which this research adds to our understanding of narrative as a social act.

The Role of Narrative

In Chapter 3 I argued that narrative was a site of intersection of language, thought and culture and that as such it needed to be understood as a 'primary act of mind' (Hardy, 1977) in which we bring together personal and social understandings of the world. In many ways, these children are using similar strategies to make sense of narratives encountered in different media. That these strategies themselves involve not just a great deal of individual retelling both of the narratives which are central to any of the activities and of many others, but also such a high proportion of 'collective remembering' (Middleton and Edwards, 1990) is surely no coincidence. It is more a sign that it is their understandings of and familiarity with narrative on which the children are drawing, rather than any similarities inherent in the media. They are learning about narrative from their encounters with narrative in whichever medium, rather than being taught by television how to read print or vice versa. This would help to explain why the commonalities are more powerful for the children than the very real differences between television and reading; narrative as a driving force transcends the boundaries and limitations of each medium so that the children's underlying awareness of narrative enables them to use what they know as they work together to fulfil the various tasks, and at the same time it provides a vehicle for their explanations and predictions.

Just One Study — How Significant Can It Be?

I would suggest that this research is significant both in its bringing together of ideas about reading, literary theory and media studies through an examination of the role of reader, text and community which draws on insights from each of these traditions, but also because in doing so, and in showing the large number of ways in which children make sense of narratives in each medium by using similar strategies, this can offer new evidence that narrative is indeed of crucial importance for the primary classroom. However, it is also important to remember the actual nature of the research and to consider the limitations of my chosen approach.

One major issue which needs to be considered here is how far this study manages to offer a 'thick description' (Geertz, 1973). In Chapter 1, I quoted Geertz's definition of thin description as showing 'what the wide-awake, uncomplicated person takes [the world] to be' (Geertz, 1983, p. 86). A thick description attempts to go beyond this, to provide a multi-layered, detailed account that moves beyond the surface. Does this study provide such an account?

I believe that the answer to this is that it does — providing I add the caveat that what I am trying to describe is not the children's whole lives, but the ways in which they make sense of print and television narratives as revealed through their informal encounters with me in the classroom and through the more structured activities we undertook together. That is, this is a thicker description than would have been offered by an account based just on isolated encounters with the children, since I have been able to set the data obtained in the course of completing the various activities alongside my wider knowledge of the children and their lives at school. However, the description I am able to provide is not the same as that which would have been offered by an ethnography of the children's lives; it is a partial account influenced by ethnographic tradition. This does not invalidate my work, but sets it in a clearer context of school-based case-study work.

Nor does the fact that this is a case study prevent it from having a wider significance. Obviously such a small-scale study cannot be seen to be statistically relevant, nor did it set out to be so. However, Mitchell (1984) has argued that the value of case studies is not that they provide typical examples, but that they can provide telling cases, that is, cases in which the particular circumstances around the case make

> . . . previously obscure theoretical relationships suddenly apparent [. . .] they are the means whereby general theory may be developed. (Mitchell, 1984, p. 239)

I would argue that this research provides just such a telling case, in that it brings together for the first time theoretical perspectives from a range of traditions and thus illuminates the common threads within these. However, this is also a telling case because it offers new insights into children's behaviour when reading print and television in a way which allows future research to continue to develop a more substantial body of theory around the ideas developed here.

The children in this study are in no way special; they could be seen as very ordinary. They have no particularly outstanding characteristics: they are not especially intelligent or precocious; they get confused, they argue and contradict each other. And yet in this very ordinariness they do have insights; they do make leaps forward in understanding; they do work together to develop some remarkable collaborative interpretations; and thus they enable us to see the ways in which children can use the same strategies to make sense of narrative in different media. It is in the light of this belief that this study does indeed offer something worthwhile that I consider those specific aspects that could offer ways for extending the understandings presented here.

This study focuses on one age group; it is a picture of a particular group of children at one moment in time. It describes the ways in which this group of 8- to 9-year-olds made sense of print and television. It does not enable us to say whether this group of children could have done the same things at a younger age, whether their development is typical of children of this age or what they would be able to do if I returned to talk to them now. Although there is some evidence from work conducted elsewhere on children as television viewers (see, for example, Buckingham, 1993a) that would support my findings, no other work appears to have been done which has compared these two media in this way. It would be valuable if this work could be replicated with children of other ages in other schools around the country and overseas; such research would have the potential to provide a developmental pattern. This would also allow for exploration of the extent to which formal media education, which was not provided for the children in my study, influences children's approaches.

This research was based entirely on work done in a school setting. In future research it would be valuable to extend this to include an ethnographic, home-based investigation of children's viewing and reading practices and to interview parents and other close relations to provide a more extensive pattern. The findings of such additional and more long-term studies (which would need extensive funded research) would enrich the more limited picture it has been possible to provide through this study.

One important limitation, of which I was very conscious as I undertook the fieldwork, was that in this situation I was a researcher and not a teacher. The future development of these children was not my responsibility and I had no brief to develop their understandings through a structured programme of media education. Although this was a necessary limitation in that what I wanted to show was the children's existing understandings, it was frustrating at times to know that there were ways in which some classroom activities might have extended and developed these understandings. There are many possibilities for action research to follow from the findings of this study, in particular from the suggestions for classroom practice later in this chapter, and it would be very valuable for this work to be extended through such an approach.

One way forward, then, from this research would be more research; however, I would argue that the more important ways in which we can move forward from this study are in changing classroom practice. I believe this study has certain implications for the ways in which teachers approach the teaching of reading a range of media, and it is to these that I now turn.

Implications for the Classroom

There are many specific activities that I believe could enhance the ways in which children develop their reading abilities, but these need to be set in an overall context which values children's prior and continuing encounters with all kinds of media within and outside the classroom and seeks to extend children's understanding of these encounters. Before I suggest just a few specific activities, then, I want to argue for such a supportive classroom environment.

Creating Communities of Readers

I believe that children's reading development could be greatly facilitated in schools if more teachers were to see their task as to create communities of readers. This process would need to go beyond a narrow definition of reading to encompass the reading of a wide range of media and would need to encourage children to see themselves as partners in these communities who have their own relevant prior experiences on which to draw.

Primary school teachers have traditionally attempted to give their children a sense that reading is desirable and important, and yet often even those teachers who are themselves avid readers have been frustrated in their attempts to inspire their children to read. Despite teachers' efforts to promote reading, it has not always been seen by children as socially desirable behaviour within family or peer group; as one secondary pupil said to her old primary school teacher, 'The trouble is, miss, you can't say to your mates, "Going down the library tonight?"' (King and Robinson, 1995). To do so would often be seen as slightly aberrant behaviour.

One way in which teachers could redress this balance would be through the adoption of more consciously social reading practice. Traditionally storytime in infant classrooms has been a shared experience, though often one which has been tightly controlled by teachers in terms of the choice of texts and the extent to which children are able to intervene; those junior school teachers who do read to their classes tend to expect even less intervention from older pupils. As I have shown, the children in my study had little idea as to their own teacher's preference of reading or viewing material or as to his motivation in choosing the books which were read to the class.

Much of the other reading practice that goes on in classrooms has tended to emphasize the individual aspects of reading at the expense of more social practices; children are encouraged to read silently and even where all the class read at the same time, such reading is often viewed as individual, as can be seen by many of the names chosen for this activity, such as USSR (Uninterrupted Sustained Silent Reading) or SQUIRT (Ssh Quiet You It's Reading Time). Although it is undoubtedly important for children to develop the ability to read silently, without other more socialized reading behaviour the use of silent reading serves to heighten the problems of the child who likes reading but has no way of admitting this to peers and does little to help those who do not enjoy reading discover its potential.

In many primary classrooms, texts from other media than print (and even some printed texts such as comics) are often seen as irrelevant or inappropriate, as Hodge and Tripp (1986) reported. Those of us who have been teachers will have heard colleagues complaining about children's use of television narratives as models for their own writing. Such behaviour is understandable given the prevailing everyday attitudes to reading in our society, and yet it discourages children from drawing on what they know of narrative in a wide range of media to understand any specific text. Given that for the children in my study at least, there was a far higher degree of familiarity with televisual narratives than with books, the exclusion of these narratives from reading practice in the classroom will disempower children, particularly those who are unconfident readers and/or who come from homes where reading print is not a common occurrence. The children in my study have shown that they have the ability to draw from all the narratives they know when watching or reading a new text, and yet often children are prevented from using this ability by the assumption by teachers that different media are not interconnected.

A number of teachers have been working hard to introduce the notion of literature circles or reading workshops into schools on both sides of the Atlantic (see, for example, Harste, Short, Burke et al., 1988; Mackenzie, 1992; King and Robinson, 1995). These work by grouping small numbers of pupils into sets who agree to read a particular text together. Most of the actual reading is done individually, but the group meet regularly to discuss the text and to consider their responses to it. This helps the children to develop a more socialized approach to reading and to appreciate that different responses are not just possible but almost inevitable. As the children become more used to working in this way, they become more autonomous; gradually the class becomes a much more active community of readers where groups of children identify texts they wish to come together to read. As this autonomy grows, the teacher is able to be more of the kind of facilitator identified in Radway's research (1987), suggesting new titles and modelling responses but also allowing groups to meet without the teacher and to take responsibility for keeping the community growing. Children report a greater sense of involvement and become more self-confident; reading becomes a socially desirable behaviour for a greater proportion of the class.

Transcripts of literature circles at work show that the children are engaging in the kinds of discussions I recorded during shared experiences of texts in my research; expectations and hypotheses are shared as well as personal responses. What is important here is that the children in my research had not had the experience of working in literature circles, and yet particularly when discussing television texts were already able to work in a similar way. This would seem to have two implications. Firstly, those teachers running literature circles need to take into account the ability children bring to these, so that the circle itself can extend the children's ability as fully as possible. More importantly, though, the range of texts that are seen as appropriate for discussion, which currently tends to be dominated by printed narratives, should include narratives from other media, particularly television, if this transference of prior experience to the new situation is to be optimized. By legitimizing such texts, teachers would be both allowing children to draw on the full range of their prior experience and encouraging the same degree of critical reflection on television as on printed texts.

Such a widening of the range of texts within a context where choice and preference would be essential elements for debate within literature circles could also lead to an exploration of the existence of a canon; children could be introduced explicitly to the idea that some books and television programmes have been labelled as having particular merit and could be encouraged to read such texts before considering the judgments made by others in the light of their own experience. Thus the teacher would be able to extend the children's familiarity with a wide range of texts without automatically perpetuating value judgments about such texts. By including texts from a wide range of media children's own experience and expertise would be given a value and currency which I believe would allow a smoother transference of strategies between media and a clearer critical focus.

Activities to Enrich the Community of Readers

Within a classroom operating as a community of readers, there are many activities that could be introduced to enrich the experience, and my purpose here is not to attempt a comprehensive exploration of these; there are others who have already explored in more general terms the best ways of teaching literature (see, for example,

Benton and Fox, 1985; Corcoran and Evans, 1987) and many of their ideas are still of great value, though it may be worth considering applying them to a wider range of media. Similarly there are several books setting out approaches to media education that offer specific practices which could be used by teachers seeking to create a community of readers (see, for example, Buckingham, 1993; Fox, 1991). However, there are some specific activities which stem from my fieldwork that are worth mentioning here; these examples are designed with 8- and 9-year-old children in mind but could be adapted for older or younger pupils.

There is scope for extending children's understanding of audience and appropriateness and the role of industry. For example, the discovery arrived at here that for some children *The Golden Girls* was considered to be a children's programme could have led to some valuable work on such assumptions which could have allowed the children to explore how others would classify the programme and the basis of such a classification. This could have been extended into a more general consideration of the labels we put on particular texts and from which features these are derived. This, in turn, could lead to some specific work on genre that goes beyond the starting point here of identifying the ways in which children use genre and uses these as a way into a more careful exploration of genres of all kinds, including the chance to create texts in particular genres or to change genres.

The discussions on narrative which were a central part of my fieldwork and which would be an essential feature of a community of readers could lead into a more detailed consideration of narrative structure. Children have always been asked to write stories, but the distinguishing features of narrative have not always been explicitly explored. By focusing on such ideas as plot development, characterization, time and discourse, children's reading and creation of narratives in a range of media could be enhanced. The differences between media could then be explored through such activities as storyboarding printed texts for potential televisation or writing the book version of televisual texts.

These discussions also lead to a great deal of hypothesizing, predicting and evaluating. The encouragement of such behaviour, not just in terms of events but of characterization and motivation, could lead to valuable opportunities for considering different outlooks on life. At one point during the pilot, I tried to find out if the children had any idea that some television programmes might be disapproved of by their parents. Emma explained that in fact there were some programmes her parents would see as valuable; when pressed to explain, she said that she felt her parents would approve of *Neighbours* because 'it teaches you about life, like Scott and Charlene show you it's not good to get married too young'. Given the enthusiasm for soaps among the children I worked with, and the trend for soaps to consider the big questions of life, this would seem to be a good way to explore such questions with children and in particular the way such issues are covered in books and television.

There are many other possibilities, and many activities which are a normal part of many classrooms, that could easily be used to aid the development of a real interpretive community; what really matters is that we help all children to understand the power and potential of narratives in all our lives. All those of us involved in teaching reading need to work to improve the ways in which we build on children's prior knowledge and value their experience of all the media to which they have access. I set out in this study to answer my own questions which had arisen from a personal viewing situation, but I wanted to do so because of my concern that children in schools should have the best possible opportunities for their development as readers of all kinds of texts. This study has shown that children do operate in similar ways whether the narrative they encounter is presented through the medium of television or of print; it has also argued that this indicates the need for a more social understanding of narrative and reading in primary classrooms. Whether the shift in practice necessary to develop these findings will be welcomed by those who control the education system in this country remains to be seen. Without it, though, I believe we will continue to offer the children in many of our schools a sadly limited concept of reading and a restricted set of literacy practices.

Coda

I began this book by discussing my own response to the series *Tutti Frutti*. Recently this same programme served to highlight the ways in which as an adult I am involved in a complex network of communities of readers which serves to heighten my pleasure in reading and my involvement in socialized interpretation. Some close friends came to stay for the weekend and because other plans fell through the four of us found ourselves with an evening free at home. The friends had not seen *Tutti Frutti* and so we all agreed to watch it. The first thing this emphasized to me was that it was particularly important to me that our friends should share our pleasure in this text, so that to start with I was watching them more than the video. The sense that we were becoming involved together in the viewing experience was then increased by the way in which at one point one of our friends asked, 'How do we know that they are still on the road?' He had identified a particular point in the narrative at which a large 'gap' (Iser, 1974) had been left for the viewer to fill and, being uncertain of his own response, appealed to the group for support in his interpretation. My reply, that I knew because I was in possession of the full narrative, was not what he was asking for; he made this explicit by saying, 'Yes, I know *you* know because you've seen it before, but how do *we* know?' Discussion of the series ran through our conversations for the rest of the weekend; it had become a shared text which had acted to create a new relationship between the four of us. Here there was no need for any intervention to allow this to happen; all four of us are experienced and confident readers of a wide range of media.

For many children, the chance to grow into adults with this confidence in enjoying narrative is limited by the experiences they have at school and at home, and yet the children in my research have shown that they have the potential to develop in this way. If teachers can begin to draw on this rich experience so that children use their knowledge and understanding of narrative in all media as they take on print literacy, then we could perhaps look forward to a more fully empowered and autonomous future for these children.

Bibliography

ADAMS, M.J. (1990) *Beginning to Read: Thinking and Learning about Print*, Cambridge, Mass.: MIT Press.

AHLBERG, J. and AHLBERG, A. (1980) *Each Peach Pear Plum*, London: Picture Lions.

ALLEN, R.C. (1985) *Speaking of Soap Operas*, Chapel Hill, North Carolina: University of North Carolina Press.

ANDERSON, D. and LORCH, E. (1983) 'Looking at television: Action and reaction', in BRYANT, J. and ANDERSON, D. (1983) *Children's Understanding of Television: Research on Attention and Comprehension*, New York: Harcourt Brace Jovanovich.

ANDREWS, R. (ed.) (1989) *Narrative and Argument*, Milton Keynes: Open University Press.

ANG, I. (1985) *Watching Dallas: Soap Opera and the Melodramatic Imagination*, London: Methuen.

ANG, I. (1991) *Desperately Seeking the Audience*, London: Routledge.

APPLEBEE, A. (1977) 'Where does Cinderella live?', in MEEK, M., WARLOW, A. and BARTON, G. (1977) *The Cool Web: The Pattern of Children's Reading*, London: The Bodley Head.

BARTHES, R. (1973a) *Mythologies*, St Albans, Herts: Paladin Granada.

BARTHES, R. (1973b) *Le Plaisir du Texte*, Paris: Editions du Seuil.

BARTHES, R. (1975) *The Pleasure of the Text*, New York: Hill and Wang.

BARTHES, R. (1990) *S/Z*, Oxford: Basil Blackwell.

BAUMAN, Z. (1973) *Culture as Praxis*, London: Routledge and Kegan Paul.

BENTON, M. and FOX, G. (1985) *Teaching Literature Nine to Fourteen*, Oxford: Oxford University Press.

BORDWELL, D. (1988) *Narration in the Fiction Film*, London: Routledge.

BRITTON, J. (1972) 'Writing to learn and learning to write', in PRADL, G. (ed.) (1982) *Prospect and Retrospect: Selected Essays of James Britton*, New Jersey: Boynton/Cook.

BRITTON, J. (1977) 'The role of fantasy', in MEEK, M., WARLOW, A. and BARTON, G. *The Cool Web: The Pattern of Children's Reading*, London: The Bodley Head.

BRUNER, J. (1986) *Actual Minds, Possible Worlds*, Cambridge, Mass.: Harvard University Press.

BRUNER, J., OLIVER, R., GREENFIELD, P. (1966) *Studies in Cognitive Growth: A Collaboration at the Center for Cognitive Studies*, New York: John Wiley and Sons, Inc.

BRUNSDON, C. and MORLEY, D. (1978) *Everyday Television: 'Nationwide'*, London: BFI Publishing.

BRYANT, J. and ANDERSON, D. (1983) *Children's Understanding of Television: Research on Attention and Comprehension*, New York: Harcourt Brace Jovanovich.

BUCKINGHAM, D. (1987) *Public Secrets: EastEnders and its Audience*, London: BFI Publishing.

BUCKINGHAM, D. (ed.) (1990) *Watching Media Learning: Making Sense of Media Education*, London: Falmer Press.

BUCKINGHAM, D. (ed.) (1993) *Reading Audiences: Young People and the Media*, Manchester: Manchester University Press.

BUCKINGHAM, D. (1993a) *Children Talking Television: The Making of Television Literacy*, London: Falmer Press.

BUCKINGHAM, D. (1993b) 'Boys' talk: Television and the policing of masculinity', in BUCKINGHAM, D. (ed.) *Reading Audiences: Young People and the Media*, Manchester: Manchester University Press.

BUSSIS, A.M., CHITTENDEN, E.A., AMAREL, M. and KLAUSNER, E. (1985) *Inquiry into Meaning: An Investigation of Learning*, New Jersey: Lawrence, Erlbaum Inc.

CHAFE, W. (ed.) (1980) *The Pear Stories: Cognitive, Cultural and Linguistic Aspects of Narrative Production*, Norwood, New Jersey: Ablex.

CHALL, J. (1967) *Learning to Read: The Great Debate*, New York: McGraw Hill.

CHAPMAN, J. (ed.) (1981) *The Reader and the Text*, London: Heinemann Educational Books (for UKRA).

CHATMAN, S. (1978) *Story and Discourse: Narrative Structure in Fiction and Film*, Ithaca: Cornell University Press.

CORCORAN, B. and EVANS, E. (eds) (1987) *Readers, Texts, Teachers*, Milton Keynes: Open University Press.

CRAIG, G. (1976) 'Reading: Who is doing what to whom?' in JOSIPOVICI, G. (ed.) (1976) *The Modern English Novel*, London: Open Books Publishing.

CULLER, J. (1975) *Structuralist Poetics, Structuralism, Linguistics and the Study of Literature*, London: Routledge and Kegan Paul.

CULLER, J. (1981) *The Pursuit of Signs: Semiotics, Literature, Deconstruction*, London: Routledge and Kegan Paul.

DAVIES, M.M. (1989) *Television is Good for Your Kids*, London: Hilary Shipman.

DORR, A. (1983) 'No shortcuts to judging reality', in BRYANT, J. and ANDERSON, D. (1983) *Children's Understanding of Television: Research on Attention and Comprehension*, New York: Harcourt Brace Jovanovich.

EAGLETON, T. (1983) *Literary Theory: An Introduction*, Oxford: Basil Blackwell.

ECO, U. (1981) *The Role of the Reader*, London: Hutchinson.

EKE, R. and CROLL, P. (eds) (1992) 'Television formats and children's classifications of their viewing', *Journal of Educational Television*, **18**, 2–3.

FISH, S. (1980) *Is there a Text in this Class? The Authority of Interpretive Communities*, Cambridge, Mass.: Harvard University Press.

FISKE, J. (1987) *Television Culture*, London: Methuen.

FISKE, J. (1989) 'Moments of television: Neither the text nor the audience', in SEITER, E., BORCHERS, H., KREUTZNER, G. and WARTH, E. (1989) *Remote Control*, London: Routledge.

FOX, C. (1989) 'Divine discourses', in ANDREWS, R. (ed.) (1989) *Narrative and Argument*, Milton Keynes: Open University Press.

FOX, C. (1993) *At the Very Edge of the Forest: The Influence of Literature on Storytelling by Children*, London: Cassell.

FOX, K. (1991) *Story to Story: Language Development Through Media Education, a Teaching Pack for 8–13 Year Olds (KS2/KS3)*, Maidstone, Kent: TVS Education.

FREIRE, P. (1972) *Pedagogy of the Oppressed*, Harmondsworth: Penguin.

FREIRE, P. and MACEDO, D. (1987) *Literacy: Reading the Word and the World*, London: Routledge and Kegan Paul.

FRY, D. (1985) *Children Talk About Books: Seeing Themselves As Readers*, Milton Keynes: Open University Press.

GEERTZ, C. (1973) *The Interpretation of Cultures*, New York: Basic Books Inc.

GEERTZ, C. (1983) *Local Knowledge: Further Essays in Interpretive Anthropology*, New York: Basic Books Inc.

GENETTE, G. (1980) *Narrative Discourse: An Essay In Method*, Ithaca, New York: Cornell University Press.

GIDDENS, A. (1984) *The Constitution of Society: Outline of the Theory of Structuration*, Cambridge: Polity Press.

GILLESPIE, M. (1993) 'The Mahabharata: From Sanskrit to sacred soap. A case study of the reception of two contemporary televisual versions', in BUCKINGHAM, D. (ed.) (1993) *Reading Audiences: Young People and the Media*, Manchester: Manchester University Press.

GLASGOW UNIVERSITY MEDIA GROUP (1976) *Bad News*, London: Routledge and Kegan Paul.

GOLLASCH, F.V. (ed.) (1982) *Language and Literacy: The Selected Writings of Kenneth S. Goodman*, Boston: Routledge and Kegan Paul.

GOODMAN, K. (1969) 'Psycholinguistic universals in the reading process', in GOLLASCH, F.V. (ed.) (1982) *Language and Literacy: The Selected Writings of Kenneth S. Goodman*, Boston: Routledge and Kegan Paul.

GOODMAN, K., (1987) *Language and Thinking in School*, New York: Richard C. Owen.

HALLIDAY, M. (1979) *Language as Social Semiotic: The Social Interpretation of Language and Meaning*, London: Edward Arnold.

HARDING, D. (1977) 'Psychological processes in the reading of fiction', in MEEK, M., WARLOW, A. and BARTON, G. (1977) *The Cool Web: The Pattern of Children's Reading*, London: The Bodley Head.

HARDY, B. (1977) 'Towards a poetics of fiction: An approach through narrative', in MEEK, M., WARLOW, A. and BARTON, G. (1977) *The Cool Web: The Pattern of Children's Reading*, London: The Bodley Head.

HARSTE, J., SHORT, K. with BURKE, C. and contributing teacher researchers (1988) *Creating Classrooms for Authors: The Reading–Writing Connection*, Portsmouth, New Hampshire: Heinemann Educational Books.

HEATH, S. BRICE (1983) *Ways With Words: Language, Life and Work in Communities and Classrooms*, Cambridge: Cambridge University Press.

HEATHER, P. (1981) 'CRUS Occasional Paper 6: Young People's Reading: A study of the leisure reading of 13–15 year olds', Sheffield: Centre for Research on User Studies, University of Sheffield.

HEWITT, R. (1986) *White Talk Black Talk: Interracial Friendship and Communication Among Adolescents*, Cambridge: Cambridge University Press.

HOBSON, D. (1982) *Crossroads: The Drama of a Soap Opera*, London: Methuen.

HODGE, R. and KRESS, G. (1988) *Social Semiotics*, Cambridge: Polity Press.

HODGE, R. and KRESS, G. (1993) *Language as Ideology* (second edition), London: Routledge.

HODGE, B. and TRIPP, D. (1986) *Children and Television*, Cambridge: Polity Press.

HOLDAWAY, D. (1979) *The Foundations of Literacy*, Gosford, New South Wales: Ashton Scholastic.

HUSTON, A. and WRIGHT, J. (1983) 'Children's processing of television: The informative functions of formal features', in BRYANT, J. and ANDERSON, D. *Children's Understanding of Television: Research on Attention and Comprehension*, New York: Harcourt Brace Jovanovich.

HUTCHINS, P. (1969) *Rosie's Walk*, London: The Bodley Head.

INGHAM, J. (1982) *Books and Reading Development: The Bradford Book Flood*, London: Heinemann Educational Books, on behalf of the British National Bibliography.

ISER, W. (1974) *The Implied Reader: Patterns of Communication in Prose Fiction from Bunyan to Beckett*, Baltimore: John Hopkins University Press.

JAGLOM, L. and GARDNER, H. (1981) 'The pre-school television viewer as anthropologist', in KELLY, H. and GARDNER, H. (1981) *Viewing Children Through Television*, San Francisco: Jossey-Bass.

JOSIPOVICI, G. (ed.) (1976) *The Modern English Novel*, London: Open Books Publishing.

KELLY, H. and GARDNER, H. (1981) *Viewing Children Through Television*, San Francisco: Jossey-Bass.

KEMP, G. (1986) *Mr Magus Is Waiting For You*, London: Faber and Faber/Thames Television.

KING, C. and ROBINSON, M. (1995) 'Creating communities of readers', *English in Education*, Summer.

LEAVIS, F.R. (1962) *The Great Tradition* (first edition 1948), London: Chatto and Windus.

LE GUIN, U. (1981) 'It was a dark and stormy night; or, Why are we huddling about the campfire?' in MITCHELL, W. (ed.) *On Narrative*, Chicago: University of Chicago Press.

LITTLEFAIR, A. (1991) *Reading All Types of Writing*, Milton Keynes: Open University Press.

LOWERY, S. and DE FLEUR, M. (1988) *Milestones in Mass Communication Research: Media Effects*, New York: Longman.

LULL, J. (1990) *Inside Family Viewing: Ethnographic Research on Television's Audiences*, London: Comedia, Routledge.

MACKENZIE, T. (ed.) (1992) *Readers' Workshops: Bridging Literature and Literacy; Stories from Teachers and Their Classrooms*, Toronto, Canada: Irwin.

MATHIOT, M. (1979) *Ethnolinguistics: Boas, Sapir and Whorf Revisited*, The Hague: Mouton Publishers.

MEEK, M. (1982) *Learning to Read*, London: The Bodley Head.

MEEK, M. (1988) *How Texts Teach What Readers Learn*, Stroud: Thimble Press.

MEEK, M., WARLOW, A. and BARTON, G. (1977) *The Cool Web: The Pattern of Children's Reading*, London: The Bodley Head.

MEYER, M. (ed.) (1983) *Children and the Formal Features of Television: Approaches and Findings of Experimental and Formal Research*, Munich: KG Saur.

MIDDLETON, D. and EDWARDS, D. (eds) (1990) *Collective Remembering*, London: Sage Publications.

MITCHELL, J. (1984) 'Case studies', in ELLEN, R. (ed.) (1984) *Ethnographic Research: A Guide to General Conduct*, London: Academic Press.

MITCHELL, W. (ed.) (1981) *On Narrative*, Chicago: University of Chicago Press.

MOORES, S. (1993) *Interpreting Audiences: The Ethnography of Media Consumption*, London: Sage Publications.

MORLEY, D. (1986) *Family Television: Cultural Power and Domestic Leisure*, London: Comedia Press.

MORLEY, D. (1992) *Television, Audiences and Cultural Studies*, London: Routledge.

MORRIS, J. (1981) 'Stylistic variation in texts for young children', in CHAPMAN, J. (ed.) *The Reader and the Text*, London: Heinemann Educational Books (for UKRA).

MOSS, G. (1989) *Un/Popular Fictions*, London: Virago.

MOYLE, D. (1972) *The Teaching of Reading*, London: Ward Lock Educational.

MUNRO, J. (1954) *Janet and John Teachers' Manual*, London: Nisbet.

NEALE, S. (1980) *Genre*, London: BFI Publishing.

PALMER, P. (1986) *The Lively Audience: A Study of Children Around the TV Set*, London: Allen and Unwin.

PRADL, G. (ed.) (1982) *Prospect and Retrospect: Selected Essays of James Britton*, New Jersey: Boynton/Cook.

PROPP, V. (1968) *The Morphology of the Folk Tale* (first edition 1928), Austin, Texas: University of Texas Press.

RADWAY, J. (1987) *Reading the Romance: Women, Patriarchy and Popular Literature*, London: Verso.

READING IS FUNDAMENTAL INC (publishers and authors of this leaflet) (1985) *TV and Reading*, USA.

RICHARDS, C. (1993) 'Taking sides? What young girls do with television', in BUCKINGHAM, D. (ed.) (1993) *Reading Audiences: Young People and the Media*, Manchester: Manchester University Press.

RICHARDS, I.A. (1973) *Practical Criticism: A Study of Literary Judgment* (first edition 1929), London: Routledge and Kegan Paul.

ROBINSON, M. (1995) 'An investigation of children reading print and television narratives', unpublished PhD thesis, University of London Institute of Education.

ROSEN, H. (n/d) *Stories and Meanings*, Sheffield: NATE.

ROSEN, H. (1994) 'The whole story?', *NATE News*, Summer.

RUMELHART, D. and MCCLELLAND, J. (1986) *Parallel Distributed Processing: Explorations in the Microstructure of Cognition: Vol 1*, Cambridge, Mass.: MIT Press.

SALOMON, G. (1981) *Communication and Education: Social and Psychological Interactions*, Beverley Hills: Sage Publications.

SALOMON, G. (1983) 'Beyond the formats of television: The effects of student preconceptions on the experience of televiewing', in MEYER, M. (ed.) (1983) *Children and the Formal Features of Television: Approaches and Findings of Experimental and Formal Research*, Munich: KG Saur.

SAMPSON, E. (1989) 'The deconstruction of the self', in SHOTTER, J. and GERGEN, K. (eds) (1989) *Texts of Identity*, London: Sage Publications.

SAPIR, E. (1949) *Culture, Language and Personality: Selected Essays*, Berkeley: University of California Press.

SARLAND, C. (1991) *Young People Reading: Culture and Response*, Milton Keynes: Open University Press.

SAUSSURE, F. DE, (1974) *Course in General Linguistics* (first edition 1916), London: Fontana.

SCHOLES, R. (1985) *Textual Power: Literary Theory and the Teaching of English*, New Haven: Yale University Press.

SCHOLES, R. (1989) *Protocols of Reading*, New Haven: Yale University Press.

SCHONELL, F. (1951) *The Psychology and Teaching of Reading*, Edinburgh: Oliver and Boyd.

SEITER, E., BORCHERS, H., KREUTZNER, G. and WARTH, E. (1989) *Remote Control*, London: Routledge.

SENDAK, M. (1981) *Outside Over There*, London: The Bodley Head.

SHOTTER, J. and GERGEN, K. (eds) (1989) *Texts of Identity*, London: Sage Publications.

SMITH, F. (1978) *Understanding Reading: A Psycholinguistic Analysis of Reading and Learning to Read* (2nd edition), New York: Holt, Rinehart and Winston.

SMITH, F. (1988) *Joining the Literacy Club: Further Essays into Education*, Portsmouth, New Hampshire: Heinemann.

TANNEN, D. (1980) 'A comparative analysis of oral narrative strategies: Athenian Greek and American English', in CHAFE, W. (ed.) (1980) *The Pear Stories: Cognitive, Cultural and Linguistic Aspects of Narrative Production*, Norwood, New Jersey: Ablex.

TOLKIEN, J. (1966) *The Tolkien Reader*, New York: Ballantine Books.

TOPPING, K. and WOLFENDALE, S. (eds) (1985) *Parental Involvement in Children's Reading*, London: Croom Helm.

TUNSTALL, J. (ed.) (1970) *Media Sociology: A Reader*, London: Constable.

TRELEASE, J. (1984) *The Read-Aloud Handbook*, Harmondsworth, Middlesex: Penguin.

VOLOSINOV, V. (1973) *Marxism and the Philosophy of Language*, New York: Seminar Press.

VYGOTSKY, L. (1962) *Thought and Language* (first edition 1934), Cambridge, Mass.: MIT Press.

VYGOTSKY, L. (1978) *Mind in Society: The Development of Higher Psychological Processes*, Cambridge, Mass.: Harvard University Press.

WALSH, J. PATON (1987) *Gaffer Samson's Luck*, Harmondsworth, Middlesex: Puffin Books, Penguin Books Ltd.

WARLOW, A. (1977) 'What the reader has to do', in MEEK, M., WARLOW, A. and BARTON, G. (1977) *The Cool Web: The Pattern of Children's Reading*, London: The Bodley Head.

WATERLAND, L. (1988) *Read With Me: An Apprenticeship Approach to Reading* (second edition), Stroud: Thimble Press.

WELLS, G. (1987) *The Meaning Makers*, London: Hodder and Stoughton.

WHITEHEAD, F., CAPEY, A. and MADDREN, W. (1975) *Children's Reading Interests (Schools Council Working Paper 52)*, London: Evans/Methuen Educational.

WHORF, B. (1956) *Language, Thought and Reality: Selected Writings*, Cambridge, Mass.: MIT Press.

WILLIAMS, R. (1958) *Culture and Society 1780–1950*, London: Chatto and Windus.

WILLIAMS-ELLIS, A. (1989) *The Enchanted World (Part 2)*, London: Macmillan.

WINN, M. (1985) *The Plug-In Drug* (second edition), Harmondsworth: Viking Penguin.

WINNICOTT, D. (1971) *Playing and Reality*, London: Tavistock Press.

Appendix — List of Transcripts

Index

Adams, 14, 15, 16, 18, 19, 28
Anderson and Lorch, 27
Ang, 32, 60, 119, 139, 171
Applebee, 98, 100
appropriateness, 80–2, 88–93, 105, 107–10
audience, 3, 4, 26, 29, 30, 33, 34, 56, 58, 73, 75, 81, 82, 89, 105, 110, 141, 185
aural information, 133, 145, 151

Baba Yaga, 136, 143, 150, 156, 157, 158, 159, 164, 174, 175, 178
Barthes, 2, 3, 21–2, 27, 31, 52
Benton and Fox, 185
Berelson, 29
body language, 125, 127
book choice, 56, 68, 69, 70, 96
Bordwell, 29, 30
Britton, 52–3, 97–8, 116, 130
Brookside, 10, 11, 83, 103
Bruner, 40, 41, 47, 49, 136
Bryant and Anderson, 28
Buckingham, 10, 28, 29, 32, 34, 60, 67, 81, 89, 90, 92, 93, 95, 97, 99, 105, 108, 144, 153, 166, 169, 181, 185
Bussis et al., 15, 36, 177

canon, 20, 22, 35, 36, 51, 61, 176, 184
cartoon, 32, 58, 86, 95, 99, 101, 105
categorisation, 81, 82, 84, 89, 100, 106
censorship, 65, 69
Chall, 14
Chatman, 52, 147
choice, 26, 38, 40, 44, 56–63, 65–70, 73, 76–8, 82, 96, 112, 114, 158, 169, 175, 183–4
classroom, 179–80, 182–5
cliffhanger ending, 149
closed texts, 21
codes, 21, 23, 25, 27, 30, 31, 147, 172

cognitive development, 7, 28
collaboration, 168, 172, 173, 174
collaborative interpretation, 179, 181
collaborative retelling, 168, 173
collective remembering, 168, 180
common sense, 2, 3, 4, 9, 12, 14, 39, 137, 176
communication, 33, 37
community, 13, 14, 16, 17, 18, 19, 23, 24, 25, 26, 27, 28, 29, 30, 31, 32, 33, 34, 35, 36, 37, 50, 51, 54, 56, 60, 61, 66, 70, 75, 78, 82, 109, 152, 176, 177, 178, 179, 180, 184, 185
community of readers, 24, 182, 185–6
competencies, 13, 21, 27, 36, 52, 55, 62, 71–2, 80, 111, 174
computer games, 92
conceptual development, 106
conciêntização, 18
connotation, 13, 27, 40
conscientization, 18
construct theory, 15
content analysis, 29, 33
Corcoran and Evans, 185
Craig, 52
cues, 15, 30, 32, 99, 109, 115, 131–3, 135–6, 139, 142, 144, 147–8, 150–2, 154, 158–9, 161, 178–9
Culler, 21–2, 24, 45, 46, 53–4, 97, 129
culture, 2–5, 11–14, 20, 22, 26, 27, 29–31, 33, 34, 36–44, 48–51, 54, 72, 77–8, 106, 110–11, 176, 179–80

Davies, 11
direct quotation, 138, 139, 142–4
discourse, 1, 12, 44, 45, 46, 53, 111, 124, 125, 126, 135, 156, 162, 176, 185
documentary, 53, 58, 65
Dorr, 28, 94, 97, 99